W9-AFD-319

The Study of Dying

What is it really like to die? Though our understanding about the biology of dying is complex and incomplete, greater complexity and diversity can be found in the study of what human beings encounter socially, psychologically and spiritually during the experience. Contributors from disciplines as diverse as social and behavioural studies, medicine, demography, history, philosophy, art, literature, popular culture and religion examine the process of dying through the lens of both animal and human studies. Despite common fears to the contrary, dying is not simply an awful journey of illness and decline; cultural influences, social circumstances, personal choice and the search for meaning are all crucial in shaping personal experiences. This intriguing volume will be of interest to clinicians, professionals, academics and students of death, dying and end-of-life care, and anyone curious about the human confrontation with mortality.

ALLAN KELLEHEAR is Professor of Sociology at the University of Bath.

The Study of Dying

From Autonomy to Transformation

Edited by

ALLAN KELLEHEAR
University of Bath

CAMBRIDGE
UNIVERSITY PRESS

Hartness Library System
Vermont Technical College
One Main Street
Randolph Center, VT 05061

CAMBRIDGE UNIVERSITY PRESS

Cambridge, New York, Melbourne, Madrid, Cape Town, Singapore,
São Paulo, Delhi

Cambridge University Press
The Edinburgh Building, Cambridge CB2 8RU, UK

Published in the United States of America by Cambridge University Press, New York

www.cambridge.org
Information on this title: www.cambridge.org/9780521739054

© Cambridge University Press 2009

This publication is in copyright. Subject to statutory exception
and to the provisions of relevant collective licensing agreements,
no reproduction of any part may take place without
the written permission of Cambridge University Press.

First published 2009

Printed in the United Kingdom at the University Press, Cambridge

A catalogue record for this publication is available from the British Library

Library of Congress Cataloguing in Publication data
The study of dying : from autonomy to transformation / [edited by] Allan Kellehear.
       p.   cm.
   ISBN 978-0-521-51767-6
   1. Death–Social aspects.   2. Death–Psychological aspects.
   I. Kellehear, Allan, 1955–   II. Title.
   HQ1073.S786 2009
   306.9–dc22   2009025803

ISBN 978-0-521-51767-6 hardback
ISBN 978-0-521-73905-4 paperback

Cambridge University Press has no responsibility for the persistence or
accuracy of URLs for external or third-party Internet websites referred to
in this publication, and does not guarantee that any content on such
websites is, or will remain, accurate or appropriate.

Therefore learn, know yourself and see
Look how I am, and thus shalt thou be
                    From The Kalendar and Compost of Shepherds
                                        Guy Marchant (1493)

Contents

Figures

Tables

Contributors

Michael Ashby is Professor of Palliative Care in the School of Medicine at the University of Tasmania and Director of Palliative Care, Royal Hobart Hospital, Hobart.

Marie-Aurélie Bruno is a Ph.D. student at the Coma Science Group, Cyclotron Research Centre, University of Liège.

Douglas Davies is Professor of Theology and Religion at Durham University. He is the author of *The Theology of Death* (2008).

Clare Gittings is Learning Manager in the Learning Department at the National Portrait Gallery, London. She is a visiting lecturer in the Death and Society M.Sc. programme at the University of Bath and an editorial-board member of the international journal *Mortality*.

Bruce Greyson is the Chester F. Carlson Professor of Psychiatry and Neurobiological Sciences and Director of the Division of Perceptual Studies at the University of Virginia. He is co-author of *Irreducible Mind: Towards a Psychology for the 21st Century* (2007).

Glennys Howarth is Professor of Sociology in the Department of Social and Policy Sciences at the University of Bath. She is currently Director of the Centre for Death and Society.

Allan Kellehear is Professor of Sociology and Head of the Department of Social and Policy Sciences at the University of Bath. He is the author of *A Social History of Dying* (2007).

Siri Kristine Knudsen is Associate Professor and Head of the Animal Department, Faculty of Medicine, University of Tromsø. She has specialized in the pathophysiology of death and animal welfare and how these particularly relate to hunting activities.

Steven Laureys is Clinical Professor in the Coma Science Group at the Department of Neurology and Cyclotron Research Centre, Sart Tilman University Hospital and University of Liège. He heads the Coma Science Group and is author of *The Neurology of Consciousness* (2008).

Didier Ledoux is Head of Clinics at the Coma Science Group and Intensive Care Department, Sart Tilman University Hospital, Liège.

Fran McInerney is Associate Professor in Aged Care, School of Nursing and Midwifery, Australian Catholic University, Australia. Her forthcoming book *Mass Media Representations of Requested Death at the End of the Twentieth Century* is to be published in 2009.

Geoffrey Scarre is Professor of Philosophy at Durham University. In recent years he has taught and published mainly in the areas of moral theory and applied ethics. His latest book is *Death* (2007).

Julie-Marie Strange is Senior Lecturer in Modern British History at the University of Manchester. She is author of *Death, Grief and Poverty in Britain* (2005) and currently directing an Economic and Social Research Council project: 'Families Need Fathers? Emotion and Paternity in Working-Class Culture, 1880–1914'.

John Skelton is Professor of Clinical Communication at Birmingham University College of Medicine and Dentistry. He is the author of *Language and Clinical Communication: This Bright Babylon* (2008).

Preface

What is it like to die? If the contributors to this volume are to be believed, much depends on who you ask. Dying is no one thing, no single experience, no easy stereotype of decline or failing. Dying is not encompassed by what we know about illness even though illness is a common route to death. Dying is not always about decline and hopelessness though both decline and despair are commonly associated with the end of life. Dying can be quick or slow, heroic or degrading, emblematic of a life or unexpectedly transforming. Dying people can display control and autonomy or fear and dependency. Dying is like living because dying people are living people – they are not dead, yet.

In these ways, the human experience of dying is complex, diverse, surprising and full of possibility. This book brings together a collection of scholars and clinicians whose aim is to demonstrate some of this complexity to the reader. Their meditations, examples and reviews remind us not to be too quick to stereotype dying as simply sad and bad. The aim of this volume then, is to dare us to pause and think again, and to re-examine our common fate more carefully, more thoughtfully, even more hopefully.

I begin this book with an overview of what the social and behavioural studies have observed about dying. I summarize their observations and opinions into 'themes'. I have then asked each contributor from medicine or the social sciences and humanities to explore what their own discipline has observed about dying, noting how, if at all, these social and behavioural themes apply to their own areas. The early chapters examine some of the clinical and biological processes involved in dying and death. These writers remind readers of the underlying organic and animal basis of our final dying moments that lead to death itself. But just minutes or hours before those often-uniform organic processes take place, individual and social meanings of dying can express themselves in a mesmerizing diversity of ways.

Most of this book, then, is specifically looking at how people behave just minutes, hours or days before their death and how that conduct is influenced by an array of physical, psychological, cultural and spiritual factors triggered by the fact that they will die very shortly. In addition to these descriptions and observations about dying are other meditations and observations about dying as we have recorded these in our art or literature, on screen or inside Western theologies, philosophies or histories. In this broad way this book is less about 'death and dying' and more about 'living with dying'. And in this way too, this is the first major multidisciplinary review devoted specifically to the topic of dying both as a lived experience and as a process of meaning-making in the shadow of imminent death.

Of course, there are limits to what we can do in such an early, introductory volume. We limit ourselves to mainly Western literature and experience. Our art chapter, for example, provides highlights rather than an exhaustive review of artistic representations of dying from the Classical period to the present. We do not attempt to look at hunter-gatherer or prehistoric art. Our religion chapter is devoted to Judaeo-Christian thinking and not, for example, Islamic or Shintoist ideas about dying. We have not attempted a chapter on children's views about dying. There is obviously much more to say and far more to describe. There is far more to debate and challenge. There is much to think about.

But if this collection of essays stimulates a more critical, thoughtful, more global set of meditations – and research – about our common fate, then both professional and philosophical aims of this book will have been ably achieved. The specific, multidisciplinary study of dying is an important, recent area of scholarship. We hope we have been able to demonstrate, in this collection of reviews and observations, the basic elements of our knowledge about this experience as it currently stands. And we hope through the book's ability to provoke important discussion about what we know about dying, or perhaps more importantly about the gaps in our current understandings, that it will stimulate far more work by far more people in the future.

1 | What the social and behavioural studies say about dying

ALLAN KELLEHEAR

In the popular mind, the serious study of the dying experience is often traced to Elizabeth Kübler-Ross's best-selling work *On Death and Dying* (1969). Nevertheless, important academic work by sociologists Barney Glaser, Anselm Strauss, Renee Fox, or physician John Hinton among others, had in fact pioneered this field well before the appearance of the best-selling psychiatrist. Although the study of dying is very much a post-1945 research development with important theoretical and empirical gains made in the 1960s, the field has continued to struggle to attract researchers over the years.

Certainly the growing concerns over aged care and hospice care have brought their share of interest in the dying experience but much of the research effort has focused on carers' experiences and views, social, psychological or medical problems of dying, and health service delivery issues. Specific research on dying as a particular form of social life and experience that goes beyond, yet providing context to illness and its associations, receives far less attention even today. Yet that wider experience is important to understand.

Assumptions or implicitly held views about dying drive diverse policies and lobbies about care – from euthanasia, hospice and palliative care to other policies about aged care or the legal or medical determination of death. These assumptions are also commonly the basis of other profession-based theories about the limits to counselling, psychotherapy or spiritual and pastoral interventions. Many of our assumptions about the dying experience are just that – common assumptions characterized by little empirical support. Other assumptions are actually derived empirically but from highly selective sources and traditions of social literature about the dying experience. The aim of this opening chapter is to critically review the major literature studying dying conduct and to identify and make explicit their different theoretical insights, limitations and future possibilities.

I believe that it is self-evidently important that clinicians, academics and policy-makers are explicit about the model of dying that is at the centre of their particular advocacy, course of action or arguments. To date, most literature from these occupational areas has *not* demonstrated this kind of frankness, leading some to believe that a certain consensus exists about the social experience of dying. As I will argue in this review, no such consensus about the dying experience exists.

The review is organized around seven themes that directly emerge from the empirical literature on dying behaviour. I characterize them according to their theoretical emphasis and do not for a moment argue that they are immune from overlap or social complexity, often rehearsed even by the authors themselves. I acknowledge that dying from cancer, or elderly dying in nursing homes, is mediated by social determinants such as gender, class or education for example. Dying behaviour often reflects the different lifestyles and values of the person at the centre of that conduct. The elderly for example, like all dying people, are not a homogenous group (Wass et al. 1978–9; Meares 1981). Notwithstanding these qualifications, a systematic review of the literature about dying conduct nonetheless suggests seven reoccurring insights. These consist of theories about dying as agency, linearity, oscillation, disengagement, disintegration, disenfranchisement and transformation.

The theme of agency: dying as personal control

By far the most common view of dying is that dying people are in control of their fate, that they are active players in the last scenes of their lives. This is a major theme in the literature on suicide, making explicit the role of agency in determining not only the mode of dying but also its timing (Durkheim 1952; Alvarez 1970; Sagan 1987). Suicidal behaviour appears to be strongly associated with the aged and particularly with social influences such as modernization (Makinen 2002), affluence (Andersson and Moniruzzaman 2004), individualism (Sourvinou-Inwood 1981) and social fragmentation, dependency and alienation (Seale and Addington-Hall 1994, 1995). But studies of illness dying display no less emphasis on personal control than do studies of suicide.

In terminal illness, the most common phrase disguising the idea of agency is the 'good death', a signature term that describes a series of individual actions that portrays dying persons as controllers of their affairs. As Houlbrooke (1998: 184–219) describes it for many Europeans: on feeling that one will die soon one makes a will, dividing the estate fairly, making some provision for the poor, accepts visits from priests and doctors, says one's prayers and goodbyes and dies surrounded by friends and family at home and in bed. Such descriptions of the good death are replete in the literature from early Europe (Sussman et al. 1970; Boase 1972; Souvinou-Inwood 1981; McManners 1985; Jalland 1996), in European populations of more recent times (Fox 1959; Hinton 1967; Kalish 1970; Saum 1975; Jaffe and Jaffe 1977; Kastenbaum 1979; Marshall 1980; Kellehear 1990; Young and Cullen 1996; McNamara 2001; Kaufman 2005) and in some non-European populations (Counts 1976; Lifton 1979).

Away from studies that have emphasized preparations initiated by the dying are other studies also emphasizing the control exerted by the dying but referring to their abilities to maintain identity (Matthews 1976, 1979). Planning for their demise, informal willing, organizing others for a life beyond the dying person's lifespan and card-carrying with medical and social information are illustrations of this identity maintenance, particularly by older women. Active negotiations with physicians and other healthcare workers, the use of advanced directives or the pursuit of advanced technological interventions are also well-described signs of agency and control while dying (Kaufman 2005). Other researchers emphasize the more informal ability of the dying to conduct 'impression management' to manipulate medical and nursing staff to gain favours, attention or maintain positive relationships with hospital staff (Weisman and Hacket 1965; Watson 1976; Hinton 1971).

Sometimes, dying people are viewed as active contributors to the social and even physical life of others as they volunteer for experimental medical research that will not necessarily benefit them but others who come after them (Fox 1959; Parsons et al. 1974). Even physical stamina and control are emphasized by some studies. The physician Witzel (1975), in his medical investigation of 360 dying people, for example, emphasizes how the majority of the dying maintain their consciousness and social relations until quite late in the course of their dying.

Agency theories of dying commonly portray dying people as individuals in control of their destiny. Most of the empirical support for this idea usually comes from historical studies of dying among the middle classes – whether from Souvinou-Inwood's aristocratic descriptions of dying in Ancient Greece, McManner's study in the Enlightenment, or Jalland's study in the Victorian period (although, see Young and Cullen 1996, and Strange 2005, for important exceptions). In any case, contemporary social studies of people dying in modern hospitals are portraits of dying under modern healthcare and are therefore consistently reports of dying from degenerative diseases associated with affluence and long life expectancy – cancer, heart disease or neurological decline such as motor neuron disease or dementia. Whether these are medical studies from authors such as Hinton or Witzel, or sociological studies from authors such as Fox, Glaser and Strauss, or Seale, the overwhelming majority of the empirical support for this image of dying comes from regional circumstances of comparative affluence. These are also the backgrounds of most of the writers and researchers, and this may also partly explain the descriptive bias or selective vision in much of the narrative from these studies and commentary.

Nevertheless, studies of dying that emphasize control tell us how the dying reciprocate their social obligations in life right to the very end. Dying people prepare for death often by getting their social and legal affairs in order before they die. They use professional people such as priests, lawyers or doctors to help ease their passage. The deliberations of these dying people reinforce and reproduce the ideological interests of the day – they do not ignore a lifetime's investment in work, family or religion. Rather, dying people reinforce their importance to themselves and their networks by affirming their relevance right up to the very end of life. Theories of agency locate these activities, obligations and responsibilities in a dying person who is usually conscious enough and has time enough to execute them.

The theme of linearity: dying as a journey

Among anthropologists and sociologists, the idea of dying as a journey is an old one that can be traced to an early study by Van Gennep (1969). Van Gennep's classic work on the rites that people undergo during the life course is one of the earliest works to highlight the fact that the life course is not biologically determined but rather socially constructed by the community. Puberty rites, for example, are not based on the physical appearance of sexual maturity but on a desire to separate initiates from the asexual world and to integrate them into the sexual one. The criteria for initiation are often based on a diversity of social determinants, age or gender for example. Van Gennep theorizes that individuals in the community underwent a series of rites that both separated them from some experiences and groups (children, single adults or warriors, for example) and incorporated them into others (adulthood, married people or as elders, for example). These rites were characterized as rites of separation, transition or liminality, and incorporation.

In the original work, Van Gennep devotes only one chapter (Chapter 8) to death, and most of that chapter addresses funerals. Van Gennep (1969: 146) notes that in matters to do with death, rites of transition and incorporation dominated. He fails to realize that a principal reason why rites of separation appeared to be less apparent may have to do with the fact that most of these probably occur during dying itself. In the 1960s, sociologists Glaser and Strauss took it upon themselves to conduct these observations of dying as a 'trajectory' (1968: 6) or 'status passage' (1971: 8). These phrases were based on Glaser and Strauss's view of hospital dying as a journey that involved family and hospital staff making a time-related series of assessments about the dying person's behaviour during their final illness.

Assessment of the dying person's physical and psychological decline, the occasional reversibility of that decline, or the duration and pace of that decline, among other factors, were important to chart for family and staff because these indicated what each party should do in relation to dying. Dying became a process and series of 'critical junctures' that others could employ to help them determine what to do next. In other words, viewing dying as a narrow passageway that leads individuals from 'living person' to 'dead person' was an important social device for care management by family and healthcare staff. In this way, theorizing dying as linearity – moving from point 'A' to end-point 'Z' becomes an interactive assessment by carers to note aspects of dying that were important *to them rather than the dying person*. In this way, the concept of status passage inherits its community concerns and priorities from the earlier anthropological idea of rite of passage.

We see this continuing obsession with the idea of living and dying as journeys because they always serve the same community functions – when is the right time to leave, go elsewhere or become something

else? What are the 'signs' that we or they should look for in making
the decision or decisions about what to do *next* (Gustafson 1972;
Lofland 1978; Pollack 1980; and recently Small et al. 2007)? In psychiatry, we have witnessed the staging process of this journey described
in emotional terms – people feel certain emotions at different stages
of the dying process. These emotions can act as points of orientation
for carers to know where the dying person is in the overall process of
dying (Kübler-Ross 1969, 1974; Germain 1980). Such stage theories –
both social and psychological – have led to the observation that the
way people are expected to die and the way they actually do die are
commonly divergent (Weisman 1972: 148). If theories of dying that
emphasize control represent selective vision of the observers, theories
of dying as linearity commonly represent vested interests of carers no
less. The dying experience is filtered to the extent that it can, or cannot, tell carers what to do next. Going beyond this criterion is a road
less travelled by researchers.

The theme of fluctuation: dying as oscillation

Once the literature on dying moves away from the hospital setting
and particularly from an epidemiology of cancer dying towards dying
in old age, the picture of dying grows unsteady. Although there is
some debate about the association between increased life expectancy
and increased quality of life, it is apparent that the prevalence of acute
and chronic illness remains related to social determinants (Crimmins
2004: 81). That picture of chronic illness in old age makes the parallel picture of dying in old age an equally fluctuating one (Moss et al.
2003: 160; Lunney et al. 2003).

The pattern of terminal decline in the elderly is one characterized
by cycles of health and illness, decline and improvement. Despite the
fact that most people who develop cancer are over the age of fifty,
most people over that age don't actually die of cancer (Hall et al.
2002). The majority of the aged die of other chronic conditions such
as dementia, heart disease, diabetes or chronic obstructive airway
diseases (Moss et al. 2003: 160). The actual cause of death for many
of these people is organ failure (kidney, liver or heart) or 'frailty'
(Lunney et al. 2003). In a major study of 4,000 people over the age
of sixty-five, Lunney et al. (2003) found that people with organ failure had a 'fluctuating' pattern of dying with cycles of disability and

improvement. Those with 'frailty' experienced poor function over the whole year and were more inclined to have shorter periods of improvement and longer periods of obvious decline.

In both styles of dying, the determination of 'dying' is difficult and unpredictable (Lloyd 2004: 238). For aged care staff in nursing homes and other related facilities there is reportedly great ambiguity and conflict over how 'dying' is defined let alone identified (Sidell and Komaromy 2003: 51–2). But ageing is not the only form of dying that exhibits a frequent oscillation between decline and improvement. HIV/AIDS also exhibits these kinds of fluctuations. The emergence of effective antivirals to manage but not cure HIV makes the identification of 'dying' in this population also extremely difficult and complex. The theories about dying as fluctuation, when combined with the epidemiology of ageing, makes this particular style of dying no small matter. AIDS now affects 40 million people worldwide with some 25 million people already dead from the virus (WHO 2005). The life expectancy of someone with HIV – from first contracting the virus to its progression to AIDS – is approximately ten years (Fleming 2004). Like growing old then, the awareness of dying is gradual, mediated by bouts of serious, increasing but episodic illness and disability.

In theory, the idea of dying as oscillation is able to accommodate a complementary notion of agency, and sometimes it is highly apparent that, in the case of professional people with HIV/AIDS in affluent contexts, they actually are able to display this element of control. In reality, however, most people with HIV/AIDS live and die in poverty in the developing nations of the world, especially in Africa. Consequently, both life and death for people in these economic situations do not exhibit great degrees of agency. For people dying in poverty from malaria or tuberculosis, the presence of control is possible as a traditional partnership exercised with family and community. But the stigma and shame of AIDS dying often leaves such dying people with much less support (Takahashi 1998; Songwathana and Manderson 2001; Liddell et al. 2005).

In the case of the elderly, particularly the large group of elderly in nursing homes and those suffering from dementia, the idea of personal agency soon disappears under the weight of institutionalization and the social consequences of custodial care (Kitwood 1993; Giacalone 2001). However, Small et al. (2007) argue that the idea of journey and agency may not disappear entirely because the theoretical debates and empirical investigations about the fate of self in dementia remains contentious and inconclusive (see Small et al. 2007: 120–7).

It is also possible to integrate the idea of 'dying as journey' into this current idea of 'dying as oscillation' but usually only retrospectively since the so-called journey of ageing and dying is poorly recognized in care institutions (Mackinley 2005), clinical diagnoses (Sullivan 2002; Page and Komaromy 2005) or sometimes even by the aged themselves (Bytheway 1995). In this conceptual way, theories of dying as fluctuation are distinct from those about agency or journey because they represent a style of dying very much shaped and distorted by multiple disease causation, economic marginality and stigma. It may be that the so-called fluctuating or oscillating experience of dying is in fact a direct reflection of the ambivalence of a wider culture towards public displays of economic, aesthetic and bodily decay.

Whatever the relationship between the wider culture and the dying, it is also true that dying, from the point of view of these studies, is not a continuous physical, psychological or social journey with one overall sense of identity or purpose. Dying, as an identity and as a physical experience, is not always an uninterrupted trajectory of decline. Dying can be, and is often, an intermittent experience determined by the disease process and the social roles and circumstances that prevail in end-of-life situations.

The theme of disengagement: dying as withdrawal

When dying people steadily decline, noticeably and incrementally, sometimes in ageing or in the last few days or hours of life, this process is often characterized as a form of disengagement. These dying people are described by others as withdrawing their attentions from the affairs of the wider world, including family and self-care, appearing to surrender to tiredness, weakness or dependency in general. These theories of disengagement were originally developed to account for patterns of withdrawal by the aged (Cumming and Henry 1961; Damianopoulos 1961), but they have subsequently been incorporated into the more broadly applied idea of 'social death' (Sudnow 1967; Kalish 1968, 1972; Humphries 1981).

Fulton (1977) includes family in his idea of 'disengagement', arguing that as families disengage from their dying, hospital staff tend to increasingly engage themselves with the dying either in stepping up their watchfulness over the declining days or hours or in their nursing attentions in the final hours. Kalish (1968, 1972) argues that disengagement is a valid description of what actually happens to many dying people because many of them are simply too old or sick to desire their usual engagement. He argues, as indeed do Cumming and Henry, that activity is *not* the opposite of disengagement but rather engagement. The old and dying may still be active, but this may not represent genuine social or emotional engagement on their part.

Of course, the problem with this view, as with many psychodynamic interpretations of other people's behaviour, is that we cannot easily distinguish between speculation about active conduct that represents 'engagement' and other so-called active conduct that disguises 'disengagement'. In practical terms, this means that we have no idea what proportion of active dying people are 'really' disengaged because they are indistinguishable from other active 'engaged' people.

Other defenders of disengagement theories have argued that disengagement may well be an appropriate response to a cohort or group experience (Marshall 1975). In other words, when everyone is getting married or getting their first jobs there is a widespread feeling that things are 'right' and 'appropriate' for that time of life. In just this way, Marshall (1975: 1140) argues that many residents in nursing homes and aged care facilities feel that dying is an appropriate part of their lives since most of them will share the same fate. This social process of 'legitimation' permits their withdrawal to be viewed as a supported, understood and even a learned response to declining health or severe illness (Blauner 1966: 383). But there have been other less accommodating critics of disengagement theories.

Scoggins (1971) and Hochschild (1975), for example, believe that disengagement is a response to society withdrawing from their sick and elderly. Disengagement theories ignore the social determinants for health (age, sex, class, etc.) that may also apply to other social experiences such as withdrawal. Disengagement may also not be disengagement but re-engagement with other activities, values or concerns. Disengagement may be a superficial and misleading ascription to major changes from one part of life (working, grandparenting, for instance) to another part of one's life more adaptive to frailty (gardening, reading, increased television viewing, as examples).

Scoggins is particularly critical of disengagement theories, challenging the assumption that withdrawal is both inevitable and satisfying for the dying and their network. Scoggins (1971: 143) argues that the elderly in particular are being rejected as non-functional, inefficient and ugly, and 'retirement' is society's permission to 'disengage'. Disengagement may be a response to social rejection and segregation (see also Hockey and James 1993).

However, it is difficult to distinguish here the criticism about social response to ageing, by both the aged and the wider society, and what actually happens when people are near death – at any age. Hochschild (1975: 559), a critic of disengagement theories for the aged, readily admits that for dying people, 'distance from death ... was the one most conducive to social and economic disengagement of a mutual (me–them) kind'. In the context of the current review, it may be no coincidence that the language and ideas of 'disengagement', 'withdrawal' or 'surrender' have been greeted with suspicion, criticism and even rejection over more readily received and preferred notions of dying as 'agency' and 'personal control'.

We cannot fairly separate that critical response from its possible sociological basis. Philosophically and methodologically, we must accept that all studies of dying come from researchers and carers who enjoy basic levels of health, and not from the dying themselves. Furthermore, most of these studies are conducted by members of the Western middle classes – a culture famous for its anxious attachments to personal control and individual autonomy (Lasch 1980; Vidich 1995). A certain degree of withdrawal as a response to serious illness should come as no surprise to anyone, but the ambivalent academic response to that reality makes a balanced assessment of its social conditions contentious. This too should come as no surprise given the cultural character of the research leadership into dying over the past half-century.

From theories of disengagement, we learn that dying may not only be a slow withdrawal of bodily energies but also a slow withdrawal of social engagement and interest as well. Even in societies or personal situations where dying receives optimum support, few dying people can sustain – or seem even to desire to sustain – an active social involvement to their last breath. At some point in the dying process there often comes a time when it is important for the dying person to pay attention to what comes next after all seems said and done. When this process begins too early for the comfort of some researchers or carers, the reasons for this withdrawal may then commonly become objects of suspicion and contention.

The theme of disintegration: dying as collapse

Probably the best known recent work describing dying as a form of collapse is Sherwin Nuland's *How We Die* (1993). That book is part of a tradition of medical and sociological writings portraying the human body as a failing, disintegrating machine that both the dying person and their social network observe as helpless onlookers at the end of life. Lawton (2000), McNamara (2001) and Armstrong-Coster (2004) describe from their interview-based studies of dying people the dismay and distress dying people and their families undergo when their bodies fail. 'Dirty dying' is how Lawton describes the combination of leaking, painful and difficult bodies that no longer respond to personal control by their owners. These ethnographic accounts are part of wider clinical and social studies of dying as collapse.

Aminoff and Adunsky (2004), for example, document dying in a geriatric department of a large US hospital as mostly an 'unstable' set of 'medical conditions' where most have pressure sores, are malnourished and are not emotionally 'calm'. Most of these people also underwent 'an invasive medical procedure' in the last week before dying, and some 15 per cent were screaming during that time. The Report on Dying in America (Last Acts 2002) observed that one third to one half of all nursing-home residents were in moderate to excruciating daily pain and that they frequently died in these conditions or attached to life support. Physical collapse – fall-related injuries, self-inflicted injuries or physical impairment – dog the aged and contribute to their demise (Moniruzzaman and Andersson 2005). In cancer dying under geriatric care, some 85 per cent are estimated to die in some form of delirium (Sullivan 2002), with many elderly dying characterized by dementia. Dementia is a huge worldwide problem with 0.5 per cent of the world population affected, and 6.1 per cent over the age of sixty-five (Wimo et al. 2003). Brock and Foley (1998), in their study of over 1,000 people over the age of sixty-five, found that a day before death, three-quarters of the dying aged were non-ambulant, one third incontinent, and 40 per cent had difficulty recognizing family.

In the countries seriously affected by HIV/AIDS, the emphasis on dying as a form of collapse continues. People dying from AIDS are vulnerable to a wide range of infections, but they are also prone to malignant tumours, colitis, severe shingles, thrush, pneumonias, lymphoma, Kaposi's sarcoma and profound wasting, premature greying, wrinkling and ageing (Reichert et al. 1985; Schoub 1999: 25). One of the earliest studies of dying was conducted by David Sudnow (1967) and was entitled *Passing On: The Social Organization of Dying*. However, unlike the longer and more social view of dying assumed by ethnographers Lawton, McNamara or Armstrong-Coster, most of Sudnow's 'dying' were comatose. All these studies and theories about dying focus on disintegration and bodily failure and their social and psychological consequences for dying persons, family and staff. Seale (1998) argue that an integral part of the experience of dying is to understand the vulnerability of our bodies. Dying in the modern world is about coming to terms with our fragile, decaying bodies, sooner or later, and developing social and psychological defences against this contradiction to our human 'reflexive subjectivity'.

It is no surprise that clinical researchers and writers such as Nuland or Aminoff and Adunsky should focus our attention on the problem of bodily decay. Much of this is about providing a popular and professional corrective to the higher profile given to psychological, social but often 'disembodied' treatments about dying as 'journey' or as control. Theories and studies of dying as disintegration remind us that dying is also a practical physical matter, and sometimes this can be quite shocking. Other theorists and researchers that stress these aspects of dying do so because, as Aminoff and Adunsky do, they wish to draw attention to problems in the quality of service provision for people who are dying.

For sociological researchers and theorists, however, the emphasis on disintegration and collapse represents a desire to develop an understanding of the sociology of the body that charts how cultural ideas about 'fighting cancer' or 'heroism' in death and dying are imbedded in both social *and* physical experiences of struggle (Seale 1995, 1998). Although this brings a certain medical balance to more abstract understandings of the experience of dying, it does so at the cost of strengthening the unfortunate research stereotype of dying as always an illness-related experience. Theories of indeterminacy are an important departure from this stereotype.

The theme of indeterminacy: disenfranchised dying

A number of social theorists have argued that modernity is a period characterized by the disappearance of 'dying'. This judgement has exhibited two important phases. First, we recall the 1960s and early 1970s literature on the denial or taboo of death voiced from numerous writers from Elizabeth Kübler-Ross and Geoffrey Gorer to Barney Glaser and Anselm Strauss. Some writers, such as Philippe Ariès, make this claim the centre of their work, arguing that in the twentieth century death had become 'hidden'. In several works, Ariès (1974, 1975, 1981) argues that, in the late twentieth century, deception had become formalized, and most dying people died in ignorance of their fate because of the pervasive medical practice of not disclosing poor life expectancy. Death and dying had become medicalized, private, supervised and hidden away.

A continuing focus on illness-related dying, especially cancer dying, encouraged sociologists to follow the social changes that occurred to dying people in this very specific context of formal health care. Since the early writings and criticism of the 1960s there have been major changes to medical responses to dying, including more openness about diagnosis and prognosis and the rapid rise and establishment of the hospice and palliative-care movement. This has led to sociologist Tony Walter (1994) including these changes under the rubric of what he calls the 'revival of death'. However, it is only by focusing on illness-related dying that one can speak about any sort of 'revival' of dying because in just about every other scenario of dying social recognition of dying remains absent or obscure. This is the second way that dying is understood to have disappeared.

Gil Elliot (1972) argues that most people who fight in wars are not regarded as 'dying people' because if they were this would be the 'century' of dying since, compared to previous times, this is the most violent period in history. Elliot, and Marcuse before him (1969), were some of the first writers to theorize that social classification of dying rests in the hands of the prevailing authority of the day and that authority is *not* medicine but rather the state. 'Authority never lets you know when you are to die, except when you are a convicted

murderer. But when authority is the murderer there is no official notification' (Elliot 1972: 74).

Adler (1991: 33) echoes this criticism and argues that the lack of
recognition of dying in nursing homes for the aged reflects the power-
lessness of the residents who are placated, infantilized, ignored,
labelled and denigrated. Elias (1985) argues that this marginaliza-
tion of the old and dying does not simply extend to those in nursing
homes but is fundamental to the experience of ageing and dying. The
disenfranchisement of dying has its basis in the disenfranchisement of
life as an elderly person. Takahashi (1998) applies these observations
to those with HIV/AIDS, arguing that the stigma of AIDS functions
to single out the infectious, the poor and the deviant. This gives a
kind of social permission to reject, discriminate and rationalize self-
protective behaviour. People living with HIV are people living with
a 'chronic illness'. Although these 'deaths' and this 'illness' is widely
recognized, 'dying' is not recognized. Public-health recognition and
response to AIDS dying is meagre or non-existent (Kellehear 2005).
Even in contemporary hospital situations, outside of hospice and palliative care, 'dying' as a form of recognized conduct is uncommon. As
Nuland (1993: 265) himself admits, 'we live today in the era not of
the art of dying, but of the art of saving life.'

Agamben (1998), Noys (2005), Kellehear (2007) and Walter
(2008) argue that in all the recent clamour to scrutinize illness dying
we have forgotten the larger numbers of dying people in vegetative
states, coma, poverty, dementia and incarceration. Much of our modern dying is disenfranchised – not recognized by medical, political
or international authorities but occurring anyway and in far greater
numbers than appear in hospices or cancer wards. Few studies exist
that theorize, less describe, dementia dying, AIDS dying in poverty,
or dying in concentration camps.

Theories of indeterminacy suggest that much modern dying is
unrecognized, sometimes even by the dying themselves, and more
often by the authorities responsible for them. This indeterminacy may
be caused by impaired cognitive function or a misplaced desire for
cure, health or release. It may also be caused by state reclassification
of the dying as people who are chronically ill, detainees, or simply
'poor people in ill health' – non-specific labels convenient for multiple and changing interpretations by others. In these organizational
and cultural ways, dying must be state-endorsed to gain cultural and

professional recognition and support. Because of this modern development, knowledge about non-illness dying is poor, the population so affected by this culture of disenfranchisement under-researched.

These research circumstances mean that we do not know how many of the world's dying do indeed 'prepare for death' or what proportion of the dying seem 'in control' or receive support from health and social-care professionals. Without studies of the disenfranchised dying we do not know how much dying behaviour as journey, control, oscillation, withdrawal or collapse is really only associated with affluence, physical decline or chronic illness and how much is associated with an identity threatened with its own extinction.

The theme of transcendence: dying as transformation

The experiences of the dying are not confined to episodes of illness, coma or sudden collapse. Neither are they simply linear, oscillating or withdrawing social processes. Some experiences of dying appear to transcend these experiences and pathways to arrive at another social place where both consciousness and social interaction are altered in substantial ways. In studies of the near-death experience (NDE) (Moody 1975, Ring 1980, Sabom 1982), some people who experience a close brush with death from accident, surgery or severe illness claim to remember a diversity of psychological and social experiences. These range from out-of-body experiences, tunnel sensation, encountering a white light or being of light, and reviewing their own lives, to meetings with deceased relatives and friends. Most of the time, these encounters and experiences are associated with feelings of intense euphoria, love and peace. There are some reports of negative NDEs, but, to date, very few of these have been documented (Greyson and Evans-Bush 1992). Some of these elements also appear to be long-standing in our history (Zaleski 1987) and cross-cultural, except perhaps for experiences of life review and the sensation of being propelled through a dark tunnel (Kellehear 1996; Fox 2003). These experiences have much in common with deathbed visions.

Deathbed visions are usually reports from dying people or carers about the dying person's last few hours or minutes (Osis and Haraldsson 1977; Barret 1986; Barbato et al. 1999). Common among these reports are observations by healthcare staff or family about the dying person conversing with invisible companions by their bedside.

Sometimes dying people rise in their beds, claiming at the same time to be greeted by deceased friends or relatives. Within hours or minutes of these scenes the dying person takes their final breath. Once again, most of these experiences are described by the dying person as positive, wonderful and comforting. Dying persons who experience NDEs or deathbed visions commonly report less or no fear of their impending death. Indeed, the reports by those who have experienced NDEs suggest that many do not wish to return to life and commonly report disappointment on finding they have been resuscitated.

There have been numerous attempts to explain these experiences as mere hallucination (see Blackmore 1993 for a good summary of these). However, much of these medical explanations tends to be reductionist, philosophically naive and biased (see Zaleski 1987; Kellehear 1996). Nevertheless, it is important to note that currently no critical position in these matters can be easily or summarily dismissed, and so a clear and unchanging medical or religious interpretation of these psychological and social experiences is not currently possible. For the purposes of this chapter, let it be sufficient to say that, putting ultimate explanations aside, dying is mostly viewed by this line of research as an important transformative experience for the dying person.

It is transformative in two ways. First, both those who experience NDEs and those who report deathbed visions report that they are no longer concerned with the physical rigours of severe illness or physical dying. They are able to see beyond these bodily trials to a more important set of values, goals or social experiences. They report a promise of better things, including a genuine future for themselves beyond death. Second, for those who do not die soon after their NDEs, there are numerous reports and studies of transformation of their social lives – changes in work, occupation, family and marriages, educational priorities and interpersonal styles, and a greater interest in spiritual matters (see Ring 1984, 1991; Sutherland 1992).

The studies of NDEs and deathbed visions of the dying highlight an important aspect of studies of dying that is commonly overlooked. The fact is there *can* be positive experiences associated with dying. Although the prevalence of near-death experiences is estimated to be around 10 per cent of all people who experience cardiac arrest (Van Lommel 2004), these are not the only positive experiences associated with dying. Other research on dying, too, often overlooks the positives. For example, some people find the experience of dying to be one that brings them closer to their loved ones, ironically enhancing and enriching the time they have left (Kellehear 1990: 92–104). The study of dying, similar to the study of grief and bereavement, is overburdened with the professional stereotype that these experiences are always negative experiences characterized by problems. Although dying, like grief, can be a complex, changing and often difficult experience, it is the studies of NDEs and deathbed visions that we thank for reminding us that dying is more than problems. Dying, like life itself, can still surprise us with the unexpected and the positive, often even in what seems to be our darkest hour.

Summary and concluding reflections

When people start to die, particularly under circumstances of grave illness, many of them become actively engaged in social, family and legal preparations for death. Usually these activities characterize an early stage of dying, at least when they are well enough to make them or have received enough warning about their impending death. The wide range of networks, and often the sheer size or number of material possessions that a person has, make these preparations both necessary and desirable. In a way, preparing to die helps dying people also cope with an uncertain circumstance – 'uncertain' in the sense that even with the fullest medical knowledge of their condition one can never be entirely sure of the exact hour when death will come.

To cope with the same uncertainty, but from the carer's point of view, dying has also been theorized not simply as control but as a 'journey' or 'passage' through stages of physical, emotional or social decline. The research charting and mapping this 'journey' has helped carers plan, control and respond to the dying person in a timely way. In this sense, theories of linearity demonstrate that dying is a social journey – not a path merely taken by one but, rather, by the many around the one.

And while dying is often viewed as an unbroken journey, an inevitable descent to death, especially in the last hours or days, this is also not always true. Much dying, as theories of fluctuation well demonstrate, show us that dying can be an oscillating social and physical experience, especially outside of portraits of dying from cancer. However, at some time, usually later rather than earlier, people withdraw from life before or in parallel to their physical decline. Dying as a form of identity is seldom psychologically and socially totalizing or persistent over time. Other identities take priority or become secondary depending on the relationships and time being encountered. Dying is no different from other forms of social life and identity in this respect.

It is also important to recognize that what we know about dying is mainly through the lens of illness. This is our largest concentration of studies of dying. In this way, all our above observations are contingent and uncertain because we have little understanding about the comparative prevalence of illness dying in relation to other forms of dying.

And although most of our studies of dying suggest a broad picture of decline, sickness, decay and withdrawal, it is also true that we have numerous, thoughtfully designed studies of dying that suggest unexpected and positive experiences at the end of life. Though the prevalence of mystical experiences during the dying process is modest, it is nevertheless important to note that in control or in collapse, at the end of the journey or just before its end, in illness or even in personal crisis before it, dying has sometimes been reported to be uplifting. Dying can be traumatic and frightening, but others have reported transcendence, insightfulness and peace. There is much we do not know. A review of the social and behavioural studies of dying suggests that caution and humility before our data is still good advice.

On the other hand, we must admit that our current picture of dying, as this emerges from the past half-century in the Western world, tells us quite a bit about those who research this important topic. The dominating social picture of dying is one of affluence. This social picture is consistently carer-oriented, ambivalent, threatened, stereotypically medical, state-defined and frequently negative. This is no simple coincidence. Our social and behavioural studies persistently demonstrate the obsessions, anxieties and bias of the researchers behind them – celebrating and highlighting control, order and professional care but exhibiting ambivalence and fear towards examples of decay, withdrawal and contagion.

Researchers commonly find death irksome, obsessively documenting the negative characteristics of dying, particularly bodily decline and collapse. However, often this same literature protests or refuses to acknowledge those who, faced with medically related or age-related tiredness, cultural isolation or a desire not to live anymore, choose to, or surrender to, the desire to withdraw. Despite the repeatedly observed disengagement of the elderly and ill dying, many social researchers resist the conclusion that disengagement might ironically represent agency and control and may not be a response, or solely a response, to societal rejection.

Clearly, there are many missing pieces to our contemporary understanding of dying. We need more research into poverty experiences of dying and experiences of ageing and dying, and more personal perspectives of what it is like to die from dying persons themselves. There is a need to seriously investigate non-illness forms of dying, particularly dying in incarcerated circumstances of imprisonment, suicide or war. There is also much we do not know but could know more about through ethnographic studies of dying in brain-dead, persistent vegetative or comatose states. Furthermore, the problem-based concerns of both cancer medicine and palliative care have provided much useful information about symptom management, public health management and social management of illness-related troubles but little in the way of description and understanding about positive aspects of dying.

Related to this problem are the sharp divisions in the literature between a material view of dying that emphasizes social and bodily decline and other literature that examines unusual psychological and social experiences associated with that bodily decline. The polarization of views about NDEs and deathbed visions – as hallucinations or evidence for human survival beyond death – has produced a completely divided research literature. Those in palliative care, for example, seldom research the paranormal, while researchers of NDEs or deathbed visions seldom interest themselves in other social, psychological or medical aspects of dying more broadly. These divisive politics and practices deprive us all of a more unified understanding of the relationships between decline and transcendence and between carers' views of the 'journey' of dying and the dying person's view of their 'journey'. In the pursuit of understanding the meaning of death we can ill afford such petty 'sectarianism'. The study of dying, if approached with critical intelligence and humility, has much to teach us about courage, resilience, support and even hope – but only if we pool together our different insights in this new and promising field.

References

Adler, U. (1991) *A Critical Study of the American Nursing Home: The Final Solution*, New York: Edwin Mellon.

Agamben, G. (1998) *Homo Sacer: Sovereign Power and Bare Life*, Palo Alto, Calif.: Stanford University Press.

Alvarez, A. (1970) *The Savage God: A Study of Suicide*, New York: Bantam.

Aminoff, B.Z. and Adunsky, A. (2004) 'Dying Dementia Patients: Too Much Suffering, Too Little Palliation', *American Journal of Alzheimer's Disease and Other Dementias*, **19** (4): 243–7.

Andersson, R. and Moniruzzaman, S. (2004) 'Relationship Between Economic Development and Suicide Mortality: A Global Cross-Sectional Transition Perspective', *Public Health* **118** (5): 346–8.

Ariès, P. (1974) *Western Attitudes Towards Death*, London: Johns Hopkins University Press.

   (1975) 'The Reversal of Death: Changes in Attitudes Towards Death in Western Societies', in D.E. Stannard (ed.), *Death in America*, Philadelphia, Pa.: University of Pennsylvania Press, pp. 134–58.

   (1981) *The Hour of Our Death*, London: Allen Lane.

Armstrong-Coster, A. (2004) *Living and Dying with Cancer*, Cambridge: Cambridge University Press.

Barbato, M., Blunden, C., Irwin, H., Reid, K. and Rodriguez, P. (1999) 'Parapsychological Phenomena Around Death', *Journal of Palliative Care* **15** (2): 30–7.

Barret, W. (1986) *Death Bed Visions*, Wellingborough: Aquarian Press.

Berman, M.I. (1966) 'The Todeserwartung Syndrome', *Geriatrics*, **21**: 187–92.

Blackmore, S.J. (1993) *Dying to Live: Science and the Near-Death Experience*, London: Grafton.

Blauner, R. (1966) 'Death and Social Structure', *Psychiatry*, **29**: 378–94.

Boase, T.S.R. (1972) *Death in the Middle Ages*, London: Thames & Hudson.

Brock, D.B. and Foley, D.J. (1998) 'Demography and Epidemiology of Dying in the US with Emphasis on Deaths of Older Persons', in J.K. Harrold and J. Lynn (eds.), *A Good Dying: Shaping Health Care for the Last Months of Life*, New York: Haworth Press, pp. 49–60.

Bytheway, B. (1995) *Ageism*, Buckingham: Open University Press.

Counts, D.R. (1976) 'The Good Death in Kaliai: Preparations for Death in Western New Britain', *Omega*, **7** (4): 367–72.

Crimmins, E.M. (2004) 'Trends in the Health of the Elderly', *Annual Review of Public Health*, **25**: 79–98.

Cumming, E. and Henry, W.E. (1961) *Growing Old: The Process of Disengagement*, New York: Basic Books.

Damianopoulos, E. (1961) 'A Formal Statement of Disengagement Theory', in E. Cumming and W.E. Henry (eds.), *Growing Old: The Process of Disengagement*, New York: Basic Books, pp. 210–18.

Durkheim, E. (1952) *Suicide*, London: Routledge & Kegan Paul.

Elias, N. (1985) *The Loneliness of the Dying*, Oxford: Blackwell.

Elliot, G. (1972) *Twentieth Century Book of the Dead*, London: Allen Lane.

Fleming, P.L. (2004) 'The Epidemiology of HIV and AIDS', in G.P. Wormser (ed.), *AIDS and Other Manifestations of HIV Infection*, San Diego, Calif.: Elsevier, pp. 3–29.

Fox, M. (2003) *Religion, Spirituality and the Near-Death Experience*, London: Routledge.

Fox, R.C. (1959) *Experiment Perilous*, Philadelphia, Pa.: University of Pennsylvania Press.

Fulton, R. (1977) 'The Sociology of Death', *Death Education*, 1: 15–25.

Germain, C.P. (1980) 'Nursing the Dying: Implications of Kübler-Ross' Staging Theory', in R. Fox (ed.), *The Social Meaning of Death*. Special issue of *Annals of the American Academy of Political and Social Sciences*, **447**: 46–58.

Giacalone, J.A. (2001) *The US Nursing Home Industry*, Armonk, NY: M.E. Sharpe.

Glaser, B.G. and Strauss, A.L. (1968) *Time for Dying*, Chicago, Ill.: Aldine.

(1971) *Status Passage*, London: Routledge & Kegan Paul.

Greyson, B. and Evans-Bush, N. (1992) 'Distressing Near-Death Experiences', *Psychiatry*, **55**: 95–110.

Gustafson, E. (1972) 'Dying: The Career of the Nursing Home Patient', *Journal of Health and Social Behaviour*, **13**: 226–35.

Hall, P., Schroder, C. and Weaver, L. (2002) 'The Last 48 Hours in Long Term Care: A Focussed Chart Audit', *Journal of the American Geriatrics Society*, **50**: 501–6.

Hinton, J. (1967) *Dying*, Harmondsworth: Penguin.

(1971) 'Assessing the Views of the Dying', *Social Science and Medicine*, **5**: 37–43.

Hochschild, A.R. (1975) 'Disengagement Theory: A Critique and Proposal', *American Sociological Review*, **40**: 553–69.

Hockey, J. and James, A. (1993) *Growing Up and Growing Old: Ageing and Dependency in the Life Course*, London: Sage.

Houlbrooke, R. (1998) *Death, Religion and the Family in England, 1480–1750*, Oxford: Clarendon Press.

Humphries, S.C. (1981) 'Death and Time', in S.C. Humphries and H. King (eds.), *Mortality and Immortality: The Anthropology and Archaeology of Death*, London: Academic Press, pp. 261–83.

Jaffe, L. and Jaffe, A. (1977) 'Terminal Candor and the Coda Syndrome: A Tandem View of Fatal Illness', in H. Feifel (ed.), *New Meanings of Death*, New York: McGraw-Hill, pp. 196–211.

Jalland, P. (1996) *Death in the Victorian Family*, Oxford: Oxford University Press.

Kalish, R.A. (1968) 'Life and Death: Dividing the Indivisible', *Social Science and Medicine*, 2: 249–59.

(1970) 'The Onset of the Dying Process', *Omega*, 1: 57–69.

(1972) 'Of Social Values and the Dying: A Defense of Disengagement', *The Family Co-ordinator*, 21 (1): 81–94.

Kastenbaum, R. (1979) 'Healthy Dying: A Paradoxical Quest Continues', *Journal of Social Issues*, 35 (1): 185–206.

Kaufman, S.R. (2005) *And a Time to Die: How American Hospitals Shape the End of Life*, Chicago, Ill.: University of Chicago Press.

Kellehear, A. (1990) *Dying of Cancer: The Final Year of Life*, Chur: Harwood Academic Publishers.

(1996) *Experiences Near Death: Beyond Medicine and Religion*, New York: Oxford University Press.

(2005) *Compassionate Cities: Public Health and End of Life Care*, London: Routledge.

(2007) *A Social History of Dying*, Cambridge: Cambridge University Press.

Kitwood, T. (1993) 'Frames of Reference for an Understanding of Dementia', in J. Johnson and R. Slater (eds.), *Ageing and Later Life*, London: Sage, pp. 100–6.

Kübler-Ross, E. (1969) *On Death and Dying*, New York: Macmillan.

(1974) 'Dying – from the Patient's Point of View', *Triangle*, 13 (1): 25–6.

Lasch, C. (1980) *The Culture of Narcissism*, London: Abacus.

Last Acts (2002) *Means to a Better End: A Report on Dying in America Today*, Washington DC: Last Acts.

Lawton, J. (2000) *The Dying Process: Patient's Experiences of Palliative Care*, London: Routledge.

Liddell, C., Barrett, L. and Bydawell, M. (2005) 'Indigenous Representations of Illness and AIDS in Sub-Sahara Africa', *Social Science and Medicine*, 60: 691–700.

Lifton, R.J. (1979) *The Broken Connection: On Death and the Continuity of Life*, New York: Simon & Schuster.

Lloyd, L. (2004) 'Mortality and Morality: Ageing and the Ethics of Care', *Ageing and Society*, **24**: 235–56.

Lofland, L.H. (1978) *The Craft of Dying: The Modern Face of Death*, Beverley Hills, Calif.: Sage.

Lunney, J.R., Lynn, J., Foley, D.J., Lipson, S. and Guralnik, J.M. (2003) 'Patterns of Functional Decline at the End of Life', *Journal of the American Medical Association*, **289** (18): 2387–92.

Mackinley, E. (2005) 'Death and Spirituality', in M.L. Johnson (ed.), *The Cambridge Handbook of Age and Ageing*, Cambridge: Cambridge University Press, pp. 394–400.

McManners, J. (1985) *Death and the Enlightenment*, Oxford: Oxford University Press.

McNamara, B. (2001) *Fragile Lives: Death, Dying and Care*, Sydney: Allen & Unwin.

Makinen, I.H. (2002) 'Suicide in the New Millennium: Some Sociological Speculations', *Crisis: Journal of Crisis Intervention and Suicide Prevention*, **23** (2): 91–2.

Marcuse, H. (1969) *Eros and Civilization*, London: Abacus.

Marshall, V.W. (1975) 'Socialization for Impending Death in a Retirement Village', *American Journal of Sociology*, **80** (5): 1124–44.

   (1980) *Last Chapters: A Sociology of Ageing and Dying*, Monterey, Calif.: Brooks Cole.

Matthews, S. (1976) 'Old Women and Identity Maintenance: Outwitting the Grim Reaper', in L.H. Lofland (ed.), *Towards a Sociology of Death and Dying*, Beverly Hills, Calif.: Sage, pp. 105–14.

Matthews, S.H. (1979) *The Social World of Old Women: Management of Self-Identity*, Beverly Hills, Calif.: Sage.

Meares, R.A. (1981) 'On Saying Good-Bye Before Death', *Journal of the American Medical Association*, **246** (11): 1227–9.

Moniruzzaman, S. and Andersson, R. (2005) 'Relationship Between Economic Development and Risk of Injuries on Older Adults and the Elderly', *European Journal of Public Health*, **15** (5): 454–8.

Moody, R.A. (1975) *Life After Life*, Covington, Ga.: Mockingbird.

Moss, M.S., Moss, S.Z. and Connor, S.R. (2003) 'Dying in Long Term Care Facilities in the US', in J.S. Katz and S. Peace (eds.), *End of Life in Care Homes: A Palliative Approach*, Oxford: Oxford University Press, pp. 157–73.

Noys, B. (2005) *The Culture of Death*, Oxford: Berg.

Nuland, S.B. (1993) *How We Die*, London: Chatto & Windus.

Osis, K. and Haraldsson, E. (1977) *At the Hour of Death*, Norwalk: Hastings House.

Page, S. and Komaromy, C. (2005) 'Professional Performance: The Case of Expected and Unexpected Death', *Mortality*, **10** (4): 294–307.

Parsons, T., Fox, R.C. and Lidz, V.M. (1974) 'The Gift of Life and Its Reciprocation', in A. Mack (ed.), *Death in American Experience*, New York: Schocken, pp. 1–49.

Pollack, O. (1980) 'The Shadow of Death over Aging', in R. Fox (ed.) *The Social Meaning of Death*. Special issue of *Annals of the American Academy of Political and Social Sciences* **447**: 71–7.

Reichert, C.M., Kelly, V.L. and Macher, A.M. (1985) 'Pathological Features of AIDS', in V.T. Devita, S. Hellman and S.A. Rosenberg (eds.), *AIDS: Etiology, Diagnosis, Treatment and Prevention*, Philadelphia, Pa.: JB Lippincott & Co, pp. 111–60.

Ring, K. (1980) *Life at Death: A Scientific Investigation of the Near-Death Experience*, New York: Coward, McCann & Geohegan.

(1984) *Heading Towards Omega: In Search of the Meaning of the Near-death Experience*, New York: William Morrow and Co.

(1991) 'Amazing Grace: The Near-Death Experience as Compensatory Gift', *Journal of Near-Death Studies*, **10**: 11–39.

Sabom, M.B. (1982) *Recollections of Death: A Medical Investigation*, New York: Harper & Row.

Sagan, L.A. (1987) *The Health of Nations: True Causes of Sickness and Well-Being*, New York: Basic Books.

Saum, L.O. (1975) 'Death in the Popular Mind of Pre-Civil War America', in D.E. Stannard (ed.), *Death in America*, Philadelphia, Pa.: University of Pennsylvania Press, pp. 30–48.

Schoub, B.D. (1999) *AIDS and HIV in Perspective: A Guide to Understanding the Virus and Its Consequences*, Cambridge: Cambridge University Press.

Scoggins, W.F. (1971) 'Growing Old: Death by Instalment Plan', *Life-Threatening Behaviour*, **1** (2): 143–7.

Seale, C. (1995) 'Heroic Death', *Sociology*, **29** (4): 597–613.

(1998) *Constructing Death: The Sociology of Dying and Bereavement*, Cambridge: Cambridge University Press.

Seale, C. and Addington-Hall, J. (1994) 'Euthanasia: Why People Want to Die Earlier', *Social Science and Medicine*, **39** (5): 647–54.

(1995) 'Dying at the Best Time', *Social Science and Medicine*, **40** (5): 589–95.

Sheehy, D.P. (1973) 'Rules for Dying: a Study of Alienation and Patient–Spouse Role Expectations During Terminal Illness', *Dissertation Abstracts International*, **33**: 3777.

Sidell, M. and Komaromy, C. (2003) 'Who Dies in Care Homes for Older People?' in J.S. Katz and S. Peace (eds.), *End of Life in Care Homes: A Palliative Approach*, Oxford: Oxford University Press, pp. 43–57.

Small, N., Froggatt, K. and Downs, M. (2007) *Living and Dying with Dementia*, Oxford: Oxford University Press.

Songwathana, P. and Manderson, L. (2001) 'Stigma and Rejection: Living with AIDS in Southern Thailand', *Medical Anthropology*, **20** (1): 1–23.

Sourvinou-Inwood, S. (1981) 'To Die and Enter the House of Hades: Homer, Before and After', in J. Whaley (ed.), *Mirrors of Mortality: Studies in the Social History of Death*, London: Europa, pp. 15–39.

Strange, J.M. (2005) *Death, Grief and Poverty in Britain, 1870–1914*, Cambridge: Cambridge University Press.

Sudnow, D. (1967) 'Passing On: The Social Organization of Dying', Upper Saddle River, NJ: Prentice-Hall.

Sullivan, M.D. (2002) 'The Illusion of Patient Choice in End of Life Decisions', *American Journal of Geriatric Psychiatry*, **10** (4): 365–72.

Sussman, M.B., Cates, J.N. and Smith, D.T. (1970) *The Family and Inheritance*, New York: Russell Sage.

Sutherland, C. (1992) *Transformed by the Light*, Sydney: Bantam.

Takahashi, L.M. (1998) *Homelessness, AIDS and Stigmatization*, Oxford: Clarendon Press.

Van Gennep, A. (1969) *The Rites of Passage*, Chicago, Ill.: University of Chicago Press.

Van Lommel, P. (2004) 'About the Continuity of Our Consciousness', in C. Machado and D.A. Shewmon (eds.), *Brain Death and Disorders of Consciousness*, New York: Kluwer Academic Publishers, pp. 115–32.

Vidich, A.J. (ed.) (1995) *The New Middle Classes: Lifestyles, Status Claims and Political Orientation*, New York: New York University Press.

Walter, T. (1994) *The Revival of Death*, London: Routledge.

—— (2008) 'The Sociology of Death', *Sociology Compass*, **2**: 10.

Wass, H., Christian, M., Myers, J. and Murphey Jr, M. (1978–9) 'Similarities and Dissimilarities in Attitudes Towards Death in a Population of Older Persons', *Omega*, **9** (4): 337–54.

Watson, W.H. (1976) 'The Ageing Sick and the Near Dead: A Study of Some Distinguishing Characteristics and Social Effects', *Omega*, **7** (2): 115–23.

Weisman, A.D. (1972) *On Dying and Denying: A Psychiatric Study of Terminality*, New York: Behavioural Publishing.

Weisman, A.D. and Hacket, T.P. (1965) 'Predilection to Death', in R. Fulton (ed.), *Death and Identity*, New York: John Wiley, pp. 293–329.

Wimo, A.B., Winblad, B., Aguero-Torres, H. and Von Strauss, E. (2003) 'The Magnitude of Dementia Occurrence in the World', *Alzheimer Disease and Associated Disorders*, **17** (2): 63–7.

Witzel, L. (1975) 'Behaviour of the Dying Patient', *British Medical Journal*, **2**: 81–2.

World Health Organization (2005) *AIDS Epidemic Update 2005*, Geneva: UNAIDS.

Young, M. and Cullen, L. (1996) *A Good Death: Conversations with East Londoners*, London: Routledge.

Zaleski, C. (1987) *Otherworld Journeys: Accounts of Near-Death Experiences in Medieval and Modern Times*, New York: Oxford University Press.

2 | *The dying animal: a perspective from veterinary medicine*

SIRI K. KNUDSEN

Dying and death in animals encompass a wide variety of dissimilar circumstances ranging from the wild animal being eaten alive by a predator to the well-nourished old domestic cat carefully being put to sleep by an overdose of anaesthesia. The same veterinarian that euthanizes the beloved pet may also be involved in culling hundreds of cattle due to disease outbreak that will be buried in the ground by bulldozers. Consequently, the available scientific literature on dying in animals is probably more versatile compared to human studies where the focus is predominantly on chronic, 'slow' dying in hospitalized situations.

The animal and veterinary literature has largely assumed dying as a form of biological collapse. An essential question when discussing dying in any species is at which point of biomorphosis does the dying process start? Cells in the body die even during foetal development, and throughout life the body is in a constant 'battle' between cell growth, cell repair and cell death (e.g. Speakman 2005). However, young, growing or even middle-aged healthy individuals are usually not perceived as 'dying'. It is when the advanced signs of ageing become evident that we are reminded that the final stage of life is approaching. Dying of old age, however, is not that common in the animal kingdom. The majority of animals live under such harsh environmental conditions that they die earlier or they are slaughtered for food or for other purposes before reaching an advanced age. In protected environments, though, animals may reach high age, for instance in the laboratory, zoo or the home, as is the case with an increasing number of domesticated pets in developed countries. Interestingly, these old animals develop many of the typical age-related diseases seen in humans, for instance cancer. However, rather than dying unassisted, many elderly sick pets are euthanized to relieve them from pain and distress.

In this chapter I will focus on two major themes of dying in animals, i.e. criteria of death and the aspects of 'painless' dying. As determination of death in animals is closely linked to the criteria of death in humans I will first give a concise overview on how death is determined and assessed in human medicine.

Criteria for death in humans

Definition of death has changed over the centuries depending on cultural, religious, philosophical and ethical views as well as on technological and biomedical advances. In biology, death was traditionally determined by behavioural signs such as termination of movement and respiration (Knudsen 2005) and by more advanced hallmarks such as *livor, rigor, pallor* and *algor mortis* (discolouration, stiffness, paleness and coldness) and finally putrefaction (Arnold et al. 1968; Lamb 1996). Implementation of manual resuscitation techniques in the seventeenth century seeded growing public confusion as to whether a person was dead or only apparently dead (Bacigalupo et al. 2007). However, it was widely accepted for a long period of time that death equalled the absence of pulse and breathing (the classical cardio-respiratory criteria of death). It was not until medicine advanced significantly during the wars and polio epidemics of the twentieth century that the common views on human death were really challenged. By the 1960s, the mechanical ventilator and advanced CPR techniques had become standard in intensive-care units (ICUs) (Rosengart 2006), and breathing and heartbeat could be restarted and maintained. What used to be 'certain death' was no longer so.

Around 1930 also, the electroencephalography (EEG) and cerebral angiography technologies were developed (Machado et al. 2007). Concisely, EEG records the spontaneous electrical potentials generated by nerve cells in the cerebral cortex through electrodes placed on the scalp. During unconsciousness, there may be a decrease or loss of normal high-frequency rhythms, appearance of abnormal patterns or abolishment of activity (popularly called 'flat-EEG') (Fisch 1991). During the 1950s, several reports appeared of patients on respirators with a flat EEG and no pupillary and pain reflexes as well as comatose patients with collapsed cerebral circulation (e.g. Machado et al. 2007). A milestone was reached when Mollaret and Goulon (1959) described the condition *coma dépassé* ('beyond coma'). However, they did not consider that their patients were dead. Jouvet (1959), though, suggested diagnosing the 'death of the central nervous system' by EEG. Following the publication in 1968 of the report 'A Definition of Irreversible Coma. Report of the Ad Hoc Committee of the Harvard Medical School to Examine the Definition of Brain Death' (Anon. 1968), a new criterion for death was established: *brain death* (BD). To diagnose BD, the Harvard criteria demanded the absence of cerebral responsiveness, induced or spontaneous movement, spontaneous respiration and brainstem reflexes, as well as the presence of a flat-EEG and a test period of twenty-four hours.

In 1981 in the USA, the President's Commission Report (Anon. 1981a) and the following Uniform Determination of Death Act (Anon. 1981b) concluded that death could be declared either due to irreversible cessation of circulatory and respiratory functions *or* all functions of the entire brain, including the brainstem. More detailed clinical guidelines were compiled (Anon. 1981c) recommending that if clinical neurological examination and confirmatory EEG were carried out, BD could be diagnosed after six hours, except in patients with drug intoxication, hypothermia, young age or shock. In the absence of confirmatory EEG, a period of at least twelve hours was recommended. With respect to cardio-respiratory death, the period of observation was set to only a few minutes.

The first nation that adopted BD as a legal definition of death was Finland in 1971 (Randell 2004). Over the past three decades, more than eighty countries have followed, predominantly adopting the principles of the President's Commission (e.g. Zamperetti et al. 2004). In the UK, however, the Conference of Medical Royal Colleges and Their Faculties (Anon. 1976) suggested that BD diagnosis should be based on death of the brainstem and this has been adopted in the legal system of the UK and several of its former colonies (Randell 2004; Baron et al. 2006).

The primary mode of determining BD is clinical neurological examination. Unresponsiveness to painful stimuli and absence of all cranial nerve reflexes have to be demonstrated and the underlying cause of the brain damage has to be known (Hammer and Crippen 2006). Several ancillary procedures to assist the diagnosis exist, but the diagnostic practice varies considerably among different countries (Hammer and Crippen 2006). Apnoea test is mandatory in most countries, but the guidelines on how to perform the test vary (Zamperetti

et al. 2004). All countries that have adopted the 'whole brain' definition recommend the use of EEG (Facco et al. 2002; Wijdicks 2002).
Several have, however, emphasized the technical pitfalls and clinical
limitations when using the EEG (for review, see Knudsen 2005), and
it is not considered a definite indicator of death since it only monitors
the activity in the cerebral cortex and not the brainstem function.
Cerebral angiography is regarded the most reliable method to diagnose BD, since a loss of blood perfusion to the brain is incompatible with sustained brain viability (e.g. Poularas et al. 2006). Also,
various other imaging techniques (CT [computed tomography], PET
[positron emission tomography], MRI [magnetic resonance imaging],
TCD [transcranial doppler]) can be used to assess cerebral circulation
(Hammer and Crippen 2006), but only the conventional angiography is recognized as a confirmatory test by most countries (Randell
2004). However, these tests are expensive and greatly depend on
operator capability and skill and are only applicable in large hospitals
(Baumgartner and Gerstenbrand 2002; Facco et al. 2002).

Despite widespread implementation and the apparent lay community acceptance, BD has constantly been a topic of passionate debate
in the scientific community. During the 1990s, calls were increasingly
made to abandon BD (e.g. Truog and Fackler 1992; Halevy and Brody
1993). In 1995, the Institute of Medicine in the USA concluded that
despite certain theoretical and practical shortcomings, BD diagnosis was so successful and well accepted that there was no need for
any revisions (cited in Bernat 2006). However, BD has continued to
provoke a significant amount of correspondence in the medical literature (e.g. Powner et al. 1996; Youngner et al. 1999; Karakatsanis
and Tsanakas 2002; Wijdicks 2002; Shemie et al. 2003; Truog and
Robinson 2003; Verheijde et al. 2007; Evans 2007; Truog 2007).

Apparently, significant confusion and inconsistency exist among
professionals, in the media and among the general public about the
legal status and medical criteria for determining BD (Harrison and
Botkin 1999; Joffe and Anton 2006; Joffe et al. 2007; Truog 2007).
Youngner et al. (1998) demonstrated that only 35 per cent of the physicians involved with BD patients were able to correctly define and
diagnose the condition. Newspaper headlines of brain-dead patients
being 'kept alive' awaiting decisions on organ donation or court rulings are common, and expressions such as '*life-sustaining* therapy',
'BD *leads* to death', 'BD is a *life-threatening* condition' can be found

in the scientific literature, even in publications that strongly advocate BD (for review, see Zamperetti et al. 2004; Joffe et al. 2007; Whetstine 2007; Truog 2007). The strongest indication that the legislative status of BD is not comprehended by society may be that BD cases are almost exclusively referred to as 'patients', 'individuals' or 'donors' but very seldom as 'corpses'. These examples lead us to the kernel of the debate: does BD equal death?

The President's Commission proposed that when the brain is dead there is a 'loss of integrated control of the organism' and the body is only a rapidly disintegrating collection of organs with no capacity to work 'as a whole' (Anon. 1981b). This rationale has been the most widely accepted view among BD proponents (for review, see, for example, Zamperetti et al. 2004; Bernat 2006). There seems to be general agreement that BD is an extremely advanced point of no return, and there are no documented cases where a person who has been diagnosed with BD has ever regained any degree of consciousness. After initiation of BD, dramatic physiological events usually follow if no supportive therapy is given, including cardiac arrest and organ failure. In the earliest reports, cardiac arrest ensued quickly (minutes or hours) after the initial insult (e.g. Randell 2004). However, reports of BD cases who do not develop cardiac collapse and where biological integration have been upheld for weeks, months and even years if provided with the necessary support therapy have later been published (Shewmon 1998; Youngner et al. 1999; Baumgartner and Gerstenbrand 2002; Shemie 2007). BD patients have even successfully gestated foetuses to term (Powner and Bernstein 2003). The 'whole-brain' criterion does not define how much of the neuron population that has to die in order to diagnose BD (e.g. Bernat 2006), and it has been questioned as to why so much emphasis is placed on brainstem reflexes while neuro-endocrine and autonomic functions, important for biological survival, are ignored (Truog and Robinson 2003; Zamperetti et al. 2004; Truog 2007). Several have strongly advocated that the BD concept confuses the fact that a person is dying with the claim that he or she is already dead (e.g. Shewmon 2001; Truog and Robinson 2003; Zamperetti et al. 2004; Joffe et al. 2007; Serani-Merlo 2007; Whetstine 2007).

Only a year before the publication of the Harvard report, the first successful heart transplantation was performed, and kidney transplantations had been carried out since the mid-1950s. The concept of BD is viewed by some as created solely for utilitarian purposes (e.g. Taylor 1997; Kerridge et al. 2002; Evans 2007), and analyses of the Harvard deliberation have demonstrated that the transplant lobbies exerted significant influence (for review, see Kellehear 2008). Though most scientists seem to acknowledge that the growing transplantation practice in the 1950s–1960s led to added relevance of BD, many argue that the prime driving force in formulating the BD concept was concerns on what to do with the unfortunate patients rather than 'to get organs' (e.g. Belkin 2003; Machado 2003; Randell 2004; Zamperetti et al. 2004; Machado et al. 2007). As Truog (2007) points out, withdrawal of ventilation was regarded homicide in 1968, and a definition of BD as death was needed in order to withdraw therapy. However, there have been significant changes in end-of-life care since 1968. According to Truog (2007), 60–90 per cent of deaths in ICUs in the USA today are as the result of life-support withdrawal. Therefore, the definition of BD as death now has highest relevance for organ transplantation, as a wildly implemented principle has been the 'dead donor rule', which aroused after doubts were cast in the 1960s whether donors were in fact dead (e.g. Truog and Miller 2008). Recently, the option to use organs harvested from 'non-heart-beating donors' has emerged (e.g. Verheijde et al. 2007). This has ignited the debate in the scientific community and calls are again increasing to abandon the current definitions of human death (Evans 2007; Joffe et al. 2007; Shemie 2007; Truog 2007; Verheijde et al. 2007; Whetstine 2007; Bernat 2008; Truog and Miller 2008; Veatch 2008).

Determination and evaluation of death in domestic animals

Evaluation of death in domestic animals in veterinary practice usually takes place during companion and laboratory animal euthanasia and livestock slaughtering. No official criteria of death, like those in humans, have been formulated for animals, except those adopted by the International Whaling Commission for whales (for review, see Knudsen 2005). The American Veterinary Medical Association provides a much generalized guideline: 'death must be confirmed by examining the animal for cessation of vital signs, and consideration given to the animal species and methods of euthanasia when determining the criteria for confirming death' (AVMA 2007).

Pet and laboratory animal euthanasia

Resorting to euthanasia in animals with diseases that seriously and irreversibly compromise the quality of their lives is generally accepted in veterinary medicine. However, as advanced treatment alternatives are becoming more available, particularly in small-animal practice, the balance of the benefits of keeping the animal alive versus the decreasing quality of life is constantly challenged (Coombes 2005; Passantino et al. 2006; Milani 2008). Also, there is increasing concern over 'convenience euthanasia', i.e. owners who request euthanasia of unwanted but healthy animals (Rollin 2003; Manette 2004; Morgan and McDonald 2007).

In the veterinary clinics, pet animals such as cats and dogs are almost exclusively euthanized pharmaceutically by an overdose of intravenously administered barbiturate, which depresses the central nervous system in descending order beginning with the cerebral cortex, with loss of consciousness progressing to anaesthesia (AVMA 2007). Vocalization, muscle twitches and terminal gasps may occur in unconscious animals as well as urination and defecation in the agonal phase. The anaesthesia progresses to apnoea, followed by cardiac arrest, and death is almost exclusively determined using cardiorespiratory criteria.

Laboratory rodents are either euthanized in the same way as pets, or carbon dioxide (CO_2), cervical dislocation or decapitation are used. A more detailed description of CO_2 is provided below in the section on slaughter animals. Cervical dislocation is widely used in small rodents. The technique is also applied during mass slaughter of poultry (AVMA 2007). Decapitation is used to euthanize rodents in research settings, in particular to obtain anatomically undamaged brain tissue (AVMA 2007). Both methods lead to rapid (5–20 seconds) disruption of cortical function in mice and rats as measured by EEG and evoked responses (ERs) (Vanderwolf et al. 1988; Cartner et al. 2007).

Slaughter animals

Due to increased awareness of problems in the slaughter industry, the effect of different slaughter techniques was studied extensively by means of EEG and ERs (somatosensory evoked potential [SEP] and visual evoked potential [VEP]) in ruminants, pigs and poultry during the 1980–90s (for review, see Knudsen 2005). At slaughter, the moment of death is regarded as being less important than the moment of insensibility, i.e. when the animal no longer responds to noxious stimuli. When disregarding some types of ritual slaughter (see below), industrial slaughter in most countries consists of a two-step process: stunning and bleeding. The EC Council Directive 93/119 (Anon. 1993) defines stunning as 'Any process which, when applied to an animal, causes immediate loss of consciousness which lasts until death.' Regardless of stunning method, bleeding before further carcass processing is mandatory in all European countries (Anon. 1993). Blackmore and Delany (1988) defined technical death of slaughter animals as 'irreversible insensibility due to cerebral anoxia, usually due to severance of both common carotid arteries or the vessels from which they arise'. Interestingly though, in a recent report by the European Food Safety Authority (EFSA 2004: 43, 'Determination of Death'), reference was made to a principle in UK law on animal experimentation, stating that 'an animal shall be regarded as continuing to live until the permanent cessation of circulation or the destruction of its brain' (Anon. 1986a). It is indicated in the EFSA report that this UK principle has been implemented from the EU Council directive that regulates animal experimentation (Anon. 1986b), but this principle cannot be found in that directive. However, the EFSA report extrapolates the UK principle to slaughter without any further scientific references and concludes, 'Therefore, from slaughter or killing point of view, death can be recognized from the absence of cardiac activity (e.g. pulse or heart beat) when bleeding has ceased or destruction of brain' and 'Brain death in animals can be recognized from the absence of brain stem reflexes' (EFSA 2004). However, as far as I know, the concept of 'brain death' has not been implemented in any current slaughter regulations and has no practical application as slaughter animals are not consider dead until they have been bled (Anon. 1993). The EC directive of 1993 will be revised in the nearest future. Whether BD then will be legally recognized as death in slaughter animals remains to be seen. Taking into account that stunning methods, which ideally may cause death due to severe brain damage, in practice often fail to do so (see below), bleeding will likely still be obligatory in the slaughter industry and, in practice, exsanguinations will be the definition of death.

Some stunning methods only induce temporary loss of consciousness (e.g. CO_2 and electricity), and stunned animals have the potential to regain normal brain and bodily functions if not bled rapidly. Sticking should therefore be performed quickly after the stun, and, in this process, the major blood vessels supplying oxygenated blood to the brain must be severed to ensure rapid onset of death (EFSA 2004). Cattle and sheep are commonly bled by cutting the common carotid arteries and the external jugular veins. Pigs are usually bled by chest sticking with incision of the major blood vessels that arise from the heart. Poultry are either neck-cut or decapitated.

Under the 1993 EC directive on slaughter (Anon. 1993), member states have retained the right to authorize religious slaughter (halal and kosher) without pre-stunning in their own territory. Many, including France, Germany and the UK allow religious slaughter without stunning. In the Scandinavian countries, though, slaughter without stunning is forbidden, and no exception is given for ritual slaughter. In cattle, Daly et al. (1988) found that after *Shechita* slaughter (neck cutting without previous stunning), spontaneous brain activity persisted for an average of 75 seconds (range 19–113 seconds) and mean time to SEP abolishment was 77 seconds (range 32–126 seconds). After chest sticking of pigs, the time to loss of brain responsiveness was found to range between 14 and 23 seconds (mean 18), while isoelectric electrocorticogram (ECoG) developed within 22–30 seconds (Wotton and Gregory 1986).

Electrical stunning is widely used in poultry, pigs and sheep. In red-meat animals (e.g. ruminants and pigs), the electrodes are placed on either side of the head (transcranial application), while in poultry head-to-body application is used (commonly in electrified water baths). In red-meat animals, seizure activity is produced, recognized by tonic-clonic convulsions and a great increase in the EEG magnitude and frequency, which are interpreted as incompatible with a coherent brain function based on anecdotal studies of human generalized seizures. In poultry, electrical stunning produces only low-frequency polyspike EEG activity, which is not necessarily associated with unconsciousness, and a current magnitude that prevents the brain from responding to an external applied stimulus is therefore recommended (Gregory and Wotton 1987; Gregory 1991; EFSA 2004). As reviewed in Knudsen (2005), the clinical signs of adequate electrical stunning are that the animal should immediately collapse and go rigid (tonic). In red-meat animals, the hind legs are flexed under the body, the forelegs initially become stiff but may straighten out, the eyes become fixed, the head bends backwards and respiration should stop. After 15–20 seconds, a clonic (kicking) phase sets in, and the animal will gradually relax and make walking movements with its legs. Bleeding should take place before the clonic phase sets in. When poultry is stunned with electricity, the neck will be arched, the head directed vertically and rapid body tremors will usually appear in the tonic phase. Additionally, the eyes will be open, the wings held close to the body and the legs will be rigidly extended.

In ruminants and horses, the most widely used stunning method is the captive bolt pistol, which is also used on pigs and poultry. Captive bolt guns are powered by gunpowder or compressed air, and there are two types available: penetrating and non-penetrating. The non-penetrating fires a mushroom-headed blunt bolt causing concussion at impact with the skull, while the penetrating fires a sharp-rimmed bolt design to penetrate and cause damage deep into the brain (e.g. Daly and Whittington 1989; Finnie 1993; Finnie et al. 2002). Both types are normally fired on the forehead. However, if the presence of horns prevents frontal stunning, sheep and goats may be shot from behind using the penetrating bolt, but this is less effective and should there-fore be followed by immediately bleeding (EFSA 2004). Adequate restraint is important to ensure proper placement of the captive bolt, and it may therefore be difficult to apply in field conditions outside the slaughterhouse (EFSA 2004).

The non-penetrating captive bolt is permitted for use not only in calves and small ruminants but also in adult cattle and horses in some countries (AVMA 2007). In other countries, including Norway, this method is not allowed during slaughter (Anon. 1995). Scientific investigations of the effectiveness of this method are scarce. Finnie (1995) reported 100 per cent immediate unconsciousness in twelve adult cattle based on behavioural observations and the neurotrauma produced. Several studies of calves have shown approximately 80 per cent immediate effect and that the duration of unconsciousness is relatively short based on EEG and behavioural observations (for review, see EFSA 2004). In a field study of about 1,200 cattle, it was reported that 20–30 per cent of the animals needed re-stunning (Moje 2003, cited in EFSA 2004). In lambs, Finnie (2000) reported that the efficiency of the method equalled the penetrating captive bolt, but no data are available for adult sheep. EFSA does not recognize the non-penetrating captive bolt as an independent killing method and recommends that bleeding should start within 12 seconds (EFSA 2004).

EFSA has also concluded that the *penetrating* captive bolt should not be used as a sole method of killing horses (EFSA 2004). AVMA (2007), though, consider it an acceptable method. However, no peer-reviewed scientific publications are available on the use of captive bolt pistols in horses to support either view. Regardless, EFSA (2004) states, 'When performed correctly, captive bolt stunning is an effective method of stunning horses and loss of consciousness is immediate.'

The only study apparently available on the use of penetrating captive bolt in pigs demonstrated that it causes much less brain damage in this species compared to sheep (Finnie 2003), but both EFSA and AVMA endorse the use of the method in pigs (EFSA 2004; AVMA 2007).

The penetrating captive bolt is the most commonly used method for cattle. In calves it produces immediate delta and theta waves tending to a flat-EEG, and it is assumed that the animal is unconscious by analogy to similar EEG changes described in man (Lambooy and Spanjaard 1981; Blackmore and Newhook 1982). In adult cattle, Daly et al. (1988) found that ERs were immediately abolished after penetrating captive bolt stunning, while EEG delta waves occurred after 4–17 seconds developing in to a flat-EEG after 21–58 seconds in 37 per cent of the animals, while in the remaining animals flat-EEG did not develop until after bleeding started (after 60 seconds). Despite the potential efficiency of penetrating captive bolt stunning, practical information shows that mis-stuns occur relatively frequently (EFSA 2004). If the site of stunning is more than 4–6 centimetres from the ideal position, the stunning efficiency is reduced by 60 per cent (Daly 1987). Grandin (1998) reported that of eleven federally inspected beef plants in the USA, only four were able to render 95 per cent of the cattle insensible with a single shot. In a UK study, it was reported that as many as 53 per cent of young bulls had to be re-shot twice or more before being declared unconscious (Daly and Whittington 1992).

Indicators of successful captive bolt stunning are that the animal should immediately collapse to the floor with its hind legs flexed into the body. It may also draw in its forelegs, but they straighten after a short period of time (Blackmore and Delany 1988). The animal must not show normal rhythmic breathing. The muscles of the body are contracted, the back is usually arched, and kicking may be seen after the initial muscle contraction phase. Good stunning produces relaxation of the jaw and, consequently, the tongue will hang out when the animal is hoisted (Gregory 1991). The head should be completely relaxed, the ears should drop and the eyeballs have a fixed position. The animal should not react to noxious stimuli (Grandin 1980).

The rapid depressant, analgesic and anaesthetic effects of CO_2 gas are well established (AVMA 2007), and the method is commonly used in pig and poultry slaughter. Inhalation of CO_2 induces respiratory and metabolic acidosis and hence neuronal inhibitory and anaesthetic effects. Signs of effective CO_2 stunning are similar to the traditional reflexes used to judge the depth of surgical anaesthesia. The duration of unconsciousness depends upon the duration of exposure. Prolonged exposure to high concentrations (greater than 70 per cent) causes death (EFSA 2004). In the slaughterhouse, pigs are usually taken into a chamber filled with 70–80 per cent CO_2 and kept there for 45–60 seconds (Anon. 1993, 1995). In a field study, Nowak (2002, cited in EFSA 2004) found that after exposure to 80 per cent CO_2 for 72 seconds, 83 per cent of the pigs showed a positive corneal reflex, 9 per cent reacted to painful stimuli, and EEG recordings indicated latent consciousness. To increase the concentration and exposure time (greater than 90 per cent and 2–3 minutes, respectively) have been suggested to improve CO_2 stunning of pigs (EFSA 2004). However, the acceptability of this method on welfare grounds will likely still be controversial because unconsciousness is not induced immediately and the animals may have to endure respiratory distress for a certain time period (15–30 seconds in 80 per cent CO_2) prior to the loss of brain responsiveness (for review, see EFSA 2004). Also, the adverse effects of initial exposure and subsequent inhalation of CO_2 have been demonstrated in many species of animals, including humans. In laboratory rats and mice, CO_2 even at 20 per cent is aversive (Leach et al. 2001).

According to the EFSA (2004), a disconcerting fact is that the significance of various kinds of spinal reflexes and automatisms in stunned slaughter animals has not been completely elucidated. Pedal reflexes have been observed for more than two and five minutes after electrical stunning in sheep and cattle respectively (Blackmore and Newhook 1982). Palpebral reflexes, which are not under cortical control, have been recorded for up to 200 seconds in sheep after exsanguination, and, in the case of ineffective electrical stunning, the reflex can be inhibited while the cerebral cortex is still functional (Blackmore and Delany 1988). The presence of a corneal reflex indicates physiological brainstem activity and not cortical function, and, consequently, it does not accurately distinguish between consciousness and unconsciousness (Anil 1991) and it has been evoked in calves for up to 44 seconds after the EEG has become iso-electric (Blackmore and Delany 1988). Anil and McKinstry (1991) reported that as corneal reflexes were recorded although there were no concomitant ERs, brainstem reflexes should not be relied on as indices of recovery in electrically stunned sheep.

Registration of respiration or rhythmic breathing is widely used as a criterion to judge the effect of stunning in slaughter plants. However, stunned animals may exhibit periodic respiratory gaps, which have been recorded in cattle and sheep for up to six minutes (Blackmore and Delany 1988). Walking movements are usually considered as a sign of sensibility, but this is not an absolute criterion. It may be seen even when the head has been separated from the body ('the running headless chicken'), and muscular contractions, spasms and tremors are common long after animals have been bled and died (Knudsen 2005).

As the testing of insensibility in stunned animals using indirect effects, such as behavioural signs and reflexes, is a challenge in practice, much effort in industrialized slaughter plants is put into inspection and control of the stunning gears and operator routines (e.g. Knudsen 2005). The efficiency demands during industrialized slaughter do not allow for the use of advanced monitoring systems like EEG to evaluate insensibility and death in practice. And, as for humans, the data from animal EEG recordings have limitations and require some degree of subjective evaluation, but results obtained in these studies have served as guidelines to change stunning procedure requirements in recent decades. However, considerable problems exist in many slaughter plants (e.g. Grandin 1998), and data on stunning efficiency are still scarce or lacking for several species and methods (EFSA 2004).

Wildlife

In the wild, there are many reasons why an animal might die before it gets a chance to experience senescence (starvation, predation, disease, trauma, hunting, etc.). For example, the life expectancy of a bank vole (*Myodes glareolus*) in the wild is about two to six months, while in captivity these voles can live up to forty months (Speakman

2005). However, early stages of ageing may contribute to death in animals living in unprotected environments. If an animal loses a bit of its speed, predators will more easily seize it, or, if it is a predator, it may become a less successful hunter.

In biology, terms such as population 'fluctuation' and 'dynamics' are often used to describe events that literally mean that thousands of animals may die within a restricted time period due to environmental factors. When disregarding research on mortality rates and causes of death, little scientific attention has been given to dying in wildlife.

Hunting is a widespread practice globally. In the USA alone, 12.5 million people hunted more than 3.3 million animals in 2005 (Anon. 2006). There is an abundance of popular literature on hunting. However, when disregarding some types of whaling activities and the use of kill-traps (for review, see Knudsen 2005), surprisingly little scientific data exist regarding studies of the efficiency of different methods and weapons in use, including evaluation of the moment of insensibility and death as well as other animal-welfare concerns in connection with hunting.

One phenomenon related to dying in wildlife has, however, intrigued scientists for decades, namely 'death feigning', also known as tonic immobility (TI), which is a well-characterized fear response occurring during some prey–predator confrontations (e.g. Misslin 2003). TI has been observed in a wide class of animal species ranging from arthropods, crustaceans, fish, amphibians, reptiles, birds and mammals (e.g. Gallup 1974; Kaufman and Rovee-Collier 1978; Leite-Panissi et al. 2006; Hazard et al. 2008; Miyatake et al. 2008). Ratner (1967) described TI as a terminal defensive reaction that the animal turns to after going through a sequence of anti-predator defence behaviours: 'freeze, flight, fight and feign', where each step is elicited by the prey's perceived decreasing distance to the predator.

The TI response can last from seconds to hours and is characterized by the temporary suppression of the righting response, muscular tension (tonic immobility), unresponsiveness to external stimuli, including noxious ones (i.e. analgesia), but sustained awareness. Vocalization is typically depressed. In addition, Parkinson-like tremors in the extremities, changes in EEG, heart rate, respiration and core temperature have been documented (Gallup 1974; Fleischmann and Urca 1988; Leite-Panissi et al. 2006; Souza Da Silva and Menescal 2006). Some species add special 'cadaverous effects' such as defecating and releasing strong odours (Ruxton et al. 2004; Honma et al. 2006).

TI is usually reversible, but fatalities may occur. Gallup (1974) observed that death-feigning chickens occasionally suddenly collapsed and died, providing substance to the expression 'to be scared to death' (Moskowitz 2004). Death feigning may also be regarded as an integrated part of the dying process as the likelihood of getting killed while exhibiting this last resource of anti-predator defence mechanism is substantial (Sergeant and Eberhardt 1975).

TI is believed to have evolved as an anti-predator defence mechanism as some predators are triggered by movement and lose interest if their prey becomes motionless (e.g. Gallup 1974; Valance et al. 2008). However, this cannot provide a full explanation of the diversity of this reaction so widely dispersed in the animal kingdom. Sergeant and Eberhardt (1975) noted that the survival success of death-feigning ducks predated on by red foxes was largely due to the relatively gentle handling by the foxes, and they concluded that the death-feigning strategy would not function well against predators that kill or cripple more effectively. Further, death feigning is not only an anti-predator behaviour. It has been reported also *in predators* using it as a hunting strategy in order to lurk closer to the prey (Tobbler 2005).

Large wounds usually elicit major pain responses. The analgesia that is activated during TI (e.g. Souza Da Silva and Menescal 2006) likely has adaptive value benefiting the survival of the individual as the animal may endure a significant level of pain if the immobility itself fails to stop the predatory attack (Misslin 2003). In the death-feigning ducks previously mentioned, feathers were pulled out, neck musculature was mouthed and some fowls had their feet chewed off while still being alive but immobile (Sergeant and Eberhardt 1975). This analgesia likely also benefits those individuals that do not survive predator attack as the dying process will be less painful. However, this has no adaptive value as it does not benefit survival, but the pain relief may at least be viewed as a 'merciful' side effect for the dying animal.

Concluding reflections

The history of veterinary medicine is closely tied to the development of human medicine. Studies of animals have contributed significantly to our understanding of the basic biological and physiological mechanisms behind the dying process. For instance, the understanding of systemic blood circulation was based on vivisection of animals in the seventeenth century (Palladino and Noordergraaf 2000). The discovery of respiratory gas exchange in mammals, blood pressure and spinal reflexes were all based on animal studies in the 1700s, and studies of frogs in the 1920s provided new evidence on the function of neurons and neural communication (e.g. Loewi 1957; Felts 1977; Buchholz and Schoeller 2004). In modern times, most complex surgical operations (including organ-transplant techniques) as well as other advances in biomedicine have originated from animal studies.

Prior to the major advances in human medicine during the twentieth century, basically the same criteria of death were applied for both animals and humans, i.e. termination of movement and respiration, absence of heartbeat and pulse, and the gradual physical changes that occur in the dead body shortly after death having supervened (coldness, colour change, etc.). Today, these relatively simple criteria are still the most widely applied to assess death in animals. In recent decades, medical progress and law changes have opened some new possibilities for defining and diagnosing death in human beings. The introduction of the clinical state 'brain death' has led physicians now to pronounce death in an artificially ventilated body that looks alive, i.e. the heart still beats, the body is warm and most of the organs besides the brain function normally. Consequently, the modern medical literature centres to a large degree around dying in controlled circumstances. However, a large proportion of the world's people still leave life from what can be termed 'natural causes' often outside hospitals and without a physician present. Consequently, relatives as well as medical officers that have to issue death certificates normally diagnose death using the same simple criteria that are applied for all other species.

Acknowledgement

This chapter is based on the review article 'A Review of the Criteria Used to Assess Insensibility and Death in Hunted Whales Compared to Other Species', *The Veterinary Journal* (2005) 169: 42–59, published by Elsevier.

References

Anil, M. H. (1991) 'Studies on Return of Physical Reflexes in Pigs Following Electrical Stunning', *Meat Science*, **30** (1): 13–21.

Anil, M.H. and McKinstry, J.L. (1991) 'Reflexes and Loss of Sensibility Following Head-to-Back Electrical Stunning in Sheep', *Veterinary Record*, **128** (5): 106–7.

Anon. (1968) 'A Definition of Irreversible Coma. Report of the Ad Hoc Committee of the Harvard Medical School to Examine the Definition of Brain Death', *Journal of the American Medical Association*, **205** (6): 337–40.

— (1976) 'Diagnosis of Brain Death: Statement Issued by the Honorary Secretary of the Conference of Medical Royal Colleges and Their Faculties in the United Kingdom on 11 October 1976', *British Medical Journal*, **2** (6045): 1187–8.

— (1981a) *President's Commission for the Study of Ethical Problems in Medicine and Biomedical and Behavioral Research. Defining Death: A Report on the Medical, Legal, and Ethical Issues in the Determination of Death*, Washington, DC: US Government Printing Office.

— (1981b) *Uniform Determination of Death Act*, Chicago, Ill.: National Conference of Commissioners on Uniform State Laws.

— (1981c) 'Guidelines for the Determination of Death: Report of the Medical Consultants on the Diagnosis of Death to the President's Commission for the Study of Ethical Problems in Medicine and Biomedical and Behavioral Research', *Journal of the American Medical Association*, **246** (19): 2184–6.

— (1986a) *Animals (Scientific Procedures) Act 1986*, London: The Stationary Office. Available online at www.archive.official-documents.co.uk/document/hoc/321/321-xa.htm.

— (1986b) *European Council Directive 86/609/EEC of 24 November 1986 on the Approximation of Laws, Regulations and Administrative Provisions of the Member States Regarding the Protection of Animals Used for Experimental and Other Scientific Purposes*. Available online at http://europa.eu.int/eur-lex.

— (1993) *Council Directive on the Protection of Animals at the Time of Killing*. European Community. Council Directive 93/119/EC. Available online at http://europa.eu.int/eur-lex.

— (1995) *Forskrift om dyrevern i slakterier*. FOR 1995–08–28 Nr. 775, Ministry of Agriculture, Norway (in Norwegian).

— (2006) *National Survey of Fishing, Hunting, and Wildlife Associated Recreation*. US Department of the Interior, Fish, and Wildlife Service and US Department of Commerce, US Census Bureau.

Arnold, J.D., Zimmerman, T.F. and Martin, D.C. (1968) 'Public Attitudes and the Diagnosis of Death', *Journal of the American Medical Association*, **206** (9): 1949–62.

AVMA (American Veterinary Medical Association) (2007) *Guidelines on Euthanasia*, Schaumburg, Ill.: AVMA.

Bacigalupo, F., Huerta, D. and Siegmund, M.R. (2007) 'The Debate About Death: An Imperishable Discussion?' *Biological Research*, **40** (4): 523–34.

Baron, L.B., Shemie, S.D., Teitelbaum, J. and Doig, C.J. (2006) 'Brief Review: History, Concept and Controversies in the Neurological Determination of Death', *Canadian Journal of Anesthesia*, **53** (6): 602–8.

Baumgartner, H. and Gerstenbrand, F. (2002) 'Diagnosing Brain Death Without a Neurologist: Simple Criteria and Training Are Needed for the Non-Neurologist in Many Countries', *British Medical Journal*, **324** (7352): 1471–2.

Belkin, G.S. (2003) 'Brain Death and the Historical Understanding of Bioethics', *Journal of the History of Medicine and Allied Sciences*, **58** (3): 325–61.

Bernat, J.L. (2006) 'The Whole-Brain Concept of Death Remains Optimum Public Policy', *Journal of Law, Medicine and Ethics*, **34** (1): 35–43.

(2008) 'The Boundaries of Organ Donation After Circulatory Death', *The New England Journal of Medicine*, **359** (7): 669–71.

Blackmore, D.K. and Delany, M.W. (1988) *Slaughter of Stock: A Practical Review and Guide*, Manawatu: Massey University.

Blackmore, D.K. and Newhook, J.C. (1982) 'Electroencephalographic Studies of Stunning and Slaughter of Sheep and Calves: Part 3 – The Duration of Insensibility Induced by Electrical Stunning in Sheep and Calves', *Meat Science*, **7** (1): 19–28.

Buchholz, A.C. and Schoeller, D.A. (2004) 'Is a Calorie a Calorie?' *The American Journal of Clinical Nutrition*, **79** (5): 899S–906S.

Cartner, S.C., Barlow, S.C. and Ness, T.J. (2007) 'Loss of Cortical Function in Mice After Decapitation, Cervical Dislocation, Potassium Chloride Injection, and CO2 Inhalation', *Comparative Medicine*, **57** (6): 570–3.

Coombes, R. (2005) 'Do Vets and Doctors Face Similar Ethical Challenges?' *British Medical Journal*, **331** (7527): 1227.

Daly, C.C. (1987) 'Concussion Stunning in Red-Meat Species', *Proceedings of the EEC Seminar on Pre-Slaughter Stunning of Food Animals. European Conference on the Protection of Farm Animals*, Horsham, 2–3 June.

Daly, C.C. and Whittington, P.E. (1989) 'Investigations into the Principal Determinants of Effective Captive Bolt Stunning of Sheep', *Research in Veterinary Science*, **46** (3): 406–8.

(1992) *Survey of Captive Bolt Stunning in British Abattoirs*, Horsham: RSPCA.

Daly, C.C., Kallweit, E. and Ellendorf, F. (1988) 'Cortical Function in Cattle During Slaughter: Conventional Captive Bolt Stunning Followed by Exsanguination Compared with Shechita Slaughter', *Veterinary Record*, **122** (14): 325–9.

EFSA (European Food Standards Agency) (2004) *Welfare Aspects of Animal Stunning and Killing Methods*. Scientific Report of the Scientific Panel for Animal Health and Welfare. EFSA-AHAW/04–027.

Evans, D.W. (2007) 'Seeking an Ethical and Legal Way of Procuring Transplantable Organs from the Dying Without Further Attempts to Redefine Human Death', *Philosophy, Ethics, and Humanities in Medicine*, **2**: 11.

Facco, E., Munari, M., Gallo, F., Volpin, S.M., Behr, A.U., Baratto, F. and Giron, G.P. (2002) 'Role of Short Latency Evoked Potentials in the Diagnosis of Brain Death', *Clinical Neurophysiology*, **113** (11): 1855–66.

Felts, J.H. (1977) 'Stephen Hales and the Measurement of Blood Pressure', *North Carolina Medical Journal*, **38** (10): 602–3.

Finnie, J.W. (1993) 'Brain Damage Caused by a Captive Bolt Pistol', *Journal of Comparative Pathology*, **109** (3): 253–8.

—— (1995) 'Neuropathological Changes Produced by Non-Penetrating Percussive Captive Bolt Stunning of Cattle', *New Zealand Veterinary Journal*, **43** (5): 183–5.

—— (2000) 'Evaluation of Brain Damage Resulting from Penetrating and Non-Penetrating Captive Bolt Stunning Using Lambs', *Australian Veterinary Journal*, **78** (11): 775–8.

—— (2003) 'Brain Damage in Pigs Produced by Impact with a Non-Penetrating Captive Bolt Pistol', *Australian Veterinary Journal*, **81** (3): 153–5.

Finnie, J.W., Manavis, J., Blumbergs, P.C. and Summersides, G.E. (2002) 'Brain Damage in Sheep from Penetrating Captive Bolt Stunning', *Australian Veterinary Journal*, **80** (1–2): 67–9.

Fisch, B.J. (ed.) (1991) *Spehlmann's EEG Primer*, Amsterdam: Elsevier.

Fleischmann, A. and Urca, G. (1988) 'Clip-Induced Analgesia and Immobility in the Mouse: Pharmacological Characterization', *Neuropharmacology*, **27** (6): 641–8.

Gallup, G.G. (1974) 'Animal Hypnosis: Factual Status of a Fictional Concept', *Psychological Bulletin*, **81** (11): 836–53.

Gallup, G.G. and Maser, J.D. (1977) 'Tonic Immobility: Evolutionary Underpinnings of Human Catalepsy and Catatonia', in M.E.P. Seligman (ed.), *Psychopathology: Experimental Models*, New York: W.H. Freeman, pp. 334–57.

Grandin, T. (1980) 'Mechanical, Electrical and Anaesthetic Stunning Methods for Livestock', *International Journal for the Study of Animal Problems*, **1**: 242–63.

—— (1998) 'Objective Scoring of Animal Handling and Stunning Practices at Slaughter Plants', *Journal of the American Veterinary Medicine Association*, **212** (1): 36–9.

Gregory, N.G. (1991) 'Humane Slaughter', *Outlook on Agriculture*, **20** (2): 95–101.

—— (1998) *Animal Welfare and Meat Science*, Wallingford: CABI Publishing.

Gregory, N.G. and Wotton, S.B. (1987) 'Effect of Electrical Stunning on the Electroencephalogram in Chickens', *British Veterinary Journal*, **143** (2): 175–83.

—— (1988) 'Turkey Slaughtering Procedures: Time to Loss of Brain Responsiveness After Exsanguination or Cardiac Arrest', *Research in Veterinary Science*, **44** (2): 183–5.

Halevy, A. and Brody, B. (1993) 'Brain Death: Reconciling Definitions, Criteria and Tests', *Annals of Internal Medicine*, **119** (6): 519–25.

Hammer, M.D. and Crippen, D. (2006) 'Brain Death and Withdrawal of Support', *The Surgical Clinics of North America*, **86** (6): 1541–51.

Harrison, A.M. and Botkin, J.R. (1999) 'Can Pediatricians Define and Apply the Concept of Brain Death?' *Pediatrics*, **103** (6): E82.

Hazard, D., Couty, M., Richard, S. and Guémené, D. (2008) 'Intensity and Duration of Corticosterone Response to Stressful Situations in Japanese Quail Divergently Selected for Tonic Immobility', *General and Comparative Endocrinology*, **155** (2): 288–97.

Honma, A., Oku, S. and Nishida, T. (2006) 'Adaptive Significance of Death Feigning Posture as a Specialized Inducible Defence Against Gape-Limited Predators', *Proceedings of the Royal Society*, **B 273** (1594): 1631–6.

Joffe, A.R. (2007) 'The ethics of donation and transplantation: are definitions of death being distorted for organ transplantation?', *Philosophy, Ethics and Humanities in Medicine*, **2**: 28.

Joffe, A.R. and Anton, N. (2006) 'Brain Death: Understanding of the Conceptual Basis by Pediatric Intensivists in Canada', *Archives of Pediatrics and Adolescent Medicine*, **160** (7): 747–52.

Joffe, A.R., Anton, N. and Metha, V. (2007) 'A Survey to Determine the Understanding of the Conceptual Basis and Diagnostic Tests Used for Brain Death by Neurosurgeons in Canada', *Neurosurgery*, **61** (5): 1039–47.

Jouvet, M. (1959) 'Diagnostic électrosouscorticographique de la mort du system nerveux central au cours de certains comas', *Electroencephalography and Clinical Neurophysiology*, **3**: 52–3.

Karakatsanis, K.G. and Tsanakas, J.N. (2002) 'A Critique on the Concept of "Brain Death"', *Issues in Law and Medicine*, **18** (2): 127–41.

Kaufman, L.W. and Rovee-Collier, (1978) 'Arousal-Induced Changes in the Amplitude of Death Feigning and Periodicity', *Physiology and Behavior*, 20 (4): 453–8.

Kellehear, A. (2008) 'Dying as a Social Relationship: A Sociological Review of Debates on the Determination of Death', *Social Science and Medicine*, **66** (7): 1533–44.

Kerridge, H., Saul, P., Lowe, M., McPhee, J. and Williams, D. (2002) 'Death, Dying and Donation: Organ Transplantation and the Diagnosis of Death', *Journal of Medical Ethics*, **28** (2): 89–94.

Knudsen, S.K. (2005) 'A Review of the Criteria Used to Assess Insensibility and Death in Hunted Whales Compared to Other Species', *The Veterinary Journal*, **169** (1): 42–59.

Lamb, D. (1996) *Death, Brain Death and Ethics*, Aldershot: Avebury.

Lambooy, E. and Spanjaard, E. (1981) 'Effect of the Shooting Position on the Stunning of Calves by Captive Bolt', *Veterinary Record*, **109** (16): 359–61.

Leach, M.C., Bowell, V.A., Allan, T.F. and Morton, D.B. (2001) 'Degrees of Aversion Shown by Rats and Mice to Different Concentrations of Inhalational Anaesthetics', *The Veterinary Record*, **150** (26): 808–15.

Leite-Panissi, C.R.A., Ferrarese, A.A., Terzian, A.L.B., Menescal-de-Oliveira, L. (2006) 'Serotoninergic Activation of the Basolateral Amygdala and Modulation of Tonic Immobility in Guinea Pig', *Brain Research Bulletin*, **69** (4): 356–64.

Loewi, I. (1957) 'On the Background of the Discovery of Neurochemical Transmission', *Journal of the Mount Sinai Hospital, New York*, **24** (6): 1014–16.

Machado, C. (2003) 'A Definition of Human Death Should Not Be Related to Organ Transplants', *Journal of Medical Ethics*, **29** (3): 201–2.

Machado, C., Kerein, J., Ferrer, Y., Portela, L., García, C.M. and Manero, J.M. (2007) 'The Concept of Brain Death Did Not Evolve to Benefit Organ Transplants', *Journal of Medical Ethics*, **33** (4): 197–200.

Manette, C.S. (2004) 'A Reflection on the Ways Veterinarians Cope with the Death, Euthanasia, and Slaughter of Animals', *Journal of the American Veterinary Medical Association*, **225** (1): 34–8.

Milani, M. (2008) 'Death-Proofing: Preventive Measures for Difficult Times', *Canadian Veterinary Journal*, **49** (4): 405–8.

Misslin, R. (2003) 'The Defense System of Fear: Behavior and Neurocircuitry', *Clinical Neurophysiology*, **33** (2): 55–66.

Miyatake, T., Tabuchi, K., Sasaki, K., Okada, K., Katayama, K. and Moriya, S. (2008) 'Pleiotropic Antipredator Strategies, Fleeing and

Feigning Death, Correlated with Dopamine Levels in *Tribolium castaneum*', *Animal Behaviour*, **75** (1): 113–21.

Moje, M. (2003) 'Alternative Verfahren Beim Rind. Die Stumpfe Schuss-Schlag-Betäubing Une Die Elektrobetäubung', *Fleischwirtschaft*, **83** (5): 22–3.

Mollaret, P. and Goulon, M. (1959) 'Le Coma Dépassé', *Revue Neurologique*, **101** (July): 3–15.

Morgan, C. A. and McDonald, M. (2007) 'Ethical Dilemmas in Veterinary Medicine', *The Veterinary Clinics of North America: Small Animal Practice*, **37** (1): 165–79.

Moskowitz, A. K. (2004) '"Scared Stiff": Catatonia as an Evolutionary-Based Fear Response', *Physiological Review*, **111** (4): 984–1002.

Nowak, B. (2002) 'Influence of Three Different Stunning Systems on Stress Response and Meat Quality of Slaughter Pigs', School of Veterinary Medicine, Habilitation (Postdoctoral) Thesis, Hanover, Germany.

Palladino J. L. and Noordergraaf, A. (2000) 'The Changing View of the Heart through the Centuries', *Studies in Health Technology and Informatics*, **71**: 3–11.

Passantino, A., Fenga, C., Morciano, C., Morelli, C., Russo, M., Di Pietro, C. and Passantino, M. (2006) 'Euthanasia of Companion Animals: A Legal and Ethical Analysis', *Annali dell'Istituto superiore di sanità*, **42** (4): 491–5.

Poularas, J., Karakitsos, D., Kouraklis, G., Kostakis, A., De Groot, E., Kalogeromitros, A., Bilalis, D., Boletis, J. and Karabinis, A. (2006) 'Comparison Between Transcranial Color Doppler-Ultrasonography and Angiography in the Confirmation of Brain Death', *Transplantation Proceedings*, **38** (5): 1213–17.

Powner, D. and Bernstein, I. (2003) 'Extended Somatic Support for Pregnant Women After Brain Death', *Critical Care Medicine*, **31** (4): 1241–9.

Powner, D. J., Ackerman, B. M. and Grenvik, A. (1996) 'Medical Diagnosis of Death in Adults: Historical Contributions to Current Controversies', *Lancet*, **348** (9036): 1219–23.

Randell, T. T. (2004) 'Medical and Legal Considerations of Brain Death', *Acta Anaesthesiologica Scandinavia*, **48** (2): 139–44.

Ratner, S. C. (1967) 'Comparative Aspects of Hypnosis', in J. E. Gordon (ed.), *Handbook of Clinical and Experimental Hypnosis*, New York: Macmillan, pp. 550–87.

Rollin, B. E. (2003) 'An Ethicist's Commentary on Veterinarians Treating Unowned Animals and Euthanizing Unwanted Animals', *Canadian Veterinary Journal*, **44** (5): 363–4.

Rosengart, M. R. (2006) 'Critical Care Medicine: Landmarks and Legends', *The Surgical Clinics of North America*, **86** (6): 1305–21.

Ruxton, G. D., Sherrat, T. N. and Speed, M. P. (2004) *Avoiding Attack: The Evolutionary Ecology of Camouflage, Warning Signals and Mimicry*, Oxford: Oxford University Press.

Serani-Merlo, A. (2007) 'The Vitality of Death Discussions: Comments on Bacigalupo et al., "the Debate About Death: an Imperishable Discussion?"' *Biological Research*, **40** (4): 535–7.

Sergeant, A. B. and Eberhardt, L. E. (1975) 'Death Feigning by Ducks in Response to Predation by Red Foxes (*Vulpes fulva*)' *American Midland Naturalist*, **94** (1): 108–19.

Shemie, S. D. (2007) 'Clarifying the Paradigm for the Ethics of Donation and Transplantation: Was "Dead" Really So Clear Before Organ Donation?' *Philosophy, Ethics, and Humanities in Medicine*, **2**: 18.

Shemie, S. D., Doig, C. and Belitsky, P. (2003) 'Advancing Towards a Modern Death: The Path from Severe Brain Injury to Neurological Determination of Death', *Canadian Medical Association Journal*, **168** (8): 993–5.

Shewmon, D. A. (1998) 'Chronic "Brain Death": Meta-Analysis and Conceptual Consequences', *Neurology*, **51** (6): 1538–45.

—— (2001) 'The Brain and Somatic Integration: Insights into the Standard Biological Rationale for Equating "Brain Death" with Death', *The Journal of Medicine and Philosophy*, **26** (5): 457–78.

Souza Da Silva, L. F. and Menescal-de-Oliveira, L. (2006) 'Cholinergic Modulation of Tonic Immobility and Nociception in the NRM of Guinea Pig', *Physiology and Behavior*, **87** (4): 821–7.

Speakman, J. R. (2005) 'Body Size, Energy Metabolism and Lifespan', *The Journal of Experimental Biology*, **208** (Pt 9): 1717–30.

Taylor, R. M. (1997) 'Reexamining the Definition and Criteria of Death', *Seminars in Neurology*, **17** (3): 265–70.

Tobbler, M. (2005) 'Feigning Death in the Central American Cichlid, *Parachromis freidrichsthalii*', *Journal of Fish Biology*, **66** (3): 877–81.

Truog, R. D. (2007) 'Brain Death: Too Flawed to Endure, Too Ingrained to Abandon', *Journal of Law, Medicine and Ethics*, **35** (2): 273–81.

Truog, R. D. and Fackler, J. C. (1992) 'Rethinking Brain Death', *Critical Care Medicine*, **20** (12): 1705–13.

Truog, R. D. and Miller, F. G. (2008) 'The Dead-Donor Rule and Organ Transplantation', *The New England Journal of Medicine*, **359** (7): 674–5.

Truog, R. D. and Robinson, W. M. (2003) 'Role of Brain Death and the Dead-Donor Rule in the Ethics of Organ Transplantation', *Critical Care Medicine*, **31** (9): 2391–6.

Valance, D., Després, G., Richard, S., Constantin, P., Mignon-Grasteau, S., Leman, S., Boissy, A., Faure, J. M. and Leterrier, C. (2008) 'Changes in Heart Rate Variability During a Tonic Immobility Test in Quail', *Physiology and Behavior*, **93** (3): 512–20.

Vanderwolf, C. H., Buzsaki, G. and Cain, D. P. et al. (1988) 'Neocortical and Hippocampal Electrical Activity Following Decapitation in the Rat', *Brain Research*, **451** (1–2): 340–4.

Verheijde, J. L., Rady, M. Y. and McGregor, J. (2007) 'Recovery of Transplantable Organs After Cardiac or Circulatory Death: Transforming the Paradigm for the Ethics of Organ Donation', *Philosophy, Ethics, and Humanities in Medicine*, **2** (May): 8.

Veatch, R. M. (2008) 'Donation Hearts After Cardiac Death: Reversing the Irreversible', *The New England Journal of Medicine*, **359** (7): 672–3.

Whetstine, L. (2007) 'Bench-to-Bedside Review: When Is Dead Really Dead – on the Legitimacy of Using Neurologic Criteria to Determine Death', *Critical Care*, **11** (2): 208.

Wijdicks, E. F. M. (2002) 'Brain Death Worldwide. Accepted Fact but No Global Consensus in Diagnostic Criteria', *Neurology*, **58** (1): 20–5.

Wotton, S. B. and Gregory, N. G. (1986) 'Pig Slaughtering Procedures: Time to Loss of Brain Responsiveness After Exsanguination or Cardiac Arrest', *Research in Veterinary Science*, **40** (2): 148–51.

Youngner, S. J., Landefeld, C. S., Coulton, C. J., Jukinalis, B. W. and Leary, M. (1998) '"Brain Death" and Organ Retrieval: A Cross-Sectional Survey of Knowledge and Concepts Among Health Professionals', *Journal of the American Medical Association*, **261** (20): 2205–10.

Youngner, S. J., Arnold, R. M. and Schapiro, R. (1999) *The Definition of Death: Contemporary Controversies*, Baltimore, Md.: Johns Hopkins University Press.

Zamperetti, N., Bellomo, R., Defanti, C. A. and Latronico, N. (2004) 'Irreversible Apnoeic Coma 35 Years Later', *Intensive Care Medicine*, **30** (9): 1715–22.

3 | The dying human: a perspective from biomedicine

MARIE-AURÉLIE BRUNO, DIDIER LEDOUX
AND STEVEN LAUREYS

What can science and medicine say about death and dying? As Epicurus said, 'death is nothing to us' (1926). 'Death is not part of life but it is its limit' paraphrased Wittgenstein two millennia later (1961). All consciousness ends with death and therefore in death there is neither pleasure nor pain, only non-existence (similar to one's 'nothingness' before birth). Modern dying in the industrialized world takes place in a hospital setting at an old age and is caused by progressive chronic diseases. In about half of conscious patients who die in hospital, family members report moderate to severe pain at least half the time and more than one-third of deceased patients spent at least ten days in an intensive care unit with poor physician–patient communication (SUPPORT 1995). This chapter will discuss the importance of biomedical sciences in the determination of human death. It will not deal with the very important issue of the need to improve our care for dying patients (Nuland 1993; Steinhauser et al. 2000) and what is seen as a 'good death' (see Table 3.1). The interesting study of near-death experiences will be dealt with in a separate chapter. Recent neuro-imaging studies have shown the involvement of the temporo-parietal cortex in the generation of out-of-body experiences (Blanke and Dieguez 2008) and are offering a physiological, neurological account for the phenomenon, rebuffing dualistic, non-physical explanations. In the light of Kellehear's opening review, we will here mainly be confining our observations about dying to dying as a form of 'collapse and disintegration'.

A brief history of death

Historically, the seat of consciousness was widely believed to be in the heart, and the absence of heartbeat was regarded as the clinical sign of death (Laureys and Boly 2008; Pernick 1988). Neurological scientific evidence has superseded such pre-scientific thinking and has

Table 3.1. *What constitutes 'good dying'? (Adapted from Steinhauser et al. 2000).*

1. Adequate management of pain and other distressing symptoms of dying (i.e. confidence that one will not suffer).
2. Remain in control of decision-making (i.e. thinking unclouded by medication).
3. Adequately prepared for the event of death (i.e. know what to expect and plan accordingly).
4. Opportunity for personal completion (i.e. spiritual, meaning, life review, spending time with family, resolving disagreements, saying goodbye).
5. Contribute to the well-being of others (i.e. gift, time spent, knowledge and wisdom, clinical trial or research study).
6. Affirmation as a whole and unique person (i.e. not being treated as a disease but as a person in the context of one's life, values and preferences).

shown that consciousness, an emergent property of neural activity, resides in the brain (for recent review, see, for example, Laureys and Tononi 2008). For millennia, death was defined as the irreversible cessation of heartbeat and respiration, but this determination became more complicated with the invention of the artificial respirator in the 1950s.

The first to consider irreversible absence of brain function equivalent to death was Moses Maimonides (1135–1204), the foremost intellectual figure of medieval Judaism, who argued that the spasmodic jerking observed in decapitated humans did not represent evidence of life as their muscle movements were not indicative of a central control. But it was not until the invention of the positive-pressure mechanical ventilator by Bjorn Ibsen in the 1950s and the widespread use of high-tech intensive care in the 1960s that cardiac, respiratory and brain function could be truly dissociated. Severely brain-damaged patients could now have their heartbeat and systemic circulation provisionally sustained by artificial respiratory support. Such profound unconscious states had never been encountered before as until that time all these patients had died instantly from apnea.

The earliest steps towards a neurocentric definition of death were European. French neurologists Mollaret and Goulon (1959) first discussed the clinical, electrophysiological and ethical issues of what we now call brain death, using the term *coma dépassé* (that is, irretrievable coma). Unfortunately, their paper was written in French and remained largely unnoticed by the international community. In 1968, the ad hoc committee of the Harvard Medical School, including ten physicians, a theologian, a lawyer and a historian of science, published a milestone paper defining death as irreversible coma. Some years later, neuropathological studies showed that damage of the brainstem was critical for brain death (Mohandas and Chou 1971). These findings initiated the concept of 'brainstem death'(Pallis and Harley 1996) and led UK physicians to define brain death as complete irreversible loss of brainstem function: 'if the brainstem is dead, the brain is dead, and if the brain is dead, the person is dead'(Royal College of Physicians, 1995).

More than ten years prior to the Harvard criteria, anaesthesiologists who were concerned that new resuscitation and intensive-care technologies designed to safe lives appeared sometimes to only extend the dying process, sought advice from Pope Pius XII. The Pope ruled that it remains for the doctor to give a definition of the 'moment of death' and that there is no obligation to use extraordinary means to prolong life in hopelessly ill patients (Pius XII 1957). Hence, withholding or withdrawing life-sustaining treatments in *acute* irreversible massive brain damage became morally accepted.

A modern definition of death

The currently most accepted definition of death is the 'permanent cessation of the critical functions of the organism as a whole' (Bernat 1998). The organism as a whole is an old concept in theoretical biology (Loeb 1916) that refers to its unity and functional integrity – not to the simple sum of its parts – and encompasses the concept of an organism's critical system (Korein and Machado 2004). Critical functions are those without which the organism as a whole cannot function: control of respiration and circulation, neuroendocrine and homeostatic regulation, and consciousness. Death is defined by the irreversible loss of all these functions (Graham et al. 2005). The tiresome debate whether this loss is a process (Morison 1971) or an event (Kass 1971) is seemingly unsolvable. For what follows, death, is regarded as the discontinuous event (linguistically it can be understood only as an event, Shewmon and Shewmon 2004) that separates the continuous process of dying from subsequent disintegration. The radical transition from life to death has been proposed to follow a supercritical Hopf bifurcation, that is, a bifurcation presenting a combination of continuity and discontinuity known from chaos and dynamical systems theory (Alligood et al. 1997). It is important to stress that the term 'clinical death' (the popular term for cardiorespiratory arrest) is not equal to death and should in our view better be avoided.

The anatomy of death

The brain-centred definition of human death has two formulations called whole-brain and brainstem death. Both are defined as the irreversible cessation of the organism as a whole but differ in their anatomical interpretation instantiating this concept. The whole-brain formulation requires the bedside demonstration of irreversible cessation of all clinical functions of the brain and is the most widely accepted. The brainstem formulation regards irreversible cessation of clinical functions of the brainstem as not only necessary but also sufficient for the determination of death. Pallis (1995), one of the most eloquent advocates of brainstem death, argues that the brainstem is at once the through-station for nearly all hemispheric input and output, the centre generating arousal (an essential condition for consciousness) and the centre of respiration.

Brain death is classically caused by a brain lesion (for example, massive traumatic injury, intracranial haemorrhage or anoxia) which increases intracranial pressure to values superior to mean arterial blood pressure and hence causes intracranial circulation to cease and damages the brainstem due to herniation. Using the brainstem formulation of death, however, unusual but existing cases of catastrophic brainstem lesion (often of haemorrhagic origin) sparing the thalami and cerebral cortex can be declared brain death in the absence of clinical brainstem function, despite intact intracranial circulation. Hence, a patient with a primary brainstem lesion (who did not develop raised intracranial pressure) might be declared dead by the UK doctrine but not by the US doctrine (Laureys 2005a). Theoretical cases where a multi-focal brainstem lesion would selectively impair all brainstem function that can be clinically assessed but would preserve some residual (clinically undetectable) function of the ascending reticular activating system sufficient to warrant some residual fluctuating form of awareness could lead to a diagnostic error. By definition, confirmatory examinations such as functional imaging (Laureys et al. 2004) or electrophysiology would be needed to identify these cases some authors have coined as 'super locked-in syndrome' (Laureys et al. 2005a; Graham et al. 2005; Bernat 2002a).

Anatomopathology in brain-death patients receiving maximal artificial means of support will inevitably end up showing the so-called 'respirator brain': surface vasocongestion due to venous engorgement, thrombosis in cortical veins and sinuses, subarachnoid haemorrhage and cortical congestion, and haemorrhage will be observed after about twelve hours of a non-perfused state (Leestma et al. 1984). After about a week, an autolysed liquefied brain will pour from the opened skull (Leestma 2001).

Medical tests for death

How do physicians declare a patient dead? The clinical assessments for brain death are based on the loss of all brainstem reflexes and the demonstration of continuing apnea in a persistently comatose patient (see Table 3.2). The clinical set of tests for whole-brain and brainstem death are identical. There are two sets of tests, neurological and cardiopulmonary, depending on whether or not the patient has mechanical ventilation. In patients who are mechanically ventilated, validated neurological tests will assure irretrievable absence of brain (in practice merely brainstem) function. In non-ventilated patients, physicians will evaluate the irretrievable absence of heartbeat and breathing.

Irrespective of the fact that one uses neurological or cardiopulmonary criteria, death has four possible times to occur: first, when the circulatory or cerebral critical function stops; second, when this critical function is first examined and known to have stopped; third, when the loss actually becomes irreversible; and, finally, when this irreversibility is known by the physician (Lynn and Cranford 1999). The exact duration required for the absence of circulation and respiration has evoked controversy related to the Pittsburgh protocol (University of Pittsburgh Medical Center 1993) for non-heartbeating donors. It is now debated that after five minutes of asystole the heart will not auto-resuscitate and the patient can be declared dead according to cardiopulmonary criteria given that artificial resuscitation would not

Table 3.2. *The 'gold standard' guidelines for the diagnosis of brain death (The Quality Standards Subcommittee of the American Academy of Neurology, 1995).*

- Demonstration of coma.
- Evidence for the cause of coma.
- Absence of confounding factors, including hypothermia, drugs, electrolyte and endocrine disturbances.
- Absence of brainstem reflexes.
- Absent motor responses.
- Apnea.
- A repeat evaluation in six hours is advised, but the time period is considered arbitrary.
- Confirmatory laboratory tests are only required when specific components of the clinical testing cannot be reliably evaluated.

be attempted (National Academy of Sciences Institute of Medicine 1997). In this specific context, death according to neurological criteria will occur only many minutes later, when the brain has totally infracted from anoxic damage (Lynn 1993; Menikoff 1998).

Brain death can be diagnosed with an extremely high rate of probability within hours to days of the original insult (Wijdicks 2001a). Brain-dead patients are, by definition, comatose (that is, never show eye-opening, even upon noxious stimulation), and apneic and necessarily require controlled artificial ventilation. They will, at best, only show slow body movements generated by residual spinal activity: finger jerks, undulating toe flexion sign, triple flexion response, Lazarus sign, pronation–extension reflex and facial myokymia may be present in up to a third of patients (Saposnik et al. 2000; Saposnik et al. 2005).

The absence of whole-brain function in brain death can be confirmed by means of cerebral angiography (non-filling of the intracranial arteries), transcranial Doppler ultrasonography (absent diastolic or reverberating flow), nuclear imaging (absence of cerebral blood flow – 'hollow skull sign') or EEG (absent electrical activity). Cerebral angiography and transcranial Doppler sonography (Ducrocq et al. 1998) can be used with very high sensitivity and 100 per cent specificity to document the absence of cerebral blood flow in brain death (Wijdicks 2001c). Similarly, radionuclide cerebral imaging such as single photon emission CT (computed tomography) (Conrad and Sinha 2003) and PET classically show the so-called hollow skull sign confirming the absence of neuronal function in the whole brain (see Figure 3.1). The electroencephalography (EEG) in brain death shows absent electrocortical activity (that is, isoelectric recording) with a sensitivity and specificity of 90 per cent (Buchner and Schuchardt 1990). It is the most validated and, because of its wide availability, preferred confirmatory test for brain death implemented in many countries' guidelines (see Figure 3.2).

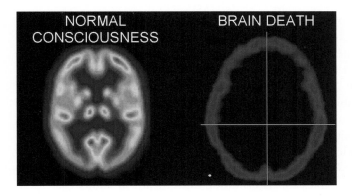

Figure 3.1. Differences in resting brain metabolism measured in normal consciousness and in brain death. The image in brain death shows a 'hollow skull sign' tantamount to a 'functional decapitation'. Adapted from Laureys, *Nature Reviews Neuroscience*, 2005.

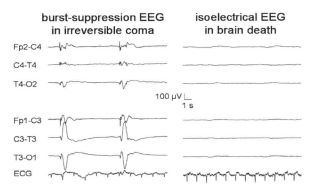

Figure 3.2. Changes in the electroencephalography (EEG) when coma evolves to brain death.

Validity of brain death

The first (and only) prospective study validating the neurocentric
criteria of death was the NIH-sponsored (US National Institute of
Health) multi-centre US Collaborative Study of Cerebral Death
(1977). Its aim was to identify tests that would predict cardiorespiratory death within three months despite continued ventilatory and
cardiac support. Of the 503 enrolled patients, 189 showed cerebral unresponsiveness, apnea and one isoelectric EEG, 187 of these
patients died based on cardiorespiratory criteria within three months;
the two who survived had drug intoxication. The authors recommended one re-examination at least six hours after onset of coma and
apnea (unlike the initial twenty-four hours required by the Harvard
criteria). In 1981, the President's Commission for the Study of Ethical
Problems in Medicine, and Biomedical and Behavioral Research of
the USA published *Defining Death* as their first project and recommended the use of ancillary diagnostic studies to reduce the duration
of the requisite period of observation (President's Commission for the
Study of Ethical Problems in Medicine, and Biomedical and Behavioral
Research 1981). The American Academy of Neurology (AAN) published its guidelines for determining brain death in adults (see Table
3.2) in 1995 – including the very important practical description of
apnea testing – which have been used to model many institutional
policies. Clinical and para-clinical diagnostic assessments have been
didactically summarized elsewhere (Wijdicks 2001a). Since the definition of brain death, not a single patient who fulfilled its clinical criteria has ever regained consciousness (Laureys and Boly 2008).

Are we all equal in death?

Under the US Uniform Determination of Death Act (1997), a person is dead when physicians determine, by applying prevailing clinical criteria, that cardiorespiratory or brain functions are absent and
cannot be retrieved. The neurocentric definition is purposely triply
redundant to require a determination that 'all functions of the entire
brain, including the brainstem' have irreversibly ceased (Beresford
2001). The American Academy of Neurology guidelines are shown in
Table 3.2. The Canadian guidelines closely mirror these US guidelines
(Canadian Neurocritical Care Group 1999). In 1971, Finland was

the first European country to accept brain-death criteria. Since then, all EU countries have accepted the concept of brain death. However, while the required clinical signs are very uniform, less than half of the European countries require technical confirmatory tests, and approximately half require more than one physician to be involved (Haupt and Rudolf 1999). Confirmatory tests are not mandatory in many developing-world countries because they aren't available. In Asia, death based on neurological criteria has not been uniformly accepted, and there exist major differences in regulation. India follows the UK criteria of brainstem death. China has no legal criteria and there seems to exist some hesitation of physicians to disconnect the ventilator in apnoeic irreversibly comatose patients (Diringer and Wijdicks 2001). Japan now officially recognizes brain death, although the public remains reluctant – possibly this relates to the case of heart surgeon Wada who was charged with murder in 1968 after removing a heart from a patient who was allegedly not brain dead (Lock 1999). Australia and New Zealand have accepted whole-brain-death criteria (Pearson 1995).

How well do physicians follow the published medical guidelines? A recent study has compared the local medical guidelines from the top 50 US neurology and neurosurgery institutions against the gold standard of the AAN guidelines (Greer et al. 2008). All hospitals correctly defined brain death as irreversible coma with absent brainstem reflexes. Nonetheless, many centres' policies did not follow 'gold standard' guidelines on criteria related to pre-clinical testing. There was variance in attention paid to the presence of hypothermia, sedatives, paralytics or presence of severe metabolic disorders which might confound diagnosis. Although careful and standardized testing of the absence of breathing – that is, apnea testing – is critical for the diagnosis of brain death, the centres differed as to how apnea testing should be done technically. There was also variance in the number of required exams and the required time intervals between them, the use of ancillary tests and who makes the diagnosis. Ideally, this should be a trained and experienced neurologist, but the medical staffing at many US hospitals might make it difficult to make this compulsory. Such studies are important as they provide empirical information about current practices that can help to improve our clinical guidelines and provide more specificity for areas where there is too much practice variation. Decreasing variance is critical if we hope to maintain the public trust that this critical diagnosis is being made properly and without avoidable error (Laureys and Fins 2008).

Death and organ donation

Although the neurocentric definition of death originated prior to the advent of multi-organ transplantation, the demand for donors has been a major drive in the popularization and legalization of brain death. In the wake of Christian Barnard's first transplant of a human heart in 1967, Henry K. Beecher justified organ harvest from those who were 'hopelessly unconscious' in utilitarian fashion. Defining death and organ harvesting are also inextricably linked because of the 'dead-donor rule'. This rule requires patients to be declared dead before the removal of life-sustaining organs for transplantation. As a result, it is considered unethical to kill patients for their organs no matter how ill they are or how much good for others can be accomplished by doing so. To avoid conflict, transplant surgeons are excluded from performing brain-death examinations.

Some authors have recently advocated to abandon the dead-donor rule (Truog 2000; Arnold and Youngner 1993; Truog and Robinson 2003). Truog (1997), for example, proposes to take organs from hopelessly neurologically devastated or imminently dying patients who are 'beyond harm' with their informed consent (or that of their family) without first being declared brain dead. In 1995, anencephalic infants were proposed as organ donors by the American Medical Association (Council on Ethical and Judicial Affairs 1995). The potential to save dying infants and to give meaning to the anencephalic infant's family were presented as its justification (Walters et al. 1997). As a result of the ensuing outcry of protests and the unresolved scientific question of consciousness in anencephaly (see for example, Shewmon et al. 1999 on residual awareness in congenitally decorticate infants), the previous recommendation banning the policy was reasserted (Plows 1996). Similarly, vegetative patients have been proposed as organ donors (Veatch 2004, Fost 2004). The International Forum for Transplant Ethics has suggested to administer a lethal injection prior to organ harvesting in patients where the decision had been taken to withdraw life-sustaining treatment (Hoffenberg et al. 1997). Justifying arguments again were humanitarian, obviating the futile use of resources needed to keep alive an individual with no hope of recovery and to make available organs suitable for transplantation. The idea has not been accepted because it violates the dead-donor rule (Engelhardt 1998) or needs to amend the definition of death (King 1998), and opposition among the general public is thought to damage organ-donation programmes (Bakran 1998). The benefits from using vegetative living humans as organ donors do not justify the harm to society ensuing from sacrificing the dead-donor principle (Bernat 2001). Despite the current shortage of donors, our definition of death should not serve to facilitate transplantation. In the public eye, the acceptance of multi-organ donation depends on the certainty of the diagnosis of death and the confidence in the dead-donor rule (Bernat 2001). An irreproachable assessment of death is an unconditional prerequisite for organ donation, with no one fearing that organs will be harvested inappropriately. Such transparency is necessary for the successful continuation – and growth – of organ-donor programmes.

Opponents to a brain-centred definition of death

Some physicians (Shewmon 2001), philosophers (Seifert 1993) and ultra-conservative Catholic theologians (Cabeza et al. 1997) have criticized the brain-centred definition and advocate a circulatory formulation of death defined by the irreversible cessation of circulation. Alan Shewmon, its most persuasive proponent, cites two lines of data to support this contention. In his view, a living body possesses not an integra*tor* but integra*tion*, a holistic property deriving from the mutual interaction among all parts (Shewmon 2001). He has presented thought-provoking cases of brain-dead children and adults who were treated aggressively and at least fifty had their circulation maintained for many months or longer (Shewmon 1998). There have also been pregnant brain-dead patients where intensive care was requested to be continued until the foetus was mature enough to be born (Kantor and Hoskins 1993; Loewy 1987; Feldman et al. 2000). The most exceptional is the successful maintenance of a pregnant brain-dead woman from seventeen to thirty-two weeks of gestation (Bernstein et al. 1989). These findings have been used by Shewmon (1998) to show that the neurocentric concept of death is inherently counterintuitive, for how could a dead body continue visceral organ functioning for extended periods, grow or gestate infants?

In response to the integration-regulation criticism, Bernat (2002b) has counter-argued that the circulatory formulation has the inverse problem of the higher brain formulation. While the higher brain formulation generates a criterion that is necessary but insufficient for death, the circulatory formulation generates a criterion that is sufficient but unnecessary for death (Bernat 2005). The homeostatic capacities of the brain are not the sole evidence of functions of the organism as a whole. As previously stated, the functions of circulation as well as respiration and consciousness are regarded critical functions. With regard to the extremely exceptional 'chronic' cases, their chronicity merely 'indicates that their bodily decomposition has been delayed until their circulation has ceased' (Wijdicks and Bernat 1999) and reveals heroic technological support within the modern intensive care unit – 'an example of what science and technology could do, but should not do' (Crisci 1999). Brain death signifies death not *because* it is invariably and imminently followed by asystole.

The concept of brain death as irreversible loss of the capacity of the organism to function as a whole that results from the permanent loss of its critical system is not invalidated by the time lag between the diagnosis of brain death and cardiac arrest (Lang 1999). From a pragmatic point of view, the advocates of the circulatory formulation have not swayed the majority who experience an intuitive attraction to the brain-death formulation and find it sufficiently coherent and useful to wish to preserve it as public policy (Bernat 2005).

A personhood-centred definition of death

In 1971, Scottish neurologist Brierley (et al.) urged that death be defined by the permanent cessation of 'those higher functions of the nervous system that demarcate man from the lower primates'. This neocortical or higher-brain-death definition was further developed by others, mainly philosophers (Veatch 1975; Gervais 1986), and its conceptual basis rests on the premise that consciousness, cognition and social interaction, not bodily physiological integrity, are the essential characteristics of human life. The higher-brain concept produces the neocortical death criterion, in which only the functions of the neocortex, not of the whole brain or of the brainstem, must be permanently lost. Clinical and confirmatory tests for neocortical death have never been validated as such.

Based on the neocortical definition of death, patients in a vegetative state following an acute injury or chronic degenerative disease and anencephalic infants are considered dead. Depending on how to interpret 'irreversible loss of capacity for social interaction' (Veatch 1976: 50), even patients in a permanent 'minimally conscious state' (Giacino et al. 2002), who, by definition, are unable to functionally communicate, could be regarded as dead. We have argued that despite its theoretical attractiveness to some, this concept of death cannot be reliably implemented in anatomical criteria nor in reliable clinical testing (Laureys 2005a).

First, our current scientific understanding of the necessary and sufficient neural correlates of consciousness is lacking or incomplete at best (Laureys et al. 2006; Baars et al. 2003). In contrast to brain death, where the neuroanatomy and neurophysiology are both well established, anatomical pathology, neuro-imaging or electrophysiology can, at present, not determine human consciousness. Hence, no accurate anatomical criteria can be defined for a higher-brain formulation of death. Second, clinical tests would request providing bedside behavioural evidence that consciousness is irreversibly lost. There is an irreducible philosophical limitation in knowing for certain whether any other being possesses a conscious life (Chalmers 1998). Consciousness is a multifaceted subjective first-person experience, and clinical evaluation is limited to evaluating patients' responsiveness to the environment (Majerus et al. 2005). As previously discussed, vegetative patients, unlike brain-dead patients, can move extensively, and clinical studies have shown how difficult it is to differentiate 'automatic' from 'willed' movements (Prochazka et al. 2000). This results in an underestimation of behavioural signs of consciousness and hence a misdiagnosis, estimated to occur in about one-third of chronically vegetative patients (Schnakers et al. 2006; Childs et al. 1993; Andrews et al. 1996). Physicians also frequently erroneously diagnose the vegetative state in elderly demented nursing home residents (Volicer et al. 1997). Clinical testing for absence of consciousness is much more problematic and slippery than testing for absence of wakefulness, brainstem reflexes and apnea in whole-brain or brainstem death. The vegetative state is one end of a spectrum of awareness, and the subtle differential diagnosis with the minimally conscious state necessitates repeated evaluations by experienced examiners. Practically, the neocortical death concept would also imply burying breathing 'corpses'.

Finally, complementary tests for neocortical death would request providing confirmation that all cortical function is irreversibly lost. Vegetative patients are not apallic, as previously claimed, but may show preserved islands of functional 'pallium' or cortex (Laureys et al. 2005b). Recent functional neuro-imaging studies have indeed shown limited but undeniable neocortical activation in vegetative patients disproving complete 'neocortical death' in the vegetative state (Laureys and Boly 2007). Complementary tests for proving the absence of neocortical integration necessary for consciousness are, at present, not feasible and certainly not validated. In contrast to brain death where prolonged absent intracranial blood flow proves irreversibility, the massively reduced – but not absent – cortical metabolism in the vegetative state (Laureys 2007) cannot be regarded as evidence for irreversibility. Indeed, fully reversible causes of altered consciousness such as deep sleep and general anaesthesia have shown similar decreases in brain function, and the rare patients who recover from a vegetative state have been shown to resume near-normal activity in previously dysfunctional associative neocortex (Laureys 2005b).

Finally, proving irreversibility is key to any concept of death. The clinical testing of irreversibility has stood the test of time only in the framework of whole-brain or brainstem formulations of death. Indeed, since Mollaret and Goulon (1959) first defined their neurologic criteria of death over forty-five years ago, no patient in apnoeic coma properly declared brain (or brainstem) dead has ever regained consciousness (Pallis and Harley 1996; Bernat 2005; Wijdicks 2001b). This cannot been said for the vegetative state where permanent is probabilistic, the chances of recovery depend on patient's age, etiology and time spent in the vegetative state (Multi-Society Task Force on PVS 1994). Unlike brain death, where the diagnosis can be made in the acute setting, the vegetative state can only be regarded as 'statistically permanent' after very long observation periods and even then some might exceptionally recover – even if it should be stressed that many of the anecdotes of late recovery are difficult to substantiate and that we often do not know how certain the original diagnosis was.

End-of-life decisions

The debate on the need to withhold or withdraw 'futile' life-prolonging treatments and the notion of 'death with dignity' was started by intensive-care physicians (not ethicists or lawyers) in the mid-1970s (Cassem 1974). As discussed above, a person who is brain dead is dead: disconnecting the ventilator will not let him or her die. At present, almost half of all deaths in intensive care follow a decision to withhold or withdraw treatment (Smedira et al. 1990). There is no moral or legal distinction between withholding or withdrawing (Gillon 1998). The moral values that underlie these guidelines are the principles of autonomy, beneficence, non-maleficence and justice (Beauchamp and Childress 1979). Informed competent patients should consent to any treatment they receive and have the right to make choices regarding their bodies and lives. The primary factor determining the level of treatment for an incompetent patient should reflect the patient's personally expressed wishes for treatment in this situation. It should be noted that the principle of autonomy was developed as a product of the Enlightenment in Western culture and is not yet strongly emphasized outside of the USA and Western Europe – for example, in Japan (Asai et al. 1999). In the Western world, the main challenge for autonomy as justifying a right to refuse life-prolonging treatment comes from the vitalist religious view (mainly from orthodox Jews, fundamentalist Protestants and conservative Roman Catholics) which holds that only God should determine when life ends.

In the past, physicians interpreted beneficence to mean promotion of continued life, almost at any cost. With the advancement of medical technology, medicine is now ethically obliged not to promote life at all costs in a paternalistic way but rather to enable patients to choose what kind of life represents a 'good life' to them and what kind of life does not. Medical choices should now depend upon patients' individual values and can hence be in disagreement with physicians' personal perceptions (Layon et al. 1990). When patients can no longer speak for themselves, having someone who knew them make decisions for them seems the best reasonable compromise. However, critics have argued that surrogate decisions are flawed. Most people would not want to continue living if they were in a vegetative state (Frankl et al. 1989). Severely disabled brain-damaged patients, however, seem to want to go on living (Homer-Ward et al. 2000; Shiel and Wilson 1998; McMillan 1997; McMillan and Herbert 2004). Some studies have shown the limitations of spouses' predictions of patients' desires regarding resuscitation (Uhlmann et al. 1988), and healthy people tend to underestimate impaired patients' quality of life (Starr et al. 1986; Bruno et al. 2008a; Bruno et al. 2008b).

The principle of justice, which includes equity, demands that the individual's worth not be judged solely on social status nor on physical or intellectual attributes. Vulnerable patients such as not only the non-communicative severely brain-damaged but also the otherwise handicapped, very aged or very young should not be treated differently to healthy individuals. No person's life has more or less intrinsic value than the next. Concepts of justice should trump the claims of autonomy, based on a model of medical futility (Payne and Taylor 1997).

Medical futility is defined as that situation in which a therapy that is hoped to benefit the patient's medical condition predictably will not do so on the basis of the best available evidence – there remains discussion on exactly what probability threshold satisfies the standard of 'ethical acceptability' (Bernat 2002b).

Finally, the question remains on the mode of death. Stopping hydration and nutrition will lead to death in ten to fourteen days (Cranford 1984). Some, however, are in favour of injecting a lethal drug to hasten the dying process. This practice can currently only be envisaged in countries or states where euthanasia is legalized (for example, Belgium, the Netherlands and Switzerland) and only if patients have explicitly expressed this wish antecedently in living wills (Detry et al. 2008). Letting irreversibly unconscious patients die can, however, be the most humane option – just as abortion can be justified in, for example, cases of anencephaly, without needing to declare the foetus to be dead. This is not a purely medical matter but an ethical issue depending on personal moral values, and we should accept deviating culture- and religion-dependent viewpoints.

Conclusion

We have here considered death as a 'simple' biological phenomenon for which we construct pragmatic medical, moral and legal policies on the basis of their social acceptance (Bernat 2001). As evidenced by the views taken in other chapters of this book, our 'bench science' approach represents only one view in the complex debate on death and dying (e.g. see Kellehear 2008). What is the future of death? Improving technologies for brain repair and prosthetic support for brain functions (for example, stem cells, neurogenesis, neural computer prostheses, cryonic suspension, nanoneurological repair) might one day change our current notions of irreversibility and force medicine and society once again to revise their definition of death. Of the two bio-philosophical concepts of brain death (the 'whole-brain' and the 'brainstem' formulation) defined as the irreversible cessation of critical functions of the organism as a whole (i.e. neuroendocrine and homeostatic regulation, circulation, respiration and consciousness), the whole-brain concept is most widely accepted and practiced. Since their first use in 1959 (Mollaret and Goulon), the neurocentric criteria of death – as compared to the old cardiocentric criteria – are considered to be 'among the safest medicine can achieve' (Lang 1999). The decision whether a patient should live or die is a value judgement over which physicians can exert no specialized professional claim. The democratic traditions of our pluralistic society should permit personal freedom in patients' decisions to choose to continue or terminate life-sustaining therapy in cases of severe brain damage. Like most ethical issues, there are plausible arguments supporting both sides of the question. It is our hope that policy-makers and the medical community will improve educational and public awareness programmes on death and dying, stimulate the creation of advance directives as a form of advance medical-care planning and more actively encourage research on our care for the dying.

Acknowledgements

Steven Laureys is Senior Research Associate at the Belgian Fonds National de la Recherche Scientifique (FNRS). Marie-Aurélie Bruno and Didier Ledoux are research fellows at FNRS. Portions of this chapter were published in Steven Laureys (2005) *Nature Reviews Neuroscience*, 6: 899–909. This research is funded by the Belgian Ministry of Health, the European Commission, the James S. McDonnell Foundation, the Mind Science Foundation, the French Speaking Community Concerted Research Action and the Fondation Médicale Reine Elisabeth.

References

Alligood, K. T., Sauer, T. D. and Yorke, J. A. (1997) *Chaos: An Introduction to Dynamical Systems*, New York: Springer-Verlag.

Andrews, K., Murphy, L., Munday, R. and Littlewood, C. (1996) 'Misdiagnosis of the Vegetative State: Retrospective Study in a Rehabilitation Unit', *British Medical Journal*, **313**: 13–16.

Arnold, R.M and Youngner, S.J. (1993) 'The Dead Donor Rule: Should We Stretch It, Bend It, or Abandon It?', *Kennedy Institute of Ethics Journal*, **3**: 263–78.

Asai, A., Maekawa, M., Akiguchi, I., Fukui, T., Miura, Y., Tanabe, N. and Fukuhara, S. (1999) 'Survey of Japanese Physicians' Attitudes Towards the Care of Adult Patients in Persistent Vegetative State [in Process Citation]', *Journal of Medical Ethics*, **25**: 302–8.

Baars, B., Ramsoy, T. and Laureys, S. (2003) 'Brain, Conscious Experience and the Observing Self', *Trends in Neurosciences*, **26**: 671–5.

Bakran, A. (1998) 'Organ Donation and Permanent Vegetative State', *Lancet*, **351**: 211–12; discussion, 212–13.

Beauchamp, T.L. and Childress, J.F. (1979) *Principles of Biomedical Ethics*, New York: Oxford University Press.

Beresford, H.R. (2001) 'Legal Aspects of Brain Death', in E.F.M. Wijdicks (ed.), *Brain Death*, Philadelphia, Pa.: Lippincott Williams & Wilkins, pp. 151–69.

Bernat, J.L. (1998) 'A Defense of the Whole-Brain Concept of Death', *Hastings Center Report*, **28**: 14–23.

   (2001) 'Philosophical and Ethical Aspects of Brain Death', in E.F.M. Wijdicks (ed.), *Brain Death*, Philadelphia, Pa.: Lippincott Williams & Wilkins, pp. 171–87.

   (2002a) 'The Biophilosophical Basis of Whole-Brain Death', *Social Philosophy and Policy*, **19**: 324–42.

   (2002b) *Ethical Issues in Neurology*, Boston, Mass.: Butterworth Heinemann.

   (2005) 'The Concept and Practice of Brain Death', in S. Laureys (ed.), *In the Boundaries of Consciousness: Neurobiology and Neuropathology, Vol. 150*, Amsterdam: Elsevier, pp. 373–84.

Bernstein, I.M., Watson, M., Simmons, G.M., Catalano, P.M., Davis, G. and Collins, R. (1989) 'Maternal Brain Death and Prolonged Fetal Survival', *Obstetrics & Gynecology*, **74**: 434–7.

Blanke, O. and Dieguez, S. (2008) 'Leaving Body and Life Behind: Out-of-Body and Near-Death Experience', in S. Laureys and G. Tononi in (eds.), *The Neurology of Consciousness*, New York: Academic Press.

Brierley, J.B., Graham, D.I., Adams, J.H. and Simpsom, J.A. (1971) 'Neocortical Death After Cardiac Arrest: A Clinical, Neurophysiological, and Neuropathological Report of Two Cases', *Lancet*, **2**: 560–5.

Bruno, M., Bernheim, J.L., Schnakers, C. and Laureys, S. (2008a) 'Locked-in: Don't Judge a Book by Its Cover', *Journal of Neurology, Neurosurgery & Psychiatry*, **79**: 2.

Bruno, M.A., Pellas, F. and Laureys, S. (2008b) 'Quality of life in locked-in syndrome', in J.L. Vincent (ed.), *Yearbook of Intensive Care and Emergency Medicine*, Berlin: Springer-Verlag, pp. 881–90.

Buchner, H. and Schuchardt, V. (1990) 'Reliability of Electroencephalogram in the Diagnosis of Brain Death', *European Neurology*, 30: 138–41.

Cabeza, R., Grady, C.L., Nyberg, L., McIntosh, A.R., Tulving, E., Kapur, S., Jennings, J.M., Houle, S. and Craik, F.I. (1997) 'Age-Related Differences in Neural Activity During Memory Encoding and Retrieval: A Positron Emission Tomography Study', *Journal of Neuroscience*, 17: 391–400.

Canadian Neurocritical Care Group (1999) 'Guidelines for the Diagnosis of Brain Death', *Canadian Journal of Neurological Sciences*, 26: 64–6.

Cassem, N.H. (1974) 'Confronting the Decision to Let Death Come', *Critical Care Medicine*, 2: 113–17.

Chalmers, D.J. (1998) 'The Problems of Consciousness', *Advances in Neurology*, 77: 7–16; discussion 16–18.

Childs, N.L., Mercer, W.N. and Childs, H.W. (1993) 'Accuracy of Diagnosis of Persistent Vegetative State', *Neurology*, 43: 1465–7.

Conrad, G.R. and Sinha, P. (2003) 'Scintigraphy as a Confirmatory Test of Brain Death', *Seminars in Nuclear Medicine*, 33: 312–23.

Council on Ethical and Judicial Affairs, AMA (1995) 'The Use of Anencephalic Neonates as Organ Donors', *Journal of the American Medical Association*, 273: 1614–18.

Cranford, R.E. (1984) 'Termination of Treatment in the Persistent Vegetative State', *Seminars in Neurology*, 4: 36–44.

Crisci, C. (1999) 'Chronic "Brain Death": Meta-Analysis and Conceptual Consequences', *Neurology*, 53: 1370; author reply 1371–2.

Detry, O., Laureys, S., Faymonville, M.E., De Roover, A., Squifflet, J.P., Lamy, M. and Meurisse, M. (2008) 'Organ Donation After Physician-Assisted Death', *Transplant International*, 21(9): 915.

Diringer, M.N. and Wijdicks, E.F.M. (2001) 'Brain Death in Historical Perspective', in E.F.M. Wijdicks (ed.), *Brain Death*, Philadelphia, Pa.: Lippincott Williams & Wilkins, pp. 5–27.

Ducrocq, X., Hassler, W., Moritake, K., Newell, D.W., Von Reutern, G.M., Shiogai, T. and Smith, R.R. (1998) 'Consensus Opinion on Diagnosis of Cerebral Circulatory Arrest Using Doppler-Sonography: Task Force Group on Cerebral Death of the Neurosonology Research Group of the World Federation of Neurology', *Journal of the Neurological Sciences*, 159: 145–50.

Engelhardt, K. (1998) 'Organ Donation and Permanent Vegetative State', *Lancet*, 351: 211; author reply 212–13.

Epicurus (1926) *The Extant Remains*, trans. and ed. C. Bailey, Oxford: Clarendon Press.

Feldman, D. M., Borgida, A. F., Rodis, J. F. and Campbell, W. A. (2000) 'Irreversible Maternal Brain Injury During Pregnancy: a Case Report and Review of the Literature', *Obstetrical & Gynecological Survey*, **55**: 708–14.

Fost, N. (2004) 'Reconsidering the Dead Donor Rule: Is It Important That Organ Donors Be Dead?', *Kennedy Institute of Ethics Journal*, **14**: 249–60.

Frankl, D., Oye, R. K. and Bellamy, P. E. (1989) 'Attitudes of Hospitalized Patients Towards Life Support: A Survey of 200 Medical Inpatients', *American Journal of Medicine*, **86**: 645–8.

Gervais, K. G. (1986) *Redefining Death*, New Haven, Conn.: Yale University Press.

Giacino, J. T., Ashwal, S., Childs, N., Cranford, R., Jennett, B., Katz, D. I., Kelly, J. P., Rosenberg, J. H., Whyte, J., Zafonte, R. D. and Zasler, N. D. (2002) 'The Minimally Conscious State: Definition and Diagnostic Criteria', *Neurology*, **58**: 349–53.

Gillon, R. (1998) 'Persistent Vegetative State, Withdrawal of Artificial Nutrition and Hydration, and the Patient's "Best Interests"', *Journal of Medical Ethics*, **24**: 75–6.

Graham, D. I., Maxwell, W. L., Adams, J. H. and Jennett, B. (2005) 'Novel Aspects of the Neuropathology of the Vegetative State after Blunt Head Injury', in S. Laureys (ed.), *The Boundaries of Consciousness: Neurobiology and Neuropathology*, Vol. 150, Amsterdam: Elsevier.

Greer, D. M., Varelas, P. N., Haque, S. and Wijdicks, E. F. (2008) 'Variability of Brain Death Determination Guidelines in Leading US Neurologic Institutions', *Neurology*, **70**: 284–9.

Haupt, W. F. and Rudolf, J. (1999) 'European Brain Death Codes: a Comparison of National Guidelines', *Journal of Neurology*, **246**: 432–7.

Hoffenberg, R., Lock, M., Tilney, N., Casabona, C., Daar, A. S., Guttmann, R. D., Kennedy, I., Nundy, S., Radcliffe-Richards, J. and Sells, R. A. (1997) 'Should Organs from Patients in Permanent Vegetative State Be Used for Transplantation? International Forum for Transplant Ethics', *Lancet*, **350**: 1320–1.

Homer-Ward, M. D., Bell, G., Dodd, S. and Wood, S. (2000) 'The Use of Structured Questionnaires in Facilitating Ethical Decision-Making in a Patient with Low Communicative Ability', *Clinical Rehabilitation*, **14**: 220.

Kantor, J. E. and Hoskins, I. A. (1993) 'Brain Death in Pregnant Women', *Journal of Clinical Ethics*, **4**: 308–14.

Kass, L. R. (1971) 'Death as an Event: A Commentary on Robert Morison', *Science*, **173**: 698–702.

Kellehear, A. (2008) 'Dying as a Social Relationship: A Sociological Review of Debates on the Determination of Death', *Social Science & Medicine*, **66**: 1533–44.

King, T.T. (1998) 'Organ Donation and Permanent Vegetative State', *Lancet*, **351**: 211; discussion 212–13.

Korein, J. and Machado, C. (2004) 'Brain Death: Updating a Valid Concept for 2004', in C. Machado and D.A. Shewmon (eds.), *Brain Death and Disorders of Consciousness*, New York: Kluwer Academic/Plenum Publishers, pp. 1–21.

Lang, C.J. (1999) 'Chronic "Brain Death" Meta Analysis and Conceptual Consequences', *Neurology*, **53**: 1370–1; author reply 1371–2.

Laureys, S. (2005a) 'Death, Unconsciousness and the Brain', *Nature Reviews Neuroscience*, **6**: 899–909.

—— (2005b) 'The Neural Correlate of (Un)awareness: Lessons from the Vegetative State', *Trends in Cognitive Sciences*, **9**: 556–9.

—— (2007) 'Eyes Open, Brain Shut', *Scientific American*, **296**: 84–9.

Laureys, S. and Boly, M. (2007) 'What Is It Like to Be Vegetative or Minimally Conscious?', *Current Opinion in Neurology*, **20**: 609–13.

—— (2008) 'The Changing Spectrum of Coma', *Nature Clinical Practice Neurology*. 4(10): 544–6.

Laureys, S. and Fins, J.J. (2008) 'Are We Equal in Death? Avoiding Diagnostic Error in Brain Death', *Neurology*, **70**: E14–15.

Laureys, S. and Tononi, G. (eds.) (2008) *The Neurology of Consciousness*, Oxford: Academic Press.

Laureys, S., Owen, A.M. and Schiff, N.D. (2004) 'Brain Function in Coma, Vegetative State, and Related Disorders', *Lancet Neurology*, **3**: 537–46.

Laureys, S., Pellas, F., Van Eeckhout, P., Ghorbel, S., Schnakers, C., Perrin, F., Berre, J., Faymonville, M.E., Pantke, K.H., Damas, F., Lamy, M., Moonen, G. and Goldman, S. (2005a) 'The Locked-in Syndrome: What Is It Like to Be Conscious but Paralyzed and Voiceless?', *Progress in Brain Research*, **150**: 495–511.

Laureys, S., Perrin, F., Schnakers, C., Boly, M. and Majerus, S. (2005b) 'Residual Cognitive Function in Comatose, Vegetative and Minimally Conscious States', *Current Opinion in Neurology*, **18**: 726–33.

Laureys, S., Boly, M. and Maquet, P. (2006) 'Tracking the Recovery of Consciousness from Coma', *Journal of Clinical Investigation*, **116**: 1823–5.

Layon, A.J., D'Amico, R., Caton, D. and Mollet, C.J. (1990) 'And the Patient Chose: Medical Ethics and the Case of the Jehovah's Witness', *Anesthesiology*, **73**: 1258–62.

Leestma, J.E. (2001) Neuropathology of Brain Death', in E.F.M. Wijdicks (ed.), *Brain Death*, Philadelphia, Pa.: Lippincott Williams & Wilkins, pp. 45–60.

Leestma, J.E., Hughes, J.R. and Diamond, E.R. (1984) 'Temporal Correlates in Brain Death. EEG and Clinical Relationships to the Respirator Brain', *Archives of Neurology*, **41**: 147–52.

Lock, M. (1999) 'The Problem of Brain Death: Japanese Disputes about Bodies and Modernity', in S.J. Youngner, R.M. Arnold and R. Schapiro (eds.), *The Definition of Death: Contemporary Controversies*, Baltimore, Md.: Johns Hopkins University Press, pp. 239–56.

Loeb, J. (1916) *The Organism as a Whole*, New York: G. P. Putnam's Sons.

Loewy, E.H. (1987) 'The Pregnant Brain Dead and the Fetus: Must We Always Try to Wrest Life from Death?', *American Journal of Obstetrics and Gynecology*, **157**: 1097–101.

Lynn, J. (1993) 'Are the Patients Who Become Organ Donors under the Pittsburgh Protocol for "Non-Heart-Beating Donors" Really Dead?', *Kennedy Institute of Ethics Journal*, **3**: 167–78.

Lynn, J. and Cranford, R. (1999) 'Persisting Perplexities in the Determination of Death', in S.J. Youngner, R.M. Arnold and R. Schapiro (eds.), *The Definition of Death: Contemporary Controversies*, Baltimore, Md.: Johns Hopkins University Press, pp. 101–14.

McMillan, T.M. (1997) 'Neuropsychological Assessment after Extremely Severe Head Injury in a Case of Life or Death', *Brain Injury*, **11**: 483–90. Erratum published in Brain Injury, 11 (10): 775.

McMillan, T.M. and Herbert, C.M. (2004) 'Further Recovery in a Potential Treatment Withdrawal Case 10 Years After Brain Injury', *Brain Injury*, **18**: 935–40.

Majerus, S., Gill-Thwaites, H., Andrews, K. and Laureys, S. (2005) 'Behavioral Evaluation of Consciousness in Severe Brain Damage', *Progress in Brain Research*, **150**: 397–413.

Menikoff, J. (1998) 'Doubts About Death: The Silence of the Institute of Medicine', *Journal of Law, Medicine & Ethics*, **26**: 157–65.

Mohandas, A. and Chou, S.N. (1971) 'Brain Death: A Clinical and Pathological Study', *Journal of Neurosurgery*, **35**: 211–18.

Mollaret, P. and Goulon, M. (1959) 'Le Coma Dépassé', *Revue Neurologique*, **101** (July): 3–15.

Morison, R.S. (1971) 'Death: Process or Event?', *Science*, **173**: 694–8.

Multi-Society Task Force on PVS (1994) 'Medical Aspects of the Persistent Vegetative State, II', *New England Journal of Medicine*, **330**: 1572–9.

National Academy of Sciences Institute of Medicine (1997) *Non-Heart-Beating Organ Transplantation: Medical and Ethical Issues in Procurement*, Washington DC: National Academy Press.

Nuland, S.B. (1993) *How We Die: Reflections on Life's Final Chapter*, New York: A. A. Knopf.

Pallis, C. (1995) 'Further Thoughts on Brainstem Death', *Anaesthesia and Intensive Care*, **23**: 20–3.

Pallis, C. and Harley, D.H. (1996) *ABC of Brainstem Death*, London: British Medical Journal.

Payne, S.K. and Taylor, R.M. (1997) 'The Persistent Vegetative State and Anencephaly: Problematic Paradigms for Discussing Futility and Rationing', *Seminars in Neurology*, **17**: 257–63.

Pearson, I.Y. (1995) 'Australia and New Zealand Intensive Care Society Statement and Guidelines on Brain Death and Model Policy on Organ Donation', *Anaesthesia and Intensive Care*, **23**: 104–8.

Pernick, M.S. (1988) 'Back from the Grave: Recurring Controversies over Defining and Diagnosing Death in History', in R.M. Zaner, *Death: Beyond Whole-Brain Criteria*, Dordrecht: Kluwer, pp. 17–74.

Pius XII (1957) 'Pope Speaks on Prolongation of Life', *Osservatore Romano*, **4**: 393–8.

Plows, C.W. (1996) 'Reconsideration of AMA Opinion on Anencephalic Neonates as Organ Donors', *Journal of the American Medical Association*, **275**: 443–4.

President's Commission for the Study of Ethical Problems in Medicine, and Biomedical and Behavioral Research (1981) *Defining Death: A Report on the Medical, Legal and Ethical Issues in the Determination of Death*, Washington, DC: US Government Printing Office.

Prochazka, A., Clarac, F., Loeb, G.E., Rothwell, J.C. and Wolpaw, J.R. (2000) 'What Do Reflex and Voluntary Mean? Modern Views on an Ancient Debate', *Experimental Brain Research*, **130**: 417–32.

Quality Standards Subcommittee of the American Academy of Neurology (1995) 'Practice Parameters for Determining Brain Death in Adults (Summary Statement)', *Neurology*, **45**: 1012–14.

Report of the Ad Hoc Committee of the Harvard Medical School to Examine the Definition of Brain Death (1968) 'A Definition of Irreversible Coma', *Journal of the American Medical Association*, **205**: 337–40.

Royal College of Physicians (1995) 'Criteria for the Diagnosis of Brain Stem Death: Review by a Working Group Convened by the Royal College of Physicians and Endorsed by the Conference of Medical Royal Colleges and Their Faculties in the United Kingdom', *Journal of the Royal College of Physicians of London*, **29**: 381–2.

Saposnik, G., Bueri, J.A., Maurino, J., Saizar, R. and Garretto, N.S. (2000) 'Spontaneous and Reflex Movements in Brain Death', *Neurology*, **54**: 221–3.

Saposnik, G., Maurino, J., Saizar, R. and Bueri, J.A. (2005) 'Spontaneous and Reflex Movements in 107 Patients with Brain Death', *American Journal of Medicine*, **118**: 311–14.

Schnakers, C., Giacino, J., Kalmar, K., Piret, S., Lopez, E., Boly, M., Malone, R. and Laureys, S. (2006) 'Does the FOUR Score Correctly Diagnose the Vegetative and Minimally Conscious States?', *Annals of Neurology*, **60**: 744–5.

Seifert, J. (1993) 'Is "Brain Death" Actually Death?', *Monist*, **76**: 175–202.

Shewmon, D. A. (1998) 'Chronic "Brain Death": Meta-Analysis and Conceptual Consequences', *Neurology*, **51**(6): 1538–45.

Shewmon, D. A. (2001) 'The Brain and Somatic Integration: Insights into the Standard Biological Rationale for Equating "Brain Death" with Death', *Journal of Medicine and Philosophy*, **26**(5): 457–78.

Shewmon, D.A. and Shewmon, E.S. (2004) 'The Semiotics of Death and Its Medical Implications', *Advances in Experimental Medicine and Biology*, **550**: 89–114.

Shewmon, D.A., Holmes, G.L. and Byrne, P.A. (1999) 'Consciousness in Congenitally Decorticate Children: Developmental Vegetative State as Self-Fulfilling Prophecy', *Developmental Medicine & Child Neurology*, **41**: 364–74.

Shiel, A. and Wilson, B.A. (1998) 'Assessment After Extremely Severe Head Injury in a Case of Life or Death: Further Support for McMillan', *Brain Injury*, **12**: 809–16.

Smedira, N.G., Evans, B.H., Grais, L.S., Cohen, N.H., Lo, B., Cooke, M., Schecter, W.P., Fink, C., Epstein-Jaffe, E., May, C. et al. (1990) 'Withholding and Withdrawal of Life Support from the Critically Ill', *New England Journal of Medicine*, **322**: 309–15.

Starr, T.J., Pearlman, R.A. and Uhlmann, R.F. (1986) 'Quality of Life and Resuscitation Decisions in Elderly Patients', *Journal of General Internal Medicine*, **1**: 373–9.

Steinhauser, K.E., Clipp, E.C., McNeilly, M., Christakis, N.A., McIntyre, L.M. and Tulsky, J.A. (2000) 'In Search of a Good Death: Observations of Patients, Families, and Providers', *Annals of Internal Medicine*, **132**: 825–32.

SUPPORT (1995) 'A Controlled Trial to Improve Care for Seriously Ill Hospitalized Patients: The Study to Understand Prognoses and Preferences for Outcomes and Risks of Treatments (SUPPORT)', *Journal of the American Medical Association*, **274**: 1591–8.

Truog, R.D. (1997) 'Is It Time to Abandon Brain Death?', *Hastings Center Report*, **27**: 29–37.

   (2000) 'Organ Transplantation Without Brain Death', *Annals of the New York Academy of Sciences*, **913**: 229–39.

Truog, R.D. and Robinson, W.M. (2003) 'Role of Brain Death and the Dead-Donor Rule in the Ethics of Organ Transplantation', *Critical Care Medicine*, **31**(9): 2391–6.

Uhlmann, R.F., Pearlman, R.A. and Cain, K.C. (1988) 'Physicians' and Spouses' Predictions of Elderly Patients' Resuscitation Preferences', *Journals of Gerontology*, 43: M115–21.

UK Medical Royal Colleges (1976) 'Diagnosis of Brain Death', *British Medical Journal*, 2: 1187–8.

University of Pittsburgh Medical Center (1993) 'University of Pittsburgh Medical Center Policy and Procedure Manual. Management of Terminally Ill Patients Who May Become Organ Donors After Death', *Kennedy Institute of Ethics Journal*, 3: A1–15.

US Collaborative Study of Cerebral Death (1977) 'An Appraisal of the Criteria of Cerebral Death: A Summary Statement – A Collaborative Study', *Journal of the American Medical Association*, 237: 982–6.

Veatch, R.M. (1975) 'The Whole-Brain-Oriented Concept of Death: An Outmoded Philosophical Formulation', *Journal of Thanatology*, 3: 13–30.

—— (1976) *Death, Dying, and the Biological Revolution: Our Last Quest for Responsibility*, New Haven, Conn.: Yale University Press.

—— (2004) 'Abandon the Dead Donor Rule or Change the Definition of Death?', *Kennedy Institute of Ethics Journal*, 14: 261–76.

Volicer, L., Berman, S.A., Cipolloni, P.B. and Mandell, A. (1997) 'Persistent Vegetative State in Alzheimer Disease: Does It Exist?', *Archives of Neurology*, 54: 1382–4.

Walters, J., Ashwal, S. and Masek, T. (1997) 'Anencephaly: Where Do We Now Stand?', *Seminars in Neurology*, 17: 249–55.

Wijdicks, E.F.M. (2001a) 'The Diagnosis of Brain Death', *New England Journal of Medicine*, 344: 1215–21.

—— (2001b) *Brain Death*, Philadelphia, Pa.: Lippincott Williams & Wilkins.

—— (2001c) 'Confirmatory Testing of Brain Death in Adults', in E.F.M. Wijdicks (ed.), *Brain Death*, Philadelphia, Pa.: Lippincott Williams & Wilkins, pp. 61–90.

Wijdicks, E.F.M. and Bernat, J.L. (1999) 'Chronic "Brain Death": Meta-Analysis and Conceptual Consequences', *Neurology*, 53: 1369–70; author reply 1371–2.

Wittgenstein, L. (1961) *Tractatus Logico-Philosophicus*, London: Routledge & Kegan Paul.

4 | *The dying human: a perspective from palliative medicine*

MICHAEL ASHBY

In any consideration of death, it seems reasonable to go to the health professions that care for dying people and ask them two key global questions: first, what is dying like, and, second, what, if any, theoretical conclusions does your literature come to about the process of dying? As will be seen in what follows, this task when applied to the medical palliative-care literature, despite sounding disarmingly simple, is far from being so.

Michel Vovelle divides up the subject into three major facets: first, 'la mort subie': literally, death undergone – that is, mainly demographics; second, 'la mort vécue': death 'lived' or experienced; and third, 'discours sur la mort': what is written and theorized about death (Kselman 2004). If applied to the medical palliative-care literature, the field is now recognizing the importance of the first as the demand for service increases, makes some contribution to the second, and has tended to cite writings in the third category from other fields. Notable exceptions in this third category, where overarching issues are addressed include Saunders, Cassell, Kleinman and Cherny on the nature of suffering (Saunders 1984; Kleinman 1988; Cassel 1991; Cherny 2003); Chochinov on dignity (Chochinov 2002a, 2002b); Kearney on spirituality (Kearney 2000); and MacLeod on caring (MacLeod 2001), although much of this work is focused on the doctor–patient relationship. As Sherwin Nuland writes: 'Poets, essayists ... write about death but have rarely seen it. Physicians and nurses who see it often, rarely write about it' (Nuland 1993).

In a celebrated, albeit quirky series of radio documentaries in the 1960s, the Canadian pianist Glenn Gould once observed that if he wanted to know about something, he had a tendency to bypass the relevant experts preferring, for instance, to consult a geologist in far north Canada about spirituality rather than a theologian (Gould 1992). Just as masons were thought to have the secrets of building, doctors might reasonably be expected to be experts on death, and its secrets, because they study the body and treat its illnesses and injuries. However, medical attention and expertise about death and the process of dying is variable and limited. To those outside the profession this is perhaps a bit of a surprise. In fact in the modern era medical engagement has largely been dictated by utility and outcomes, that is, to what extent doctors think they can have effective input. Throughout the twentieth century, medicine's capacity to treat disease and injury improved, and it came to focus less on dying as it was geared to preventing death. In this technological and scientific view of the scope and possibilities of medicine, there was little or no role for doctors with the dying, and so clinical practice, teaching and research in this field were very limited. Patients and their families were seen to be neglected by doctors. This disengagement is well captured in the often quoted but unhelpful aphorism 'now is the time for masterly activity'. The modern hospice and palliative-care movement was born out of a realization that medicine, working as part of a multidisciplinary team, could indeed make a significant contribution to the final part of life, and so medicine has begun to re-engage.

This chapter will briefly review the nature and extent of the clinical challenges of end-of-life care in the presence of evolving demographic changes that result largely from increasing longevity in most parts of the world. It will be seen that this has resulted in altered disease patterns that give rise to prolonged periods of deteriorating health towards the end of life, and for many people the process of dying is longer than ever previously in human history. It will then examine the difficulties of recognition and acknowledgement of the dying process in the medical view of the world and explore new research on the limitations of the ancient art of prognostication in medicine and how absence of prognostic clarity has the capacity to inhibit the deployment of appropriate and necessary care of the dying.

It is seen that as treatment has become more effective, both medicine and the societies it serves have placed more emphasis on bodily and psychological suffering on the journey to death and less on the actual final act of death itself. The bodily preoccupations have also dominated the experience, possibly at the expense of the social and spiritual dimensions. The 'good death' literature sets an agenda for the goals of palliative medicine and challenges it to be truly holistic and multidimensional in its worldview, and multidisciplinary in its practice, but it also cautions about the danger of imposed norms.

The palliative-medicine literature is skewed towards problem-solving and does not include the patient's direct voice as much as it would like to. It is argued that, as a result of professional and wider social influences, even palliative medicine is tending to avert its gaze from death and even to re-badge itself as 'supportive' care. Palliative medicine does not therefore really tell us much about what it is like to die, as we might have expected, and there is scope for it to make more contribution to interdisciplinary work on over-arching principles or theories about death or dying. It does, however, do its best to relieve suffering and has made significant strides with this since the mid-1960s. This is, of course, its main function, for which it also has strong international community support and for which a continued quest for the best clinical and therapeutic evidence is necessary.

Demographics

Progressive ageing of the population has been underway through-out written history, and this process has been accelerating in the last century at a dramatic rate in Western developed countries. This has resulted in a shift of causes of death from acute and rapid (often infect-ive) illness, towards chronic and degenerative conditions like cancer and dementia, and this results in more prolonged periods of illness and dependency before death.

Lynn writes that most people will now have a period of around two years of poor health and progressive deterioration in health status before death. She proposes three trajectories to death: cancer (with a rapid decline – usually months – if treatment fails), organ system fail-ure (gradual decline over years with acute crises, and eventual death from one of these), and prolonged dwindling or dementia/frailty (slow decline in 'old, old' age and multi-factorial cause of eventual death). Lynn suggests that palliative care has predominantly worked with cancer but in recent years has been challenged to address the needs of patients with non-malignant diseases (Higginson and Addington-Hall 1999; Murray et al. 2006) and a greater interface with aged care (Lynn 2005; Lynn et al. 2007). The engagement of palliative-care ser-vices worldwide has therefore been largely determined so far by can-cer epidemiology and the clinical challenges of advanced cancer care, particularly pain and symptom control. Hence, the medical nature of the journey has been important for access to these specialist services rather than just dying per se.

Recognition of the dying process: 'natural' death and medicine

It is hard to say when the process of dying actually begins. From a medical point of view it is most usually seen as being at the time of diagnosis of incurable and progressive disease or injury. If you ask what most doctors mean by the word 'terminal' they mean a diagnostic category of patients who have incurable disease and whose destiny is almost certainly to die of that cause, but where death might be some time off. For most palliative-care specialists, terminal means dying this week rather than next, and the terminal phase of mode is sometimes referred to as a time when the patient is 'actively' dying.

Palliative care is infused with a notion of the 'naturalness' of death in an existential sense, that is, death is an inevitable consequence of living, and dying is a normal part of the life cycle. Palliative-care practice is based on the recognition of a natural dying process and death. The wilful obstruction of this process may well involve a futile denial of one of life's fundamental realities, and it can be argued that the consequences for the individual and for society are both unkind and wasteful. Relief of symptoms and suffering is the guiding imperative in the palliative and terminal modes. It can then be proposed that any medical intervention that is not for a comfort endpoint represents obstruction of this process and may be seen as unduly burdensome or futile. The term 'absolute futility' is used when a proposed procedure has little or no chance of achieving its immediate technical objective. If, however, there is a chance of temporary success in achieving the technical objective, but the procedure is considered to be disproportionate to the underlying clinical situation, futility may be described as relative or situational. Medical decision-making is based on proportionality; by a careful assessment of the therapeutic ratio, of desirable beneficial effects weighed against unwanted side effects. The therapeutic ratio may be unfavourable per se, or unfavourable in the circumstances, due either to prevailing factors that result from the disease or other aspects of the patient's situation. The probability of a favourable outcome from a given treatment may be low but is rarely non-existent (Ashby and Stoffell 1991).

Transitions from curative to palliative and terminal care

If modern palliative-care medicine is based on the recognition of a natural dying process and death, there needs to be a way of incorporating this recognition into decision-making and clinical practice. This can be done by adopting a framework of three phases (or modes), based on goals of care, which have been described in the management of life-threatening illness: curative, palliative and terminal (Ashby and Stoffell 1991). In the curative phase, all efforts are directed towards cure or sustainable remission. A high level of adverse effects and even a significant chance of treatment-related mortality may be accepted for curative treatment. In the palliative phase the disease is deemed to be incurable and progressive, and the goals of care are modified in favour of comfort, quality and dignity. Active treatment of the underlying disease in order to improve quality of life may still occur, and any putative prolongation of life that may occur as a result will usually be regarded as a welcome spin-off but not the prime object of the therapy in question. In the terminal phase, death is believed to be hours or days away, and no treatment-related toxicity is acceptable. Whereas artificial hydration and alimentation may well be a part of care in the palliative phase, it is not usually part of terminal care.

Decreasing levels of treatment-related toxicity are then considered acceptable as the goals of treatment change with the transition from curative mode to palliative and terminal modes of care in a life-threatening illness. In all three phases, therapeutic interventions must be proportionate to the circumstances, and, specifically, treatment-related toxicity should be reduced to virtually nil in terminal care.

The key issue becomes the cut-off between reasonable and realistic medical treatment, and its corollary of futile, intrusive or burdensome treatment that obstructs a natural dying process. In practice, the question becomes: at what level of the therapeutic ratio do we stop treatment, and what degree of influence does the setting have on decisions based on the same therapeutic ratio? When it is recognized that no further curative treatment is possible, acknowledgement of a natural dying process allows the slate to be wiped clean, and only those measures which are required for comfort and dignity are left in place or introduced as indicated. This can be done in positive rather than negative language, instead of removing each therapeutic intervention as part of an anguished opting-out process.

It is both philosophically and medically contentious to suggest that it is possible to predict accurately when a person will die. In fact, medical prognostication has recently been the subject of work by Christakis et al., which shows wide discrepancies between what doctors predict and actual survival of patients (Christakis and Lamont 2000; Glare and Sinclair 2008). Although hard and fast objective clinical criteria for the onset of the terminal phase or mode are not available, the recognition of a natural dying process is central to the ethics and practice of palliative care. Impending death, when a person is said to be 'dying' or 'actively dying', is recognized by a combination of clinical and behavioural features, although they may all go unnoticed or be denied. The objective clinical evidence consists of declining appetite, weight loss, recumbency, lassitude, physiological systems failure, disease progression and vital organ failure. There is an associated decrease in oral intake that usually ceases altogether as the patient's conscious state lapses. Although very variable and personal, the overt or covert psychological evidence may consist of anticipatory grief, emotional withdrawal and future planning that acknowledges the impending death – e.g. funeral planning, by either the person who is dying or family members.

Anxiety is often expressed about nutrition and hydration in the context of the dying process. In a small qualitative study in an in-patient palliative-care unit in Australia, a picture emerges of gradual cessation of food and drink, absence of medical provision and patient concern not being as great as that of relatives. There is no evidence of suffering by patients if adequate mouth care is given. A review of the literature indicates some disagreement in the field itself about the value of medical provision of fluids, with the balance lying in favour of non-provision. Fluid overload and absence of evidence of improved oral comfort with medical provision are widely held as the main reasons for non-provision. The sense of gradual cessation of oral intake, and adaptation, both physiological and psychological, in a 'natural' process of dying, are also strong conceptual influences in palliative care (Van der Riet et al. 2006).

Good death

In a disarmingly simple and powerful study, Steinhauser et al., in a public-health research team in Chicago have shown that if you talk to dying people, their families and carers, and health professionals, there is a striking agreement about the factors that contribute to a 'good' death. They describe a nested set of physical, personal and social attributes of life's end. Patients and families tend to fear bad

dying more than death itself. They value pain and symptom management, clear decision-making, preparation for death, completion,
contributing to others and affirmation of the whole person. They
place high priority on making contributions: gifts, time and money,
decreasing family burden, planning ahead, arranging affairs and saying goodbye. This work provides valuable evidence that many people
do indeed wish to acknowledge their dying and prepare for it, provided that they have adequate symptom control and energy to do so.
Patients also seek meaning, role and usefulness during their final illness and are keen to spare their family and carers excessive burden.
This would appear to be a dignity issue for many people.

Medical personnel tend to emphasize the biomedical aspects, but
this is understandable given their key role. The important message for
them would seem to be to locate their central professional responsibilities in the broader concerns of the patient's agenda. Most services try
hard to do this, sometimes formally in care plans where the patient's
goals and priorities are recorded to ensure that they inform all aspects
of care (Steinhauser et al. 2000).

McNamara and other sociological authors have developed a more
textured and auto-critical view of the 'good death' concept in palliative care. She undertook an ethnographic study of palliative-care
nurses and their construction of the concept. She identifies five challenges to hospice care in adopting the 'good death' ideal. These
are: the encroachment of mainstream medicine and the tendency
to 'over-treat', tensions around acceptance and readiness for death,
nurse- rather than patient-defined understandings of what constitutes
a 'good death', institutional pressures to deliver a 'good death' and
compliance and disappointment issues if this is not achieved. It is
recognized that a more realistic aim, proposed by certain palliative-
care practitioners (Komesaroff et al. 1996), may be the 'good enough'
death (Hart et al. 1998; McNamara et al. 1994; McNamara 2004).
One sense of this is that the death is with integrity, in that it is consistent with the life that the person has lived. So if that person has
lived a troubled life with, say, drug and alcohol abuse and social mar-
ginalization, it should not be a surprise if they are unable to die a
quiet and tidy 'hospice' death. The author's 'good enough' construct
was originally based on the work of the English child psychotherapist
D. W. Winnicott (1896–1971) (Ashby 2001). Winnicott talks of an
idealized form of 'good' mothering that is inherently unrealistic and

that you just need to be 'good enough', but even then someone needs to 'hold' the 'good enough mother' so she can in turn hold the infant in his/her rage (Winnicott 1986). By analogy, the 'good enough' death needs to be 'held', and someone in turn needs to hold the carer. The main reason to invoke this analogy was to explain to carers, both family and professional, that there are limitations to the capacity to relieve another person's suffering, that care seldom perfectly meets the needs and wishes of those being cared for, and that carers also need to be cared for. Carers need not feel that they have failed if they cannot help the patient, and family, to achieve an idealized 'good' death. Palliative medicine has urged other specialties to recognize their own limitations, and so it is healthy for it to do likewise with its own inevitable limitations. For this reason, the French term *accompagnement* (literally accompanying) of the dying person as a linguistic expression of palliative care seems to be apt (Abiven 1990; Hennezel 1995), a walking-with rather than heroic takeover that results in dashed expectations on everybody's part.

Palliative medicine and death 'denial'

The hospice and palliative-care movement developed as a response to the neglect of dying people by the modern healthcare systems that evolved after the Second World War in developed countries. Medicine throughout the twentieth century had become focused on cure as medical technology has progressively opened up new therapeutic options. The stunning achievements of medical science in an age of scientific optimism have led to a level of expectation in the community, which often significantly exceeds reality, particularly in common solid-tumour oncology. The medical and nursing professions often saw death as medical defeat, that perhaps their best contribution to the care of dying people was to know when to stop treatment aimed at cure, but which also often felt clinically, morally and perhaps even legally bound to treat with curative intent no matter how poor the chances of achieving a favourable outcome. Palliative care has emphasized the need to be able to 'accompany' a dying person, to be comfortable with the inability to provide a cure, the uncertainty that is inherent in terminal illness – and to recognize that there is a significant medical contribution to the care of dying people. The early pioneers in Britain deliberately went outside the mainstream National Health

Service to set up their initial prototypic hospice and home hospice services. From the beginning, these services had a focus on outreach and education, recognizing that specialist palliative-care services could not, and should not, attempt to take over and provide all the care required. This would result in an impossible load for the specialist services, de-skill the rest of the health sector and, in the process, send out a dangerous message that dying cannot be dealt with by the community and its primary care and hospital services. Consultation and shared care are often effective models to ensure that palliative-care expertise complements what is already available.

Originally, most new palliative-care initiatives around the world attempted replication, to varying degrees, of the early stand-alone British hospice and home-care model, although there was not the same level of investment in free-standing hospices, and many of the early clinical services and key positions were made at least in partnership with major teaching hospitals. These beginnings have been followed, in both the countries and many others, by a process of reintegration of palliative-care initiatives into mainstream clinical services which James and Field would argue was inevitable (James and Field 1992) and which the pioneers would probably say was their initial intention anyway (Higginson 1993). Thus, palliative-care services are now seen as being in a continual dynamic state of development within health systems that are themselves in a state of instability and rapid evolution.

In a process of mainstreaming of palliative care, it might be asked whether at least palliative medicine itself may have 'reverted to type' and become death-denying. As the agenda of palliative medicine has moved 'up the line' away from death it has tended to focus on quality of life rather than the process of dying. It is, therefore, perhaps also noticeable that the medical gaze is averted from death as a tactic, consciously or unconsciously, to win over colleagues who find a less death-centric pitch more acceptable and less confronting for patients and their families. This shift is implicit in the term 'supportive' care that refers to the deployment of certain elements of palliative care for patients, especially those with cancer, at an earlier stage of their disease trajectory when death is not yet imminent, or even being considered as a likely outcome (Viallard 2004). Even palliative-care doctors do not often spend much time with patients at or very close to the point of death. This is usually the role of nursing staff and family members and carers. If you go to the Oxford Textbook of Palliative Medicine, for instance, the only chapter on the actual process of dying is the one on terminal care which occupies fourteen pages out of 1,280 (Furst and Doyle 2005).

Research

General

Most research dwells on quality of life or the relief of specific symptoms which is not problematical in itself but has the more teleological negative consequence of projecting the view that the main medical meditation on death itself is to situate oneself clinically as far away from it as possible and to dwell firmly in the biophysical. Indeed, it is the nature of medicine to focus mechanistically on specific symptoms and physical signs. These are then subjected to a clinical diagnostic process of evaluation that results in a shortlist of possibilities, the differential diagnosis, and then specifically tailored tests and investigations are used to pinpoint the cause. This cause is then subjected to treatment with the object of eradication of the problem, and hence 'cure' is achieved. Palliative medicine is an off-shoot of this Western medical tradition, and at its most straightforward simply applies the same technique to incurable situations with the prime object of relieving pain and other symptoms that cause suffering. This is a very necessary, indeed centrally important, contribution to the effective delivery of palliative care. The sub-speciality of palliative medicine has gradually developed and gained credibility within the profession, although this is still an ongoing process. However, its growth and acceptance within its own medical world is contingent upon obeying the rules of the game. This requires, first, participation in the evidence-base medicine movement of biomedical research, and, second, an emphasis on quality of life and a shift away from death (see above).

Therapeutic research, as in the rest of medicine, is based upon methodology that emphasizes and privileges the fate of groups of patients, preferably with a control and intervention arm that examines a new treatment. This acquisition of so-called 'high-level' evidence from randomized trials is essential for testing hypotheses, particularly concerning new treatments (mainly drugs). But the knowledge has to be applied to individual patients and journeys, and such research

techniques inevitably involve some endpoint focus and thereby reduc-
tion of the capacity to relate to the totality of the experience from the
patient's perspective.

The difficulties of doing research in palliative care are well documented. Much of the work so far tends to look at effectiveness of
palliative care for populations rather than individuals. The holistic
and multidisciplinary nature of palliative care makes it hard to isolate
interventions and to measure their effects. Recruitment and retention
of patients in trials is hard, and hierarchies of evidence level, based
on the gold standard of the randomized control trial, can seem to
devalue other research, especially qualitative work. An approach to
the evaluation of qualitative studies for inclusion in guidelines has
been proposed that better fits the realities of palliative care (Aoun and
Kristjanson 2005).

Symptom prevalence

The commonest symptoms of dying cancer patients have been summarized in prevalence lists. In these general constitutional symptoms
such as lack of energy, loss of weight and poor appetite are nearly
always the most common. Pain, nausea and vomiting, dyspnoea and
anxiety are usually prominent but less commonly reported than the
constitutional symptoms (Wakefield and Ashby 1993; Teunisson
et al. 2007). This is challenging for palliative medicine as the constitutional symptoms are those that respond least well to treatment and
for which options are limited at the present state of knowledge. In one
unpublished study (Kat and Ashby), bowel incontinence came very
high up the list when a distress index was applied, possibly indicating
the high value patients place on the continence as a dignity issue.

Therapeutic approaches

Whilst it is clear that a person cannot easily attend to their social or
spiritual selves if in pain or if they have other unrelieved symptoms, it
is clear that a number of writers feel that the medical model on which
even palliative medicine is based has its limits. Lawton has concluded
from ethnographic fieldwork in hospice day-care and inpatient-unit
settings that the claims of the hospice movement have been too great,
particularly with regard to embodiment and limitations of expression

of the self and the failure to be able to do much about the social disintegration that is an inevitable part of the dying process in the hospice model of care (Lawton 2000).

Kearney has explored the use of mythology based on ancient rites of Asklepian healing as way of meeting the needs of patients in his care (Kearney 2000), and has used this novel approach in tandem with conventional Western medicine. Rod MacLeod has studied how doctors learn to care and has found that profound impacts often arise from a doctor's early experience that can shape the future capacity of the practitioner to engage with patients in a caring way (MacLeod 2001). He further recommends that patient-centred palliative-care education can make a contribution to general professional and personal growth. The medical profession can also be seen to be taking up the sorts of challenges that Lawton is setting up by attempts to holistically address suffering (Macleod 2007).

Suffering

Two prominent clinicians have attempted to develop a broader medical understanding of the nature of suffering. In a classical anti-Cartesian argument based on clinical experience gained in the early hospice movement Saunders taught about 'total' suffering and made the point that all symptoms are linked and have both physical and psychological components. She therefore urged clinicians to ensure that they paid continual attention to the emotional and spiritual influences on pain and symptoms (Cherny 2003). In a similarly holistic exhortation, Cassel has studied the nature of suffering. In a classic book bearing that title, he advocates deep knowledge of the whole person and a deep engagement by the physician in the alleviation of the suffering. He sets a very doctor-based approach, but the motivation of the polemic is clearly aimed at a medical mainstream that compartmentalizes symptomatology and tends not to take a broader view (Cassel 1991; Cherny 2003).

General descriptions of dying

Descriptions of the process of dying are sparse in the clinical literature, and most tend to emanate from qualitative studies conducted from an ethnographic point of view. An early innovative local hospice programme with the status of a demonstration project in the USA, in Missoula, Montana, gave rise to the publication of an ethnographic account of the dying processes of nine patients. They identified major themes for patients as being: the search for 'transcendent continuity', attempts to gain control, the impact of immobility and shrinking social networks, economic impact, implications and rewards of choosing home care, diminished hope, and loss of personal growth and dignity (Staton et al. 2001). Whilst their social conclusions, most notably about a 'subculture' of the terminally ill, may be questioned (Ashby 2002), and despite the uniqueness of both the project and the community it is located in, these themes resonate with other work of this sort, particularly the struggle to retain independence (Kellehear 1990; Young and Cullen 1996; Lawton 2000).

Witzel reported observations of 360 dying patients between 1965 and 1972 in Erlangen-Nuremberg, including 110 people during the last twenty-four hours of life, and another 250 during their last weeks of life. He compared their behaviours to a control group and found profound differences in attitude, with calm and resignation, little or no fear and a relative absence of desire for information before death in the dying patients. He also saw a brief period of improvement and decreased analgesic requirement before death (Witzel 1975). This observation of a lucid interval is often spoken of but little documented. There appeared to be little evidence of agitated delirium and terminal restlessness, a common feature of contemporary practice, a kind of 'storm before the calm'. Rates of cognitive disturbance in patients entering palliative care of around 20–40 per cent have been quoted, and up to nearly 90 per cent by the time of death (Breitbart and Cohen 2000; Macleod 2007). Witzel also found that his data corroborated the five stages of Kübler-Ross's classic work. Whilst the published data details are limited and the socio-cultural milieu of 1970s Germany may limit applicability elsewhere, this is an interesting study, mostly because such work, from a medical perspective, is so rare.

This relatively peaceful profile of dying thirty years ago in Germany begs the question of modern palliative-care practice. Rates of delirium and terminal restlessness and consequent sedation vary considerably around the world, and in different centres, as seen above. Reasons for this may be an ageing population, and more effective treatments leading to longer survival but more challenging quality of life issues.

However, it is also possible that one price paid for better pharmacotherapy of symptoms is that as body physiology deteriorates, significant rates of cognitive disturbance as a result of drug and metabolite
accumulation, particularly from opioids, may result (Mercadante
1999; Morita et al. 2002).

An exception to the low number of palliative-medicine-based studies of death itself is the work Michael Barbato, who has made one of
the first studies of the point of death, and who has linked his observations to the existential aspects of the experience. He is one of the few
investigators to use non-invasive electroencephalography (EEG) during the final hours of life. He concludes from a small study of twelve
patients that unconsciousness is largely due to disease factors rather
than drugs (Barbato 2001). This aspect of pharmacotherapy and the
dying deserves further study as the possibility still exists of 'locked-in'
states when sedatives, especially widely used benzodiazepine drugs
such as midazolam are used. The patient may look outwardly calm
but be trapped emotionally, and awareness is not ruled out.

Brown's ethnographic study of acute hospital deaths shows that
the actual process of dying in these settings for twenty patients in
two South Australian hospitals was suboptimal. The patients spent
considerable periods of time alone; staff were obviously troubled by
their limitations and constrained by hospital routine. Transfer to a
single room was not always done primarily to meet the patient's needs
but to spare others from exposure to a dying person. A considerable
proportion of nursing time appeared to be focused on technical care,
and there was only limited attention to emotional and spiritual need.
The study shows the need for hospitals to reorientate themselves to
the needs of dying people and to adjust the care to the individual
patient's need rather than make the patient fit the routine (Pincombe
et al. 2003).

Terminal sedation

Sedative drugs are commonly used in terminal care (when death is
believed to be imminent), in order to maintain comfort and dignity by
alleviation of agitation, anxiety and so-called terminal restlessness.
They are used proportionately to the patient's distress, and not to bring
about death (Ashby 1997). It is clear that there is a robust disagreement
within medicine itself about whether such treatment contributes to the

cause of death, and even what the therapeutic goals are or should be. There are those who contend that, within accepted palliative-care practice, patients are sedated, and death is thereby caused, either through central nervous system and respiratory depression or dehydration and starvation. Certainly, palliative-care practitioners rarely use morphine for its sedative properties at any stage of an illness, especially when patients are trying to function as normally as possible, and sedation is usually unwelcome. In terminal care, morphine may even aggravate terminal restlessness, probably due to metabolite accumulation. In terminal care, sedatives are titrated against agitation and distress but occasionally also against another symptom (e.g. pain or shortness of breath) where other measures have failed and the patient may wish to be less aware of what they are going through. If patients are conscious and competent, they are consulted about this and asked if they wish to be more sedated, but they are often unable to give this consent due to incompetence. It should also be noted that patients are usually unconscious or cognitively impaired, and therefore incompetent, at this stage. It is clearly not possible to state categorically that such sedation has no effect on time of death, but this is not really the important question, being superseded by the comfort and dignity of the person. The precise timing of death is unpredictable, and verification of the relative causal contributions to that timing of disease, physiological and pharmacological factors are not usually measurable. Outside the setting of terminal care, so-called 'pharmacological oblivion' (sedation to the point of unconsciousness) is not part of accepted palliative-care practice, unless as a temporary measure for severe organic brain disturbance, and especially not as a way of ending a patient's life.

Desire to die

It is a widely held view that suffering in the advanced stages of disease is so common and bad that suicide or assistance to die are justifiable options. There is a substantial literature on euthanasia, but only a small number of studies that explore expressions of a desire for hastened death, or patients' perceptions of how they might feel about making such a request at some point in the future. Once again there was a strong emphasis on depression, anxiety, desire for control and carer burden issues, although pain and suffering were also frequently cited (Hudson et al. 2006a; Hudson et al. 2006b).

Dignity

Chochinov has studied the topic of dignity in palliative-care patients and has proposed a model of 'dignity-conserving' palliative care (Chochinov 2002b). He points out that 'dying with dignity' has been a much-used slogan in favour of good palliative care but has been little researched. His findings in one study suggest that impaired sense of dignity is relatively uncommon (7. 5 per cent) and that loss of dignity appeared to be associated with certain types of hopelessness and depression (Chochinov 2002a). This article drew an editorial that concluded that this work, despite being based on only sixteen patients receiving specialist palliative care, 'suggest[s] that the dying process may not be as bad as many people fear – at least as regards dignity' (Agrawal and Emanuel 2002). Whilst the model could be seen to be a reworking of the existing known attributes of good palliative care, and the editorial conclusion may seem a little hasty, the work does suggest that a broad view of patient wellbeing is needed and that shortness of breath and depression may be underestimated, whilst pain may be overestimated. The work also captures seven 'subthemes': continuity of self, role preservation, maintenance of pride, hopefulness, generativity/legacy, acceptance and resilience/fighting spirit. This work once again challenges palliative care to reflect on its 'death-centredness'. Hope and continuing to live positively in the face of death seem important to many people. It might be argued that, for some onlookers, including palliative-care workers imbued with death acceptance as a guiding value, the greatest dignity is equanimity and detachment in the face of death, but for those undergoing the process continuing to battle on with life is clearly a very prominent theme, and to be seen to do so is also of social and cultural importance. Macklin has also pointed out the fragility of expanded concepts such as death with dignity from a bioethics perspective (Macklin 2003).

Quality-of-life studies

There are many tools and instruments to measure quality of life in health care, but the challenge has been to adapt them to the special setting of palliative care where deterioration is inevitable (Jordhoy 2007). Global questions about quality of life can be a helpful introduction to symptom assessment. It seems that the most use in the clinical setting is to distinguish individual symptom focus from impact on the rest of the person's sense of wellbeing. So, for instance, a clinical focus on difficult pain for a given patient may still be counterbalanced by a surprisingly good overall quality of life rating by the patient. The issue of differential reporting between patients and proxies, especially family members and carers, is also an important source of bias to be aware of (Higginson and Gao 2008).

Over-arching theories of dying

It is clear that the palliative-medicine literature has been shy of buying into the field of big ideas and theorizing about the process of dying of the kind evidenced in Kellehear's opening chapter for this volume, and most practitioners would probably feel that it is not really their place to do so. In some ways, this is a pity because such an engagement can be revealing and rewarding.

It is clear that agency and personal control are of paramount importance to death and dying in the modern world. The articulation and promotion of individual autonomy is the most valued ethical imperative in modern health ethics. Few in Western countries would dissent from this viewpoint, but it is also clear that few people die in a complete social vacuum, and there are no stages of the life cycle when it is realistic for our own wishes and desires to be the sole determinants of what happens. This is particularly the case at times of great dependency such as death. Palliative care makes a point of including the family and social context of the sick person firmly in the ambit of care and itself poses significant challenges to the notion of control, no matter how much it tries to assist and empower the patient. Palliative-care practitioners work with the reality of both the process and the fact of death, and this can be very confronting, and sometimes unacceptable to those who do not wish to, or cannot, look their dying in the face, even momentarily.

Barbato has emphasized the image of death as a journey to be undertaken and the importance of clinicians helping to ensure that the journey is not obstructed or impeded (Barbato 1998). Journeying metaphors are fairly common in clinical practice.

Stroebe and Schut's model of grief behaviour has been widely adopted and researched as a model of bereavement in which the grieving person moves back and forth from grieving behaviours to practical everyday life pursuits (Stroebe and Schut 1999, 2008). This concept has not been applied to dying people but it would seem also reasonable to acknowledge that people do seem to oscillate between facing the reality of death and continuing their lives as best they can in a positivistic manner: 'living until death' and not 'giving up', planning for the worst but hoping for the best. This tension between hope and reality, and the role of courage in palliative care is a real one as the whole enterprise of the modern hospice movement is based on an acknowledgement of the reality of impending death, and preparation for it (Nekolaichuk and Bruera 1998; Wein 2005). This fundamental aspect of palliative care is not value-neutral, drawing on its Christian religious roots, where history shows that preparation for death, and living always mindful of mortality, is seen to be an all-pervasive spiritual good (Jalland 2002).

The theme of disengagement in which dying is seen as a process permeated with a sense of withdrawal is seen in religious and artistic expressions (see, for instance, Strauss and the Four Last Songs: Das Abschied von der Erde, Tibetan Buddhism, Quaker Faith and Practice, to name but a few) but not so much in the clinical literature even though this is manifestly what is going on. A sense of disengagement seems to be a feature of the older literature. The stages described by Kübler-Ross have been somewhat unfashionable in recent years because of what was felt by many to be an overly prescriptive series of stages (Kübler-Ross 1970). However, stage theories of grief are now undergoing empirical re-evaluation in bereavement research (Maciejewski et al. 2007). In fact, early writers in the field also found similar features, particularly in terms of acceptance. Witzel's and Hinton's observations also suggest an adaptation and gradual acceptance of death that evolves as the inevitability becomes clearer (Hinton 1967; Witzel 1975). Seale et al., on the other hand, show a marked change in the UK in terms of awareness of dying but interpret this as revealing a concern to maintain control over projects of self-identity (Seale et al. 1997).

Not unsurprisingly, medicine does seem to see death as physiological disintegration, and much of it is directed towards ever less successful struggles against the process. This is also the case to some degree within palliative medicine, where restorative and rehabilitation approaches are now also not uncommon.

The most prominent theme of the Missoula study was that the dying were a disenfranchised group within society, despite their location within a caring and innovative service geared at meeting their needs. Whether this conceptualization is seen to be valid or not, it does express a deeper malaise that in a busy positivistic, individualistic, task-orientated society such as the USA (or any other OECD country), it is hard to make room for a comfortable, gradual, contemplative yet connected death. The hospice and palliative-care movement can be seen in one sense as a large collective effort against medical disenfranchisement of dying people and their families. The process of dying was seen to be sidelined by the growth of effective modern medical intervention during the middle of the twentieth century. Any favourable impacts on the social and spiritual dimensions of dying are less easy to discern. The dangers of well intentioned over 'medicalization' of the process are real.

Apart from Barbato (Barbato et al. 1999) and Kearney (Kearney 2000), the medical literature is relatively quiet on the topic of transcendence and transformation, although significant importance is attached to the search for meaning as a vehicle for healing.

Modern palliative medicine, as part of multidisciplinary palliative care, has achieved a great deal for patients who are dying. The clinical endeavours in this field have focused on areas of high distress for which treatment can be effective. The literature generated by the field has surprisingly little to say about the actual death experience itself. Despite all efforts to the contrary, the patient's voice is not heard as loudly and often as it might be. Medicine needs to be cautious lest in its zeal to overcome suffering it renders medical things that are not, and in the process over-sells and over-reaches itself, thus doing what it exhorts the rest of healthcare not to do. It needs to be continuously recontextualized in the person's and the community's lives. Palliative care was born in the full gaze of death; it is predicated on placing a high value on acknowledgement and preparation for death, which is counter-cultural even in the societies where it thrived earliest and best. Palliative medicine needs to be available to all who need it, and sometimes this may be some way from death, but it cannot afford to take its eye off the ball lest it forget the elephant that is always in everybody's room: death.

References

Abiven, M. (1990) *Pour une mort plus humaine*, Paris: Intereditions.

Agrawal, M. and Emanuel, E.J. (2002) 'Death and Dignity: Dogma Disputed', *Lancet*, **360** (9350): 1997–8.

Aoun, Samar M. and Kristjanson, L.J. (2005) 'Evidence in Palliative Care Research: How Should It Be Gathered?', *Medical Journal of Australia*, **183** (5): 264–6.

Ashby, M. (1997) 'The Fallacies of Death Causation in Palliative Care', *Medical Journal of Australia*, **166** (4): 176–7.

Ashby, M. (2001) 'Natural Causes? Palliative Care and Death Causation in Public Policy and the Law', Thesis for Degree of Doctor of Medicine, Department of Medicine: University of Adelaide.

Ashby, M. (2002) 'Review of Jana Staton, Roger Shuy and Ira Byock, A Few Months to Live, Washington DC, Georgetown University Press, 2001', *Monash Bioethics Review*, **21** (2): 37–9.

Ashby, M. and Stoffell, B. (1991) 'Therapeutic Ratio and Defined Phases: Proposal of Ethical Framework for Palliative Care', *British Medical Journal*, **302** (6788): 1322–4.

Barbato, M. (1998) 'Death as a Journey to Be Undertaken', *Medical Journal of Australia*, **168** (6): 296–7.

Barbato, M. (2001) 'Bispectral Index Monitoring in Unconscious Palliative Care Patients', *Journal of Palliative Care*, **17** (2): 102–8.

Barbato, M., Blunden, C., Reid, K., Irwin, H. and Rodriguez, P. (1999) 'Parapsychological Phenomena Near the Time of Death', *Journal of Palliative Care*, **15** (2): 30–7.

Breitbart, W. and Cohen, K. (2000) 'Delirium in the Terminally Ill' in H.M. Chochinov and W. Breitbart (eds.) *Handbook of Psychiatry in Palliative Medicine*, New York: Oxford University Press, pp. 75–90.

Cassel, E.J. (1991) *The Nature of Suffering and the Goals of Medicine*, New York: Oxford University Press.

Cherny, N.I. (2003) 'The Challenge of Palliative Medicine: the Problem of Suffering', in D. Doyle, G. Hanks, N. Cherny and K. Calman (eds.), *Oxford Textbook of Palliative Medicine*, Oxford: Oxford University Press, pp. 7–14.

Chochinov, H.M. (2002a) 'Dignity in the Terminally Ill: A Cross-Sectional, Cohort Study', *Lancet*, **360** (9350): 2026–30.

(2002b) 'Dignity-Conserving Care: A New Model for Palliative Care – Helping the Patient Feel Valued', *Journal of the American Medical Association*, **287** (17): 2253–60.

Christakis, N.B. and Lamont, E.B. (2000) 'Extent and Determinants of Error in Doctors' Prognoses in Terminally Ill Patients: Prospective Cohort Study', *British Medical Journal*, **320** (7233): 469–73.

Furst, C.J. and Doyle, D. (2005) 'The Terminal Phase', in D. Doyle, G. Hanks, N. Cherny and K. Calman (eds.), *Oxford Textbook of Palliative Medicine*, 4th edn, Oxford: Oxford University Press, pp. 1119–33.

Glare, P. and Sinclair, C. (2008) 'Palliative Medicine Review: Prognostication', *Journal of Palliative Medicine*, 11 (1): 84–94.

Gould, G. (1992) *Solitude Trilogy: Three Sound Documentaries*, Toronto: Canadian Broadcasting Corporation Records.

Hart, B., Sainsbury, P. and Short, S. (1998) 'Whose Dying? A Sociological Critique of the "Good Death"', *Mortality*, 3 (1): 65–77.

Hennezel, M. de (1995) *La Mort intime*, Paris: Robert Laffont.

Higginson, I. (1993) 'Palliative Care: A Review of Past Changes and Future Trends', *Journal of Public Health Medicine*, 15 (1): 3–8.

Higginson, I.J. and Addington-Hall, J.M. (1999) 'Palliative Care Needs to Be Provided on the Basis of Need Rather than Diagnosis', *British Medical Journal*, 318 (7176): 123.

Higginson, I.J. and Gao, W. (2008) 'Caregiver Assessment of Patients with Advanced Cancer: Concordance with Patients, Effect of Burden and Positivity', *Health Quality of Life Outcomes*, 6 (2 June): 42.

Hinton, J. (1967) *Dying*, Harmondsworth: Penguin.

Hudson, P.L., Kristjanson, L.J., Ashby, M., Kelly, B., Schofield, P., Hudson, R., Aranda, S., O'Connor, M. and Street, A. (2006a) 'Desire for Hastened Death in Patients with Advanced Disease and the Evidence Base of Clinical Guidelines: A Systematic Review', *Palliative Medicine*, 20 (7): 693–701.

Hudson, P.L., Schofield, P., Kelly, B., Hudson, R., O'Connor, M., Kristjanson, L.J., Ashby, M. and Aranda, S. (2006b) 'Responding to Desire to Die Statements from Patients with Advanced Disease: Recommendations for Health Professionals', *Palliative Medicine*, 20 (7): 703–10.

Jalland, P. (2002) *Australian Ways of Death: A Social and Cultural History 1840–1918*, Melbourne: Oxford University Press.

James, N. and Field, D. (1992) 'The Routinization of Hospice: Charisma and Bureaucracy', *Social Science and Medicine*, 34 (12): 1363–75.

Jordhoy, M. (2007) 'Quality of Life Measures: Practical Considerations', *European Journal of Palliative Care*, 14 (2): 59–63.

Kearney, M. (2000) *A Place for Healing*, Oxford: Oxford University Press.

Kellehear, A. (1990) *Dying of Cancer: The Final Year of Life*, London: Harwood.

Kleinman, A. (1988) *The Illness Narratives: Suffering, Healing and the Human Condition*, New York: Basic Books.

Komesaroff, P., Lickiss, J., Parker, M. and Ashby, M. (1996) 'The Euthanasia Controversy: Decision Making in Extreme Cases', *Medical Journal of Australia*, **162** (11): 594–7.

Kselman, T. (2004) 'Death in the Western World: Michel Vovelle's Ambivalent Epic *La Mort et l'Occident, de 1300 à nos jours*', *Mortality*, **9** (2): 168–76.

Kübler-Ross, E. (1970) *On Death and Dying*, London: Tavistock Publications.

Lawton, J. (2000) *The Dying Process*, London: Routledge.

Lynn, J. (2005) 'Living Longer in Fragile Health: The New Demographics Shape End of Life Care', *Hastings Center Report Special Report*, **35** (6): S14–S18.

Lynn, J., Shuster, J., Wilkinson, A. and Simon, L. N. (2007) *Improving Care for End of Life: A Sourcebook for Health Care Managers and Clinicians*, 2nd edn, New York: Oxford University Press.

Maciejewski, P. K., Zhang, B., Block, S. D. and Prigerson, H. G. (2007) 'An Empirical Examination of the Stage Theory of Grief', *Journal of the American Medical Association*, **297** (7): 716–23.

Macklin, R. (2003) 'Dignity Is a Useless Concept', *British Medical Journal*, **327** (7429): 1419–20.

MacLeod, R. D. (2001) 'On Reflection: Doctors Learning to Care for People Who Are Dying', *Social Science and Medicine*, **52** (11): 1719–27.

Macleod, S. (2007) *The Psychiatry of Palliative Medicine: The Dying Mind*, Oxford: Radcliffe.

McNamara, B. (2004) 'Good Enough Death: Autonomy and Choice in Australian Palliative Care', *Social Science and Medicine*, **58** (5): 929–38.

McNamara, B., Waddell, C. and Colvin, M. (1994) 'The Institutionalization of the Good Death', *Social Science and Medicine*, **39** (11): 1501–8.

Mercadante, S. (1999) 'The Role of Morphine Glucuronides in Cancer Pain', *Palliative Medicine*, **13** (2): 95–104.

Morita, Tatsuya, You Tei, Junichi Tsunoda, Satoshi Inoue and Satoshi Chihara (2002) 'Increased Plasma Morphine Metabolites in Terminally Ill Cancer Patients with Delirium: An Intra-Individual Comparison', *Journal of Pain and Symptom Management*, **23** (2): 107–13.

Murray, S. A., Boyd, K., Kendall, M., Worth, A., Benton, T. F. and Clausen, H. (2006) 'Dying of Lung Cancer or Cardiac Failure: Prospective Qualitative Interview Study of Patients and Their Carers in the Community', *British Medical Journal*, **325** (7370): 929–34.

Nekolaichuk, C. L. and Bruera, E. (1998) 'On the Nature of Hope in Palliative Care', *Journal of Palliative Care*, **14** (1): 36–42.

Nuland, S. B. (1993) *How We Die*, London: Chatto & Windus.

Pincombe, J., Brown, M. and McCutcheon, H. (2003) 'No Time for Dying: A Study of the Care of Dying Patients in Two Acute Care Australian Hospitals', *Journal of Palliative Care*, **19** (2): 77–86.

Saunders, C. (1984) 'The Philosophy of Terminal Care', in C. Saunders (ed.), *The Management of Terminal Malignant Disease*, Baltimore, Md.: Arnold Publishers, pp. 232–41.

Seale, C., Addington-Hall, J. and McCarthy, M. (1997) 'Awareness of Dying: Prevalence, Causes and Consequences', *Social Science and Medicine*, **45** (3): 477–84.

Staton, J., Shuy, R. and Byock, I. (2001) *A Few Months to Live: Different Paths to Life's End*, Washington, DC: Georgetown University Press.

Steinhauser, K. E., Christakis, N. A., Clipp, E. C., McNeilly, M., McIntyre, L. and Tulsky, J. A. (2000) 'Factors Considered Important at the End of Life by Patients, Family, Physicians, and Other Care Providers', *Journal of the American Medical Association*, **284** (19): 2476–82.

Stroebe, M. S. and Schut, H. (1999) 'The Dual Process Model of Coping with Bereavement: Rationale and Description', *Death Studies*, **23** (3): 197–224.

(2008) 'The Dual Process Model of Coping and Bereavement: Overview and Update', *Grief Matters*, **11** (1): 4–10.

Teunisson, S. C., Wesker, W., Kruitwagen, C., De Haes, H. C., Voest, E. E. and De Graeff, A. (2007) 'Symptom Prevalence in Patients with Incurable Cancer: A Systematic Review', *Journal of Pain and Symptom Management*, **34** (1): 94–104.

Van der Riet, P., Brooks, D. and Ashby, M. (2006) 'Nutrition and Hydration at the End of Life', *Journal of Law and Medicine*, **14** (2): 182–98.

Viallard, M. L. (2004) 'A Meeting Point Between Palliative and Supportive Care', *European Journal of Palliative Care*, **11** (3): 91.

Wakefield, M. and Ashby, M. (1993) 'Attitudes of Surviving Relatives to Terminal Care in South Australia', *Journal of Pain and Symptom Management*, **8** (8): 529–37.

Wein, S. (2005) 'Courage: The Heart of the Matter', *Palliative and Supportive Care*, **3** (2): 81–2.

Winnicott, D. W. (1986) *Home Is Where We Start From*, Harmondsworth: Penguin.

Witzel, L. (1975) 'Behaviour of the Dying Patient', *British Medical Journal*, **2** (5962): 81–2.

Young, M. and Cullen, L. (1996) *A Good Death: Conversations with East Londoners*, London: Routledge.

5 | *The demography of dying*

GLENNYS HOWARTH

When confronted with the notion of dying, the immediate response of people in industrial societies may be to reflect on the ravages of cancer or heart disease and to ponder the inadequacies of dying within medical regimes in hospitals as opposed to the holistic care available in hospices. If asked what it is that people die of, a list of illnesses and diseases is likely to be forthcoming. In industrial societies the list might include the 'top killers' of cancer, heart disease and stroke, in developing societies, infectious diseases such as malaria and tuberculosis and, more recently, AIDS. The picture thus created is of a dichotomy between modern industrial societies in which dying can be controlled and dying in poverty in developing countries with insufficient and inadequate medicine and healthcare. To some extent this is a valid depiction of the stark distinction to be made between rich and poor societies. It is, however, a highly simplistic portrayal that effectively conceals the vast range of dying experiences such as the slow deterioration of the body in old age and dementia or Alzheimer's disease. Moreover, it assumes that dying is, or can be, medically controlled; with enough resources and commitment, longevity can be extended and quality of life enhanced. What is hidden in this thesis is non-illness dying such as suicide. What is also concealed is state-controlled dying and the political motivations of dying as a consequence of war, programmes of 'ethnic cleansing', and privation.

In an attempt to insert some complexity into understandings of the range and nature of dying experiences, this chapter first considers the demography and the epidemiology of dying in different geographical regions of the world. In so doing, it focuses on questions of where people die, at what age, what they die of, and why. It begins with a discussion of the problems of relying on mortality statistics to gather data about dying and then goes on to consider some of the major distinctions between dying in industrial and developing societies. As such, it identifies the burden of disease and focuses on the causes and nature of dying from diseases such as cancer and heart disease as distinct from large-scale pandemics such as AIDS, malaria and tuberculosis. Theories of changes in the nature and causes of dying that have distinguished between industrial and non-industrial societies will be critiqued, and non-illness dying, which has no predilection for either industrial or developing nations, will be examined.

Mortality statistics

In seeking answers to the question of what it is that people are dying of in modern industrial societies, or, indeed, throughout the world, there are two potentially rich sources of information. The first is morbidity statistics, used by epidemiologists to understand illness within specific populations. The second is mortality statistics that supply information about the causes and rates of death. Yet neither of these can provide us with an accurate picture of global dying. This is because the prevalence of illness within a population need not be equated with dying, and, equally, mortality statistics may present information on the causes of death but these cannot easily be mapped onto the experiences of dying. Whilst the former statement – relating to morbidity statistics – may be straightforward, the latter may raise a few eyebrows, for surely knowledge of the causes of death ought to be able to provide insights into the experiences of dying. There are four main reasons why such data cannot be relied upon: insufficient data, the dependence on the International Classification of Diseases, inaccuracies in the gathering of data, and political and policy priorities.

Insufficient data

The registration of death and its causes is a legal requirement in the majority of countries in North America, Australasia, and throughout Europe and is frequently noted as a feature of civil society. In many senses it can be viewed as an accounting system whereby the state is able to keep a 'balance sheet of its members' (Prior 2001: 136) in terms of the extent of the population and the causes of death. According to World Health Organization (WHO) statistics, the figures available on causes and rates of death within North America, Australasia, and Europe are almost 100 per cent complete. This, however, is not the case for many developing countries and particularly for countries in Africa where information is scanty and unreliable. Indeed, in seventy-five

WHO member states, including 90 per cent of the countries in Africa, there is no accurate information available on causes and rates of death (Mathers et al. 2005).

Dependence on the International Classification of Diseases

Mortality statistics rely on the death-certification systems of each country which themselves draw from the International Classification of Diseases and Related Health Problems (ICD) to determine primary and underlying causes of death. Currently in its tenth revision, the ICD is structured according to the biomedical model of disease and its categories are almost exclusively clinical. There are three overriding groupings within the ICD: (I) communicable diseases, maternal and perinatal conditions and nutritional deficiencies; (II) non-communicable conditions; and (III) injuries – each of which contains a number of clinical categories, themselves then divided into specific disease types or conditions. Focusing on quantitative measures, we can learn much about the estimated numbers of deaths within each clinical category but little about the nature of dying and how the experience is influenced by social factors and individual characteristics.

There are two important points to note about the ICD: first is the categorization of death according to its biophysical nature, and second is the existence of specific rules of precedence that determine the ordering of priorities in death registration. Each of these factors will be briefly examined.

The ICD is based on anatomical categories and derives its validity from a biomedical model of sickness and death. This may appear entirely appropriate as death occurs when elements of the physical body have failed and dying is a measure of the gradual or sudden breakdown of the physiological 'machine'. However, in neglecting social factors, such as poverty, the available data is unable to provide much insight into the nature and experiences of dying. For example, an African person dying of AIDS in a famine and war-torn country will have a vastly different experience of dying from that of a North American AIDS victim supported by family and friends with sufficient financial resources to provide the latest drugs and care regimes.

A further example of the problems of focusing on physiological factors in dying and death, and one that is increasingly relevant, is the refusal to recognize old age as a cause of dying. Ageing is not a disease; it is simply the case that after decades of wear and tear organs deteriorate and eventually fail. Dying takes place gradually as people experience an increasing inability of their bodies to perform the tasks taken for granted in younger years. Nuland (1993) identifies the major debilities that will lead elderly people to their deaths in affluent industrial societies: 'atherosclerosis [hardening of the arteries], hypertension, adult-onset diabetes, obesity, mental depressing states such as Alzheimer's and other dementias, cancer and decreased resistance to infection. Many of those elderly who die will have several of them. And not only that … terminally ill people are not infrequently victims of all seven. These seven make up the posse that hunts down and kills the elderly among us' (Nuland 1993: 78). Yet this general failure of the body in old age is not an appropriate cause of death when it comes to completion of the death certificate. As a cause of death, old age was removed from the sixth revision of the ICD published in 1949.

The example of death in old age leads to discussion of the other major problem with the ICD, and that is the procedural rules that accompany its use. Death certificates require a medical practitioner to identify both the primary cause of death (Section I) and the associated or underlying causes (Section II). The primary cause is the one that led directly to death. If there is more than one, the causes are listed in such a way that the last of these is taken as the underlying cause. The ICD has rules that determine the ordering of the diseases present, and this has implications for understandings of the nature of dying within particular populations. For example, causes related to the circulatory system currently take precedence over those of other systems, whereas before 1912 it was diseases of the lung and liver that were paramount. Furthermore, changes to the automatic coding rules require that any pathology noted in Section II of the certificate take precedence over a bronchopneumonia stated in Section I (Maudsley and Williams 1996; Prior 2001: 137). Returning to the example of dying of old age, pneumonia, commonly viewed as a 'friend' of the elderly, is, according to these rules, no longer perceived in such a beneficent manner, and its significance in dying is likely to be relegated to a position below that of cardiovascular disease.

Inaccuracies in the gathering of data

Having noted some of the fundamental problems with the ICD classification process, it is relevant also to note that there are inaccuracies in the completion of the certification documentation. In industrial societies, where the data is thought to be almost 100 per cent accurate and complete, studies have demonstrated that there is considerable diagnostic and semantic discrepancy in the way in which physicians interpret and record information (Maudsley and Williams 1996). Lu et al. (2001) examined 'dummy' death certificates completed by 121 doctors and found diversity in the diagnostic categories they used. Furthermore, variations in the reliance on autopsy (which is now generally used less frequently, particularly for elderly people) mean that underlying conditions that may have been significant elements in the dying experience remain hidden. In non-industrial societies, where information on cause of death is notoriously difficult to gather, countries such as Tanzania are pioneering systems of 'verbal autopsy'. These rely on interviews with next-of-kin, conducted sometimes weeks or months after a death has occurred and do not require the input of a medical professional (Adult Morbidity and Mortality Project [AMMP] 1997); thus, their accuracy within the context of the ICD and mortality statistics may be extremely doubtful.

Political and policy priorities

A key element in the collection of data on diseases and causes of death is related to public health and the need to identify factors that can improve the health of populations. The underlying-causes section of the death certificate provides important clues to managing health and illness within societies. Thus, heart disease, cancer, stroke, respiratory disease and accidents (the five leading causes of death in industrial societies) can be sourced to patterns of diet, tobacco and alcohol use, poor exercise and so on. Governments, policy-makers, medical researchers and public-health professionals use this information to initiate research and to educate people about health risks, generating educational campaigns, for example, to reduce smoking, sunbathing and cholesterol levels and to increase exercise uptake and gym membership.

It may also be the case that there is something of a circular or self-fulfilling prophecy element in the reporting of underlying causes of death in that as societies are increasingly perceived as having high rates of fatal heart disease (requiring virulent public-health campaigns), physicians may be increasingly alert to this and consequently more likely to report its presence. In a slightly more cynical vein, Peck suggests that the 'increased interest in the accuracy in the death certification process' may be correlated with the vast amount of money available for medical research (Peck 2003: 904).

All of the factors discussed above alert us to the problems of relying on mortality statistics – which purport to inform us of the demography of death – as a source of data able to provide information about the demography, and hence the nature, of contemporary dying. With this caveat in mind, what can be gleaned from the morbidity and mortality statistics about the demography of dying? If treated carefully and without too much faith in their accuracy they can supply indications of the nature of dying experiences around the world.

Perhaps the first and most obvious observation is that there appear to be major distinctions in the causes of dying between the developed and less developed countries of the world. Life expectancy at birth for males in the UK in 2006 was seventy-nine years, compared to Zambia where it was estimated at forty-two years, and Botswana at fifty years (WHO 2006). Given the focus here on dying rather than causes of death, statistics on the prevalence and death rates attributed to HIV/AIDS in 2003 reveal that around 1 million people in North America and 600,000 in Western Europe were living with HIV/AIDS. The estimate for sub-Saharan Africa was between 25 and 28 million. In the same year, those dying of AIDS were estimated to be between 12,000 and 18,000 in North America, 2,500 and 3,500 in Western Europe and 2.2 and 2.4 million in sub-Saharan Africa (WHO 2005).

It is possible from morbidity and mortality statistics and from medical research to determine reasonably accurate information on the leading causes of death according to age – and from that data to derive some assessment of the nature of dying – within industrial societies. The five 'biggest killers' are heart disease, cancer, cerebrovascular disease (stroke), lung disease and accidents, in that order. By contrast, developing countries have high rates of death from infectious diseases, diseases caused by insanitary living conditions and poor nutrition. In seeking to explain the epidemiological discrepancies between industrial countries and those in the developing world, in 1971 Omran developed a theory of epidemiological transition.

The theory of epidemiological transition

Omran (1971) suggested a three-stage model of epidemiological transition in industrial societies in order to demonstrate that demographic

changes and mortality decline could be correlated with modernization and socio-economic progress. The first stage, the age of pestilence and famine, has been associated with pre-industrial societies
where death preys heavily on the young. The second stage, the age
of receding pandemics, shows improvements in sanitation, standards
of living, medical technology and public-health strategies. The third
stage, the age of degenerative and man-made diseases, is generally
perceived as characteristic of industrial societies from the mid- to late
twentieth century. As Olshansky and Ault argue, '[s]ince degenerative
diseases tend to kill at much older ages than infectious diseases, this
transition in causes of death is characterized generally by a redistribu-
tion of deaths from young to old' (1986: 355–6).

The following discussion will focus on two of the stages of epidemiological transition: the age of pestilence and famine and the age
of degenerative diseases. The second stage, that of receding pandemics,
is primarily an intermediary or transitory period that bridges the other
two. For each of these epidemiological stages, an outline of the categories of dying will be presented, some of the major diseases associated
with it briefly examined in terms of prevalence, and reference made
to what we know about the course of dying from those diseases and
whether death is likely to be swift or lingering. The theory of epidemiological transition will then be critiqued, arguing that it is not modernization per se that has led to changes in the nature of illness dying but,
as Kellehear (2007) argues, the move from rural to urban living.

The age of pestilence and famine

This epidemiological stage is characterized as occurring in pre-
industrial societies where there is a lack of understanding of the nature
of disease and infection, in societies that are likely to be unstable
socio-economically and whose populations are at the mercy of pandemics, natural disasters and the violence associated with war and
conflict. The period of the Middle Ages in Western Europe was such a
time and was replete with infectious diseases that proved fatal. With
little or no understanding of the etiology of disease, populations were
continually at risk from cholera epidemics, smallpox, tuberculosis and
the scourge of plagues and pandemics such as the Black Death, which
swept through Europe at intervals until the early 1700s – the most famous of which, the Black Death of the 1340s, is estimated to have killed
between 25 and 50 million people in Europe alone. There are thought

to have been three types of the disease: bubonic, pneumonic and septi-caemic plague. Infectious in different ways, the diseases attacked the lymph nodes, lungs and blood vessels respectively, with death usually occurring within a few days of the appearance of symptoms.

In the early twenty-first century, there is very little incidence of dying caused by infectious diseases and famine within the industrial world. These are, however, major causes of dying within developing countries. According to WHO research, six diseases account for 90 per cent of all deaths caused by infection. These are pneumonia, AIDS, diarrhoeal diseases, tuberculosis, malaria and measles. Diarrhoeal diseases, malaria and measles particularly target the young, and espe-cially those younger than five years of age. People dying of these dis-eases may be co-infected and suffering simultaneously from malaria, HIV, tuberculosis and diarrhoeal diseases, the latter caused by ingest-ing contaminated water or food.

Malaria

Malaria is caused by infection from parasites usually delivered by the bite of an infected mosquito. In its most acute form it is possible to die within a matter of hours as the parasite attacks the red blood cells in the body, blocking blood vessels that lead to vital organs. The ill-ness causes fever, diarrhoea, nausea and vomiting. Without treatment it can lead to kidney failure, liver infection, haemorrhage and, in its acute form of cerebral malaria, the person lapses into a coma and is likely to die within twenty-four hours. It is now extremely rare for someone to die of malaria within Europe or North America. By con-trast, it is estimated that 1 million people die in Africa each year as a consequence of malaria – most of these are children under five – with others dying, albeit in smaller numbers, in South-East Asia, the Eastern Mediterranean and Western Pacific regions (WHO 2002). The disease is preventable either with medication (as advised to Westerners visiting areas of high risk) or by adopting simple, practical measures such as the use of insecticide nets whilst sleeping. In areas where children are at most risk of infection, poverty is rife and dwellings may have little pro-tection against the mosquitoes that cause the disease (WHO 2002).

Tuberculosis

Although the disease lies dormant in the vast majority of people infected, tuberculosis (TB) is thought to cause the deaths of 1.6 million people worldwide and is a disease that primarily attacks the lungs, causing a chronic cough, blood-tinged sputum, fever, night sweats and weight loss. Treatment usually involves long-term courses of antibiotics but many of the new strains of the disease are antibiotic-resistant. People with HIV, and therefore a weakened immune system, are more likely to contract the disease and to become sick as the incapacitated immune system is unable to combat the TB bacilli. If untreated, TB can spread to the blood and lymphatic systems and from there to other parts of the body. Around 50 per cent of those with the active TB bacteria will slowly die of the disease.

According to WHO data, the largest number of new cases in 2005 was found in the South-East Asia region, but sub-Saharan Africa accounted for the largest incidence of the disease, which at that time was thought to equate to 34 per cent of all cases globally. Whilst the majority of cases are found in the developing world, TB has once again become a concern for industrial societies as it is often a companion to HIV/AIDS, resulting in a lethal combination.

HIV/AIDS

A modern pandemic, which emerged long after Omran had developed the theory of epidemiological transition, is HIV/AIDS. The disease, spread through infected bodily fluids, affects around 40 million people worldwide and has so far accounted for over 25 million deaths (WHO 2005). Once an individual has been diagnosed as HIV-positive the disease may lie dormant in the body for a number of years before progressing to full-blown AIDS. During the HIV period the disease is likely to be asymptomatic. Once the transition to AIDS has occurred the immune system comes under attack and, as a consequence, people may experience multiple illnesses, neurological problems (including dementia) and are likely to suffer a long period of dying (often over a number of years) as the body's organs gradually succumb to a range of associated diseases. AIDS is most likely to affect people in youth or middle age who are sexually and economically active, but infants may be infected at birth and via breast milk and older people infected as they come into contact with the bodily fluids of infected relatives for whom they are caring.

The burden of disease is highest in Africa and South-East Asia where poverty and social stigma add to the physiological indignities of those dying from it.

Famine

The first stage of epidemiological transition is also identified as one in which famine is prevalent. During the Middle Ages starvation was a constant threat throughout Europe. As late as the mid-nineteenth century, the potato famine in Ireland, a largely agrarian society at the time, resulted in around 1 million people dying of starvation between the years 1845 and 1852. Today, in developing countries throughout the world, famine continues to target the poor leaving them without adequate nutritional resources for bodily functioning and growth and at heightened risk of succumbing to infectious diseases. We know the types of nutritional deficiencies that result from famine, and from morbidity and mortality statistics can identify, for example, that the highest rates of protein-energy malnutrition occur in African countries or that those who die of iron-deficiency anaemia are most likely to do so in the countries of South-East Asia. Other sources of information demonstrate that famine is no stranger to many of the African nations, and Westerners, encouraged to provide funding for food aid, have a wealth of media images of the deprivation and suffering it imposes.

Dying of malnutrition is a relatively slow death and, in keeping with the characteristics of this epidemiological stage, it is especially threatening for the young, with children under five experiencing the highest risk of long-term debility and death. A lack of the proteins, vitamins and minerals that are essential for healthy growth and bodily functioning result in either a body that appears to be only skin and bone or one that is bloated with swollen limbs and belly. Malnutrition not only inhibits growth but also causes fever, diarrhoea, brain damage, chronic lethargy and increased susceptibility to infection and disease. Starving people are critically ill, and, if appropriate nutrition is not made available they will die within a matter of months, with wasted bodies and a loss of appetite (and possibly a loss of the will to live) as their stomachs shrink from lack of food.

The age of receding pandemics is assumed within the theory of epidemiological transition to be a transitory stage occurring in industrial societies during the nineteenth and early twentieth centuries when increased understanding of public-health risks, such as insanitary living conditions, contaminated water supplies and other causes of infection, together with advances in medical knowledge such as the discovery of antibiotics, resulted in the introduction of effective measures that drastically reduced the incidence of communicable diseases. Greater social, political and economic stability also supported a move away from large-scale dying as a consequence of infection and famine to a stage where dying occurs much later in life and as a result of degenerative diseases. Of course, this account neglects the distinctions between rural and urban living within industrial societies and assumptions of the impact of medical knowledge and public-health regimes fail to acknowledge differences in access and resources both between and within societies. Yet, if the stage of pestilence and famine is now largely identified as characterizing dying in developing nations, the age of degenerative diseases is thought to depict the nature of dying in industrial, developed societies.

The age of degenerative diseases

It was noted earlier that mortality rates demonstrate that the top five causes of death in industrial societies are heart disease, cancer, cerebrovascular disease (stroke), lung disease and accidents. The discussion here will consider heart disease, cancer and stroke but first it is necessary to briefly examine dying of old age and dementia.

Old age and dementia

The emphasis on the biomedical nature of death requires that although other diseases may be included as underlying causes, only one will be identified as the primary cause of death – for many elderly people this will be classified as some form of heart disease despite the fact that old age carries with it a range of illnesses and declining health. As Nuland argues,

an octogenarian who dies of myocardial infarction is not simply a weatherbeaten senior citizen with heart disease – he is the victim of an insidious progression that involves all of him, and that progression is called aging. The infarction is only one of its manifestations, which in his case has beaten out the rest. (Nuland 1993: 81)

As dying occurs in industrial societies at an increasingly older age, the body may hold within it a number of sites of disease as increasing fragility, rooted simply in the wearing out of organs, means that dying is commonly a slow, degenerative process.

Furthermore, in industrial societies where autonomy is prized, the threat of Alzheimer's disease and dementia is especially terrifying. Although these diseases can occur at any age, the risk vastly increases in later life. The worldwide prevalence of dementia was estimated in the year 2000 at roughly 200 per 100,000 in people aged sixty, rising by the age of eighty to 3,000 per 100,000 in males and almost 5,000 in females of the same age (Mathers and Leonardi 2002). A statistical analysis of dementia prevalence in countries in Europe, North America, Australasia and Japan estimated rates of 1.4 per cent in people aged from sixty-five to sixty-nine, 2.8 per cent in people aged between seventy and seventy-four, 5.6 per cent for the seventy-five to seventy-nine age group, 11.1 per cent for those aged between eighty and eight-four and 23.6 per cent in people aged eighty-five years and over (Jorm et al. 1987). More recently it has been estimated that dementia affects 35 per cent of people over the age of ninety (Brown and Hillam 2004) and that the number of people living with dementia will rise to 29 million worldwide by 2020, 63 million by 2030 and 114 million by 2050 (Wimo et al. 2003; Haan and Wallace 2004).

The slow dying from Alzheimer's or dementia involves a loss of self as memory is gradually impaired and rational thought and reasoning power lost. In later stages of the disease it is not only higher brain functions that decay but also instinctive and voluntary action. It is considered by many to be a most degrading and undignified dying that slowly strips away an individual's personality and character leaving the shell of the body behind. It is commonly referred to in the academic literature as a form of social death from which a person dies despite the fact that their body is still alive (Small et al. 2007).

As people live longer, the incidence of degenerative diseases such as heart disease, cancer, stroke, respiratory diseases and arthritis has increased, and it has been suggested that although the life span has been extended this was achieved at a high cost as the number of years of poor health has also increased, thus questioning the appropriate balance between quantity and quality of life (McCallum 1997). More recently, theorists have argued that a fourth stage of transition is occurring in industrial countries: the age of delayed degenerative diseases. This thesis suggests a 'compression of morbidity' whereby dying is a brief experience and death comes quickly, for example of a sudden heart attack in late old age (Fries 1980). Until that time, people live healthy lives as the incidence of cardiovascular disease declines as a consequence of greater knowledge of causes and the growth in personal responsibility for health.

Heart disease

Heart disease is thought to be the largest cause of death world-wide with estimates of 16.7 million lives lost in 2002 (WHO 2004). Coronary heart disease claims the lives of 7.2 million people throughout the world (WHO 2004). Although 60 per cent of these deaths occur in developing countries, it is a primary cause of dying in industrial societies where, for example, it is estimated that in the USA one in four men and one in three women die each year as a result of a heart attack. The disease is largely lifestyle-related and is linked to tobacco use, high blood pressure and high blood cholesterol. Although many people will die suddenly of a heart attack, others will die gradually, over months or years, receiving medication and treatment for disease that clogs the arteries and eventually destroys the myocardium (heart muscle).

Whilst most heart disease is associated with ageing and lifestyle, rheumatic heart disease is caused by streptococcal throat infection leading to rheumatic fever and resulting in permanent damage to the valves in the heart. There are currently 12 million people affected worldwide, two-thirds of whom are children between the ages of five and fifteen, around 300,000 of whom will die each year. In industrial societies where diseases such as these are thought to have been eradicated or easily treated through antibiotics and, if necessary, surgery, sub-groups of the population who lack information or resources to access treatment continue to be at risk. For example, in Australia, the average age at death of people suffering rheumatic heart disease was thirty-six years for the Aboriginal population and sixty-seven years for non-Aboriginals (WHO 2004).

Cancer

WHO estimates suggest that in 2007 cancer accounted for 7.9 million deaths across the globe (2008). There has been an increased incidence of the disease in the middle-income countries of South America and Asia where 70 per cent of all cancer deaths occur. Whilst the most common cancers in developing countries are liver, stomach and cervical, in industrial societies cancer sufferers are dying of prostate, breast and colon cancer. Many of these cancers are, like heart disease, associated with lifestyle choices such as tobacco and alcohol use and obesity. In the developing world in particular, they may be related to chronic infections – the human papillomavirus can cause cervical cancer and the hepatitis B virus can cause liver cancer. Other forms of cancer are a result of occupational carcinogens or may be a consequence of fallout from chemical and pesticide factory accidents such as those that occurred in the Union Carbide chemical plant in Bhopal, India, in 1984 (Boyne 2003) and Anaversa pesticide factory in Cordoba, Mexico, in 1991 (Ross 1998). Although cancers differ in their effect on the body, in terminal cases the disease obstructs the organs, inhibits metabolic processes, erodes blood vessels and destroys vital centres and biochemical balances until life can no longer be sustained (Nuland 1993: 217).

Stroke

Killing 5.5 million people each year, stroke is the third most common experience of dying and the second leading cause of death for people over the age of sixty (WHO 2004). With a high prevalence in industrial countries it is, again, associated with lifestyle choices entailed in smoking, unhealthy diet, high salt intakes, high blood pressure often caused by high levels of stress, underlying heart disease and diabetes. It is not uncommon for people to experience a series of minor strokes that gradually, possibly over years, result in sensory loss, general weakness, language and visual problems and minor paralysis.

Having outlined some of the major causes of dying in both industrial and non-industrial societies, it is now possible to add a few remarks on the adequacy of the theory of epidemiological transition.

The adequacy of theories of epidemiological transition

The theory of epidemiological transition stems from a modernization thesis that assumes that developing societies will, in time, with socio-economic advances, follow epidemiological pathways similar to those experienced in the industrial world. The data presented here, however, challenges this thesis as populations in developing societies remain large, the goals of public-health campaigns remain difficult to achieve because of lack of resources, poor transportation systems and medical resources remain scarce. This is particularly true for people living in countries with a large landmass in which small rural communities remain the norm and poverty, with its accompanying low standards of living and insanitary conditions, is rife.

The emergence of HIV/AIDS, said to have originated in Africa, is now presenting further challenges to the theory in the form of a new pandemic, relatively resistant to Western medicine and devastating populations in developing countries across the globe. With increased global mobility and the resurgence of new strains of infectious diseases (such as TB) that are increasingly resistant to antibiotics, people in industrial societies are once again at risk of dying from infectious diseases. Furthermore, the alarm generated by the emergence of diseases such as MRSA (found particularly in hospitals in industrial countries) adds to the fear that the age of pestilence may not confidently be assumed to be part of history.

At the same time, diseases associated with Stage 3 of the epidemiological transition – degenerative diseases – may be migrating to developing societies. Cancer, as has been noted, is a major killer of people in middle-income developing countries, and obesity is an increasing health concern as industrial countries export cheap and nutritionally poor food products, labour-saving technologies and electronic devices, such as televisions, which promote sedentary lifestyles in the developing world (Prentice 2006).

Although there have been a number of suggestions that there may be a fourth stage of epidemiological transition, possibly entailing a shortened period of lingering dying in old age or a later onset of degenerative diseases due to healthier living standards (Fries 1980), Barrett et al. (1998) alert us to the possibility that a further stage may entail the resurgence of infectious diseases normally associated with Stage 1. Gaylin and Kates (1997) similarly argue for a revision of the theory of epidemiological transition as the AIDS pandemic has provided us with strong evidence to suggest that progression, and one-way traffic between one stage and the next, is not so clear-cut.

In his *Social History of Dying*, Kellehear (2007) offers an alternative theory of dying that does not rely on historical periods but on ages that correspond to the characteristics of society. He proposes the Stone Age (hunter-gatherer societies), the Pastoral Age (settlement societies), the Age of the City (urban societies) and the Cosmopolitan Age (modern or postmodern societies). He refers to the current modern period as the 'Cosmopolitan Age', an age of global communications and movement, where the social distinctions of earlier periods have less influence. This thesis facilitates an understanding of the dynamics and complexities of dying experiences throughout time and across societies. In the context of the demography of dying in contemporary global societies it provides a more sophisticated explanation for an age that is characterized by a complex mix of 'wealth and poverty, long and short life expectancies, [that] confuses the popular expectations of rich and poor nations about what they hold to be true about their life and death prospects' (2007: 7–8).

Having examined and critiqued the nature of illness dying in our 'cosmopolitan age', what can be said about non-illness dying? Statistics on mortality rates include categories for deaths caused by injuries, both intentional and unintentional. The latter include those caused by road traffic accidents, poisoning, falls, fires and drowning. The former, which will now briefly be considered, include self-inflicted injuries (for example, suicide) and those caused by violence and war.

Suicide

Whilst there are a multitude of reasons for suicide – including as a response to terminal illness and degenerative disease – it can be viewed as the purest form of control over dying. It is estimated that there are around 1 million deaths by suicide annually worldwide (Chishti et al. 2003) and that the highest rates are among the elderly (Kosky et al. 1998; Lloyd 2004: 238) where it is thought to be associated with depression (O'Connell et al. 2004), possibly linked to social isolation and negative attitudes towards elderly people (He and Lester 2001). Suicide is also of concern among young, particularly male, adults, and it is often perceived as a consequence of modernization, individualism and social alienation (Seale and Addington-Hall 1994, 1995; Makinen 2002; Gilchrist et al. 2007). Countries undergoing economic transition such as those of Central and Eastern Europe and the former Soviet Union have particularly high rates among men in the age group of twenty-five to sixty and have been associated with economic insecurity (Addy and Silny 2001), lack of social cohesion and meaning, and a lack of control over individual destiny (Rutz 2001). It is likely, however, that suicide rates worldwide are underestimated as the act is commonly stigmatizing both for the individual and the surviving families and in many countries evidence for an official verdict of suicide (which forms the basis of mortality statistics) needs to be as strong as that for homicide (Howarth 2007).

Violence

Writing in 1972, Gil Elliot referred to the twentieth century as the most violent period in history and estimated something in the region of 110 million deaths as a consequence of war and privation (Elliot 1972: 221). With a focus on ethnic cleansing, Michael Mann asserted that over 70 million people died in the twentieth century as a result of ethnic conflict (2005). Strangely, these figures are rarely mentioned in the literature on dying which tends to focus on illness and medical intervention and care; examinations of violent dying are commonly left to political analysts.

Mann's thesis is that ethnic conflict is a largely modern phenomenon, a product of our civilization and of a form of democracy which, in newly democratic countries, can result in the tyrannical rule of the majority over an ethnic minority. One major feature of modern ethnic cleansing is the camp or detention centre where many millions of people have experienced disenfranchised dying. Noys (2005) differentiates between extermination and concentration camps. This is an important distinction in terms of the experience of dying as in the former people's lives are terminated quickly upon arrival at the camp; these are places of mass killings where people are herded together for immediate execution. People imprisoned in concentration or labour camps may spend years in conditions of privation and enforced slavery eventually to die of 'starvation, overwork, due to disease or through execution' (Noys 2005: 43). The most frequently cited examples of such inhumanity are those of the practices of Nazi Germany with their infamous camps such as Treblinka and Auschwitz. Such camps have been replicated throughout the industrial and developing world. Examples are easily to be found in Bosnia, Cambodia, China, Rwanda and many other countries. Incarceration in such camps leads to shameful dying (Kellehear 2007) where there is a lack of recognition of dying, a loss of identity and a total absence of community support or care. Although the US Camp Delta in Guantánamo Bay in Cuba is not a place of dying, its formal structure provides an insight into the experiences of camp inmates worldwide: 'excluded from ... international human rights law ... left utterly abandoned by the law and utterly exposed to the threat of torture or death ... left without any prospect of release' (Noys 2005: 125).

Some reflections on the themes of dying

In the opening discussion in this volume, Kellehear presents a number of themes that have emerged from the literature on dying experiences. The final section of this chapter will reflect on some of those themes, namely agency and control, linearity and oscillation and disenfranchised dying.

Studies concerned with agency and control in dying have largely focused on the experiences of people dying of cancer in industrial societies. There is a tendency to assume that the nature of dying is polarized between developed and developing societies. The dichotomy assumes that people dying in industrial countries do so over a lengthy period and thus have greater control over the process and are more likely to be able to exercise agency over their personal circumstances – for example, putting their social affairs in order and saying goodbye – if not control over the extent of pain and the timing of death. An element of this is linked to the belief that medical intervention, to some extent, releases people from the physiological burdens of dying, thus enabling them to take control of, or at least participate in decision-making about treatment and to deal with social and family matters.

In developing societies, dying is frequently negatively depicted as conforming to Stage 1 of the epidemiological transition in which people are dying of infectious diseases and are thus unable to exert agency over the experience. It is certainly true that vast numbers of people live in poverty and experience dying as a consequence of infectious diseases, entailing great pain and suffering and allowing them little time to set their affairs in order. It should also be remembered, however, that many die in old age and as a consequence of the same diseases that kill people in the West. Ironically, a similar epidemiological period in Western Europe was described (perhaps rather romantically) by Ariès (1981) as a time in which people were able to die a good death in which, aware that they were dying, they were able to exert agency, preparing themselves spiritually and emotionally and dealing with the unfinished business of their earthly existence. It is possible that this is also the experience of some individuals in developing societies, where people are more familiar with dying trajectories, living in small-scale communities where family, friends, neighbours and priests may be able to support them along the journey.

If people in developing societies are more familiar with dying, it is because it is not sequestered in the way it has been represented in industrial societies (Illich 1976; Elias 1985; Mellor 1993) where it is perceived as institutionalized, medicalized and professionally managed and where its unpleasant features are hidden in institutions and masked, where possible, by medication. With fewer health resources and less medical intervention, the dying experience in developing countries may be more linear than that in industrial societies where, as Kellehear (this volume) notes, dying entails a series of critical junctures that are used by carers to determine where the dying person is positioned along the journey and what to do next.

Oscillation is a particular feature of dying in old age and also for those dying of HIV/AIDS in industrial societies where antiretroviral drugs extend the period of dying. Multiple failures of the body in old age and lack of familiarity with the signs of dying and impending death make it difficult to be confident that one has embarked on the dying journey, and even more difficult to identify the proximity of death. This, coupled with the capacity of medical science to 'bring people back from the brink' (albeit only temporarily) results in dying of old age and AIDS in industrial societies as an experience of oscillation. Indeed, in dying of old age it is possible that people may not identify themselves as dying, merely experiencing periods of malaise or suffering from the general debility associated with an increasingly aged body.

A lack of recognition that someone is dying has been described as disenfranchised dying and is frequently perceived as a consequence of withholding information about prognosis (as first highlighted by Glaser and Straus (1965) in their work on closed and open awareness). More commonly, in industrial societies today it is associated with institutionalization. For example, when very old people are no longer able to care for themselves (and are without family willing and able to care for them) they may be placed in a nursing or residential home where they will eventually end their days. This is a period of dying as the physical body and, for those with dementia, mental faculties deteriorate and decline. Yet it is also a period when the fact of dying is rarely confronted (Johnson 2005), the institutionalization of

elderly people having the effect of hiding death in old age and disenfranchising those who are dying. This is the shameful death that
Kellehear (2007) argues has the following characteristics: erosion
of awareness of dying, erosion of support for the dying, stigmatized
dying and entailing dying as a trial or set of trials – in this context
defined as 'barriers, tests and life-threatening challenges to illness,
disability, medication, harmful social attitudes and responses of other
human beings as a consequence of a life lived too long' (Kellehear
2007: 212).

This shameful and disenfranchised dying, however, does not require
the physical disappearance of dying people into residential facilities.
It also encompasses vast numbers of people dying in extermination
camps and incarcerated in the labour camps of the modern world.

The stigmatization suffered by people dying in poverty of diseases such as AIDS can also lead to shameful and disenfranchised
dying. Indeed, in some indigenous belief systems sexually transmitted
diseases are thought to be caused by evil forces such as witchcraft
and sorcery and, not uncommonly, are perceived as punishment for
wrongdoing (Liddell et al. 2005). Relatively little is known about how
people live and die from this chronic disease.

Conclusion

Notwithstanding attempts to piece together information about the
causes and nature of dying, it remains the case that there is scant knowledge of the demographics of dying – both within industrial and non-
industrial or developing societies. Further research is needed – some
of which is currently impossible to undertake in developing countries
where we can only guess at the nature of dying and where even basic
statistics on illness and death are often unavailable. Furthermore,
although we now have studies of the experiences of people dying from
the major diseases prevalent in industrial societies, there is a paucity
of similar information for those dying in the developing world. Elliot
(1972) argues that the twentieth century witnessed the greatest number of deaths in history, the majority of which were caused by violence, in concentration and labour camps and as a result of privation
and famine. His thesis is particularly notable in that these deaths were
the outcomes of disenfranchised dying. We might now add to his list
dying of AIDS in circumstances of poverty in developing countries.

Despite (or, arguably, as a result of) the obsessive focus on estimated numbers of deaths, for example, from killer diseases in continents such as Africa, these 'balance sheets' mask the experience of dying and reveal nothing about the meanings it may hold for human beings themselves. One major reason for this is the emphasis in the Cosmopolitan Age on illness dying, a physiological experience with spiritual or emotional elements but nevertheless a primary concern of medicine and subject to medical management. The political and moral dimensions of dying are lost in this analysis as is the extent to which dying is a consequence of political power. In illness dying, as we have seen, the medical and healthcare resources available are determined by the nature of the disease and the extent to which it is recognized as a 'major killer' in wealthy, as opposed to developing societies. As significant, especially in light of the vast numbers of people, is the neglect of the experience of non-illness dying: accidents, suicide, and disenfranchised dying as a consequence of state promoted violence perpetrated in the name of nationalism and ethnic cleansing.

References

Addy, T. and Silny, J. (2001) 'Globalization in Central and Eastern Europe: Responses to the Ecological, Economic and Social Consequences', *The Ecumenical Review*, 53 (4): 493–500.

AMMP (Adult Morbidity and Mortality Project) (1997) 'Overview of Census and Verbal Autospy Methods', *Policy Implications of Adult Morbidity and Mortality: End of Phase 1 Report*, UK Department of International Development and Government of the United Republic of Tanzania, 103–5.

Andersson, R. and Moniruzzaman, S. (2004) 'Relationship Between Economic Development and Suicide Mortality: A Global Cross-Section Transition Perspective', *Public Health*, 118 (5): 346–8.

Ariès, P. (1981) *The Hour of Our Death*, London: Allen Lane.

Barrett, R., Kazawa, C.W., McDade, T. and Armelagos, G.J. (1998) 'Emerging and Re-Emerging Infectious Diseases: The Third Epidemiologic Transition', *Annual Review of Anthropology*, 27 (October): 247–71.

Boyne, R. (2003) *Risk*, Buckingham: Open University Press.

Brown, J. and Hillam, J. (2004) *Dementia: Your Questions Answered*, London: Churchill Livingstone.

Chishti, P., Stone, D.H., Corcoran, P., Williamson, E. and Petridou, E. (2003) 'Suicide Mortality in the European Union', *European Journal of Public Health*, **13** (2): 108–14.

Counts, D.R. (1976) 'The Good Death in Kaliai: Preparations for Death in Western New Britain', *Omega*, **7** (4): 367–72.

Dobson, R. (2006) 'The Number of Children Dying from Malaria Approaches a Million a Year', *British Medical Journal*, **332**: 570.

Elias, N. (1985) *The Loneliness of the Dying*, Oxford: Basil Blackwell.

Elliot, G. (1972) *Twentieth Century Book of the Dead*, Harmondsworth: Penguin.

Fries, J.F. (1980) 'Aging, Natural Death, and the Compression of Morbidity', *New England Journal of Medicine*, **303** (3): 130–5.

Gaylin, D.S. and Kates, J. (1997) 'Refocusing the Lens: Epidemiological Transition Theory, Mortality Differentials and the AIDS Pandemic', *Social Science and Medicine*, **44** (5): 609–21.

Gilchrist, H., Howarth, G. and Sullivan, G. (2007) 'The Cultural Context of Youth Suicide in Australia: Unemployment, Identity and Gender', *Social Policy and Society*, **6** (2): 151–63.

Glaser, B. and Straus, A. (1965) *Awareness of Dying*, Chicago, Ill.: Aldine.

Haan, M.N. and Wallace, R. (2004) 'Can Dementia Be Prevented? Brain Ageing in a Population Based Context', *Annual Review of Public Health*, **25** (1): 1–24.

He, Z.X. and Lester, D. (2001) 'Elderly Suicide in China', *Psychological Reports*, **89** (3): 675–6.

Howarth, G. (2007) *Death and Dying: A Sociological Introduction*, Cambridge: Polity.

Illich, I. (1976) *Limits to Medicine*, London: Marion Boyars.

Johnson, M. (ed.) (2005) *The Cambridge Handbook of Age and Ageing*, Cambridge: Cambridge University Press.

Jorm, A.F., Korten, A.E. and Henderson, A.S. (1987) 'The Prevalence of Dementia: A Quantitative Integration of the Literature', *Acta Psychiatrica Scandinavica*, **76** (5): 465–79.

Kellehear, A. (2007) *A Social History of Dying*, Cambridge: Cambridge University Press.

Kinealy, C. (1994) *The Great Calamity: The Irish Famine 1845–52*, Dublin: Gill & Macmillan.

Kosky, R.J., Eshkevari, H.S., Goldney, R.D. and Hassan, R. (1998) *Suicide Prevention: The Global Context*, London: Plenum.

Liddell, C., Barrett, L. and Bydawell, M. (2005) 'Indigenous Representations of Illness and AIDS in Sub-Saharan Africa', *Social Science and Medicine*, **60** (4): 691–700.

Lloyd, L. (2004) 'Mortality and Immortality: Ageing and the Ethics of Care', *Ageing and Society*, **24** (2): 235–56.

Lu, T.-H., Shau, W.-Y., Shih, T.-P., Lee, M.-C., Chou, M.-C. and Lin, C.-K. (2001) 'Factors Associated with Errors in Death Certificate Completion: A National Study in Taiwan', *Journal of Clinical Epidemiology*, **54** (3): 232–8.

McCallum, J. (1997) 'Health and Ageing: The Last Phase of the Epidemiological Transition', in A. Borowski, S. Encel and E. Ozanne (eds.), *Ageing and Social Policy in Australia*, Cambridge: Cambridge University Press, pp. 54–75.

Makinen, I. H. (2002) 'Suicide in the New Millennium: Some Sociological Considerations', *Crisis: Journal of Crisis Intervention and Suicide Prevention*, **23** (2): 91–2.

Mann, M. (2005) *The Dark Side of Democracy: Explaining Ethnic Cleansing*, Cambridge: Cambridge University Press.

Mathers, C. and Leonardi, M. (2002) *Global Burden of Dementia in the Year 2000: Summary of Methods and Data Sources*, Geneva: World Health Organization.

Mathers, C. D., Ma Fat, D., Inoue, M., Rao, C. and Lopez, A. D. (2005) 'Assessment of Global Cause of Death Data', *Bulletin of the World Health Organization*, **83** (3): 171–7.

Maudsley, G. and Williams, E. M. I. (1996) '"Inaccuracy" in Death Certification: Where Are We Now?', *Journal of Public Health Medicine*, **18** (1): 59–66.

Mellor, P. (1993) 'Death in High Modernity: The Contemporary Presence and Absence of Death', in D. Clark (ed.), *The Sociology of Death*, Oxford: Blackwell, pp. 11–31.

Noys, B. (2005) *The Culture of Death*, Oxford: Berg.

Nuland, S. B. (1993) *How We Die*, London: Chatto & Windus.

O'Connell, H., Chin, A., Cunningham, C. and Lawlor, B. (2004) 'Recent Developments: Suicide in Older People', *British Medical Journal*, **329**: 895–9.

Olshansky, S. J. and Ault, A. B. (1986) 'The Fourth Stage of Epidemiological Transition: The Age of Delayed Degenerative Diseases', *Millbank Memorial Fund Quarterly*, **64** (3): 355–91.

Omran, A. R. (1971) 'The Epidemiological Transition: A Theory of the Epidemiology of Population Change', *Millbank Memorial Fund Quarterly*, **49** (4): 509–38.

Peck, D. (2003) 'The Death Certificate: Civil Registration, Medical Certification, and Social Issues', in C. Bryant (ed.), *Handbook of Death and Dying*, London: Sage, pp. 899–909.

Prentice, A. M. (2006) 'The Emerging Epidemic of Obesity in Developing Countries', *International Journal of Epidemiology*, **35** (1): 93–9.

Prior, L. (2001) 'Death Certificate', in G. Howarth and O. Leaman (eds.), *Encylcopedia of Death and Dying*, London: Routledge, pp. 136–7.

Ross, J. (1998) 'Two Causes for Dying Mexican Village: Pesticides and NAFTA', *Albion Monitor*, January 19. Available online at www. monitor.net/monitor.com/9801a/mexbohpal.html (accessed 18 July 2008).

Rutz, W. (2001) 'Mental Health in Europe: Problems, Advances and Challenges', *Acta Psychiatrica Scandinavica*, **104** (Suppl. 410) (15): 20.

Seale, C. and Addington-Hall, J. (1994) 'Euthanasia: Why People Want to Die Earlier', *Social Science and Medicine*, **39** (5): 647–54.

(1995) 'Dying at the Best Time', *Social Science and Medicine*, **40** (5): 589–95.

Small, N., Froggatt, K. and Downs, M. (2007) *Living and Dying with Dementia*, Oxford: Oxford University Press.

Songwathana, P. and Manderson, L. (2001) 'Stigma and Rejection: Living with AIDS in Southern Thailand', *Medical Anthropology*, **20** (1): 1–23.

Wimo, A.B., Winblad, B., Aguero-Torres, H. and Von Strauss, E. (2003) 'The Magnitude of Dementia Occurrence in the World', *Alzheimer Disease and Associated Disorders*, **17** (2): 63–7.

World Health Organization (2002) *Reducing Risks, Promoting Health Life*, Geneva: WHO.

(2004) *World Health Report 2004, Deaths by Cause, Sex and Mortality Stratum in WHO Regions, Estimates for 2002, Statistical Annex*, Geneva: WHO.

(2005) *AIDS Epidemic Update 2005*, Geneva: UNAIDS.

(2008) 'Are the Number of Cancer Cases Increasing or Decreasing in the World?', available online at www.who.int/features/qa/15/en (accessed 1 May 2009).

6 | *Historical approaches to dying*

JULIE-MARIE STRANGE

As the introduction to this volume indicates, conceptions of dying are neither universal nor static. Contemporary theories of dying conduct highlight particular theories about the role and the status of the dying and those who interact with them in either a professional or personal context. Whilst historians have borrowed from bereavement studies and anthropology in assessing death and dying in the past, and recent inter- and cross-disciplinary collections suggest the possibilities of fruitful exchange (Charmaz et al. 1997), this literature tends to relate to understanding rites of passage regarding death and separation, in particular, grief and mourning. The history of dying as an avenue in its own right is still relatively recent (Kellehear 2007).

Nonetheless, some of the insights into dying highlighted in the social and behavioural studies are pertinent to historical models of dying. In particular, dying as 'personal control' has dominated the history of dying in Western Europe from the Middle Ages in the form of the 'good death' or the 'art of dying', a series of actions by the dying to prepare for their demise. The good death as agency has been obscured, however, by the reliance on partial accounts of dying usually derived from literature outlining how individuals *should* die or the memoirs of those left behind. It is, therefore, often the agency of participants in dying that falls under the historical gaze. Although this model remains the principal mode of approaching dying in Western culture from the Middle Ages, dying has been configured in other ways that are not necessarily exclusive.

The 'good death' model rests upon the notion that some deaths were 'bad'. This has tended to refer in a literal sense to dying processes that were severely curtailed by sudden demise or inhibited by factors such as contagion or ignorance. However, as the introduction to this volume suggests, dying behaviours can fluctuate according to status, particularly for the socially excluded. Historically, the marginal dying have included the very poor, ethnic and religious minorities and the

123

plague-infested. These roles compromise the expectations and obligations of the dying and those responsible for caring for them. This overlaps with two further notions of dying: withdrawal and disenfranchised dying. First, the preparation for, contagion of or loss of consciousness during dying creates a degree of physical and social isolation from the living. Second, the experiences of some marginal groups, such as paupers, were characterized by a lack of control and decision-making over the dying process.

Analyses of dying in the twentieth century have emphasized the idea that death represents a medical 'failure' (Ariès 1981; Prior 1989; Walter 1994). Prior to advances in curative medicine, conceptual understandings of 'bad' deaths implied that individuals could 'fail' at dying well. Again, this emphasizes matters of agency: the responsibility of the dying to manage their death properly and the scope for those around them to assign alternative meanings to dying behaviours both during and after the dying process. Notions of death as a journey have resonance historically also. In pre-Reformation Britain, dying did not end as such with physiological collapse but was extended through the journey of the soul through Purgatory. Similarly, recent surveys of dying during the Stone Age suggest that dying was conceived largely as a journey into an 'other' world (Kellehear 2007).

This chapter begins by outlining how histories ostensibly concerned with the causes of death or the rites of passage following expiration can throw light on contemporary assumptions and understandings of dying, causes of death and particular groups of the dying. Focusing on the history of dying in the West, particularly in Britain, from the Middle Ages, it outlines key themes in the history of dying, notably the 'good death' model, which represent not only one of the most striking continuities across this period but also religion, domesticity, agency and emotion. It ends by considering the limits of a historical emphasis on notions of good and bad deaths that have been underpinned by the assumptions and ideals of elite groups.

Histories of dying

The origins of historical inquiry into social and cultural attitudes towards dying are often located in the French Annales School's interest in mentalities and, in particular, the publication of Philippe Ariès's seminal *Western Attitudes Towards Death: From the Middle*

Ages to the Present (1974), later expanded into *The Hour of Our Death* (1981). Ariès suggests that the cultural history of death can be organized into key mentalities associated with specific chronological periods. Although heavily criticized since, Ariès's contribution to the history of death and dying is considerable: he engages with sensibilities of death, outlines changing conceptions of the 'art' of dying and depictions of death and reads the material culture of death as indicative of shifts from community to individual-based attitudes. This is not to suggest that historical research into death did not exist prior to Ariès. In Britain, James Steven Curl (1972) and John Morley (1971) had already published on the burgeoning death culture of the Victorian period, both historians situating it within a trajectory of an increasingly consumer society that, for Curl in particular, became more tasteless the lower one travelled down the social scale. Since the 1970s, the history of death and dying has proliferated, with death studies becoming a major growth area of academic inquiry (Walter 1994). Nonetheless, the history of dying, as opposed to death and its aftermath, remains patchy and, until relatively recently, tied to studies of demography, disease and post-mortem responses to loss.

To begin, demographic analysis has enabled historians to determine the key causes of death and to chart patterns of population growth, stability and decimation. Analyses of causes of death may not illuminate the personal and cultural meanings invested in dying experiences, but they do facilitate correlations between factors such as disease, disaster and social attitudes. As Susan Sontag's studies of the metaphors of illness in the late twentieth century demonstrate (1978, 1989), the pathology of disease is inextricable from cultural conceptions of illness and, consequently, the moral judgement of those with disease. For instance, the pandemic character of smallpox between the seventeenth century and early nineteenth century did little to prevent the stigmatization of the illness, those who suffered from it or the moral aspersions cast on their dying experience (Shuttleton 2007). In the nineteenth century, syphilis was personified in written and visual texts as Death (Guthke 1999), whilst diatribes against the sex trade and anxieties about 'respectable' women in public spaces were imagined in terms of contagion and mortality (Epstein Nord 1995). Similarly, consumption was the most rampant killer in the nineteenth century, infecting the affluent as well as the poverty-stricken. In the cultural imagination, it was associated with

Romanticism, an idealized form of melancholy, refined sensibilities and 'beautiful' death (bright eyes, a slight physique and rosy/feverish cheeks) (Ariès 1981), even to the point of being ridiculed by contemporary commentators (Braddon 1864). Yet consumption was also valued as a potentially virtuous demise that gave the dying ample opportunity to prepare for death (Jalland 1996).

Causes of death have also been mapped to consider environmental and social factors shaping the geopolitics of disease and dying. For instance, research into adult mortality statistics from the eighteenth century onward indicates that the wealthy died in equal numbers to the poor but from different, affluence-associated causes such as heart or liver disease (Razzell and Spence 2007). Mortality indices have also been utilized to make assumptions about the relative value attached to different lives and dying experiences. Infant deaths have attracted particular interest because, despite overall mortality rates going into long-term decline from around 1870, infant mortality remained disproportionately high until the First World War. Whilst demographic analysis has facilitated a range of interpretations on the reasons for high infant death rates (Lewis 1980; Marks 1996; Morgan 2002), comparisons between high birth and death rates have also encouraged some historians to draw conclusions about low levels of emotional investment in dying infants, echoing contemporary assumptions that infant life was expendable and that sickly or unwanted infants were actively encouraged to die (Rose 1986). In comparison, analysis of responses to mass and sudden deaths associated with demographic disaster, such as the Black Death which hit Britain in 1348 or the First World War in 1914–18, has thrown 'normative' dying experiences into relief whilst raising questions about how non-normative dying experiences can be invested with political and social importance (Winter 1995; Horrox 1999; Morgan 1999).

Histories of mourning and disposal focus ostensibly on the aftermath of dying. Classic studies such as Julian Litten's *The English Way of Death: The Common Funeral Since 1450* (1991) and Clare Gittings' *Death, Burial and the Individual in Early Modern England* (1984) take a long view of social, economic and cultural change to chart the rise of the undertaker and the relationship between belief, custom, social hierarchy and consumption whilst histories on burial and commemoration assess the ways in which grave space and markers reflected changing social structures, cultures of consumption and expressions of identity and cultural values (Brooks 1989; Laqueur 1993; Tarlow 1999; Snell 2003). Yet texts concerned with the funeral as a status indicator and the survival and adaptation of rural custom in an urban context invariably engage with the ways in which responses to death highlight social attitudes towards the dying. For example, the introduction and growth of coffins in the early modern period and the expanding provision of cremation in the late nineteenth and twentieth centuries mirrored shifting notions of hygiene and decay that shaped interaction with the dying as well as the dead (Gittings 1984; Jupp 2006).

Similarly, the creeping commercialization of the disposal of the dead has been tied to shifting manifestations of affective individualism. As Sarah Tarlow (1999: 174) notes, fluid affective climates are 'neither prior to nor a product of social and economic change, but an inseparable part of them'. Thus, Victorian material cultures of death permitted a greater choice in the manifestation of feeling and enabled a broader cross-section of the bereaved to express the importance of personal relationships and the uniqueness of the individual through the consumption of funeral goods. Thus, what might be deemed funeral extravagance by those who could least afford it could acquire meaning beyond its economic and status value as a means of enacting the value of the deceased's life and the significance attached to their passing (Drakeford 1998; Strange 2005). Hence it is possible to read the rites and customs of mourning as insights into relations between the deceased and the bereaved both before and after expiration. Likewise, a 'good' funeral could assign new meaning to, or make amends for, a negative dying experience.

The disposal of the dead has also been used to infer attitudes towards different groups of the dying. This is most notable with the burial of the very poor. Two pieces of legislation, the Anatomy Act 1832 (which made unclaimed pauper corpses available to anatomy schools for dissection) and the New Poor Law 1834 were designed to act as deterrents to applications for relief, but, in practice, they changed the relationship of the dying to death. Punitive measures against poverty in death stigmatized the dying and removed the comforts of a dominant model of 'good' death: given popular correlations between integrity of the corpse and resurrection, the threat of dissection ruptured assumptions about afterlife reunion with loved ones; deaths in the workhouse condemned many of the poor to die alone;

and most dying would have been aware that pauper burial would bring stigma on their loved ones (Richardson 1987).

Histories that explicitly address dying as a social, cultural and familial experience continue to take Ariès as a starting point. Acknowledging that change was often slow and that continuities might exist across centuries, Ariès nonetheless sketches epochs of significant cultural change, largely tied to notions of increased individualism, theological doctrine and Ariès's own assumptions about 'healthy' and pathological approaches to dying. Thus, the twelfth century marked an increasing anxiety in Western societies about dying well, individual and communal responsibilities for negotiating the art of dying and, in particular, the salvation of the soul. The sixteenth century witnessed a growth in erotic depictions of Death whilst the Enlightenment encouraged individualism. From the eighteenth century, the deathbed was increasingly dramatic, with anxiety about an individual soul augmented, and in some cases eclipsed, by grief, loss and memory at the death of a loved one. It was this escalation of sentiment surrounding the dying that inspired the great mausoleums, cemeteries and literature of the long nineteenth century. The 'death of the Other', as Ariès terms it, moved attitudes towards dying away from preoccupations with divine judgement to fix attention on the mourner and to recast death in a romantic-tragic frame: dying was unbearable and imprinted the bereaved with lasting melancholy. The agency of the dying to inscribe final meaning on their life was overwhelmed by the effusive feelings of the grief-stricken. The twentieth century ruined the 'beautiful' death by making it invisible, forbidden and pathological with the dying and the bereaved surrendering the organization of dying to an army of professionals.

Ariès's chronology and evaluation of shifting mentalities has attracted much criticism since publication, not least because much of his thesis is underpinned by the argument that death in the twentieth century had become 'bad' (Cannadine 1981; Dollimore 1998). Nonetheless, Ariès's identification of distinct cultural epochs is symptomatic of a tendency to organize the history of dying into 'ages', sometimes reflecting common periodization trends within history or, more particularly, shifts in popular religious belief or doctrine, demographic disaster or war. For instance, studies of mortality after the Black Death note the personification of death as a triumphant cadaver who moved amongst the living to remind them of their mortality, situating 'dying' firmly in the midst of life (Guthke 1999; Horrox 1999). Analysis of the abolition of doctrinal concepts of Purgatory during the Reformation indicates not only changed eschatological beliefs but also shifts in notions of how to die well (Horrox 1994; Harding 2002). Studies of the rise of 'affective individualism' at the end of the eighteenth century identify subtle shifts concerning the conceptual relationship between 'man' and Nature, driving a culture of death and dying that fixed on the self as opposed to a community (Gittings 1984).

The rise of micro-history has militated against grand narratives of cultural change in attitudes towards dying, with historians increasingly focusing on continuities, the amorphousness of belief and elastic notions of death and dying. Likewise, a theoretical preoccupation with diverse identities has fostered approaches that emphasize the gendered, ethnic, confessional and class-bound character of social and cultural experience. Yet, as Kellehear notes in defence of broad chronologies, the grand narrative lends 'clarity' to conceptions of change, contrasts and continuities whilst drawing attention to the 'commonalities' in human behaviour (2007: 4). Kellehear draws out a different chronology to one rooted in religious change, consumer culture or disaster to identify four representative styles of dying at different points in time: the Stone Age, when cultural understandings of dying located it principally in terms of an other-worldly journey after expiration; the Pastoral Age, when anticipation and preparation for death were highly valued; the City Age, when notions of preparation for 'good' death were superseded by a desire to manage dying; and, finally, the Cosmopolitan Age in which dying became understood in terms of shame and failure. Identifying separate ages, Kellehear emphasizes the continuities and changes between periods and attitudes, eschewing a linear narrative but observing the ways in which the meanings invested in and the organization of dying are informed by cultural heritages. Indeed, much of the history of dying appears to be typified by attempts to divest dying of fear and to bring it under some form of human control.

The good death

Some form of a 'good' death model whereby the dying and those around them endeavour to bring death within the remit of human influence and understanding appears ubiquitous across the historiography of Western death from the medieval period onward. Since the Middle Ages in Europe, the good death has referred, first, to fulfilling Christian obligations of faith and, second, to a desire to put secular affairs in order. Although the two prerequisites are usually deemed to have coexisted, the emphasis on the sacred and secular differed according to context and period. To die well necessitated some anticipation of death to allow for preparation and usually included ensuring that death took place in a domestic context.

Medieval historians' understanding of good death relies heavily on religious doctrine and ideals rather than on popular interpretation and experience. Thus, dying in the Middle Ages is defined largely by concern for the soul. Dying was shaped, before expiration, by spiritual preparation for death and salvation and, afterwards, by the endeavours of those left behind to speed the soul on its journey through Purgatory to Heaven. Commentators on dying in the twentieth century often lament the institutionalization of death in hospitals and hospices (Gorer 1965; Ariès 1981); but, in a sense, dying in previous ages was not without formal regulation but, rather, managed by a different set of professionals. In preparing for death in pre-Reformation Britain, particular emphasis was placed upon receiving the 'last rites', which located dying as a spiritual journey and established powerful links between the end of life and the Church. The dying professed allegiance to Christianity, renounced and were granted absolution from their sins and received the Sacrament (Binski 1996). As Rosemary Horrox outlines, the importance attached to formalized religious preparation for death up to the end of the fourteenth century necessitated priests sleeping within their parish at night so that they could easily be found (Horrox 1999: 93).

The perception of a highly ritualized passage from life to death was also fraught with anxieties, not least involving the timing of last rites. The dying had to be sufficiently lucid to participate in the Eucharist and sufficiently well not to vomit after receiving the Host. Horrox points to a stream of clerical advice on the ability to receive the last rites more than once in a lifetime or several days in advance of death which suggests a level of popular uncertainty and fear about getting dying 'wrong' (Horrox 1999). The dying were ostensibly at the centre of the good death, but the involvement of others in making preparation for death and praying for the soul of the deceased made dying a communal affair: the priest's mission to administer last rites was advertised by the ringing of a hand bell whilst family and friends attended to the dying and households prayed for the salvation of the soul (Horrox 1999: 93). The separation of physiological death from the journey of the soul extended the social organization of dying from the onset of terminal illness to after expiration and interment with ongoing prayers for the soul of the deceased.

Although the theology of salvation underwent significant changes between the twelfth century and the twentieth and confessional identities proliferated in a post-Reformation context, the medieval conception of good death established the blueprint for the Christian art of dying for almost a millennium. The key difference after the Reformation was that, in the absence of Purgatory, the organization and spiritual definition of dying were shortened to coincide with physiological understandings of expiration. This also shifted the focus of deathbeds as the dying became solely responsible for determining the fate of their soul and investing the spiritual contrition of death with significance. This is not to suggest, however, that the communal and shared aspects of dying receded. Receipt of the Sacrament, clerical prayers or both remained desirable for many dying Christians even though, in theory, the importance of the priest diminished in a post-Reformation world that emphasized the accessibility of God. Nonetheless, the dying could repent their sins and seek spiritual comfort simply through prayer with family and friends. Such practices ensured that dying remained, to a degree, a social process that was imbued with religious meaning and that the individual desire to die well held considerable significance for those left to mourn.

Research on death among elite families in Victorian Britain suggests that the 'good death' model was still pivotal to the social organization of, and cultural meanings attached to, dying in the nineteenth century (Jalland 1996). Within Evangelical religion, the good death was firmly rooted in notions of suffering for Christ and submitting the Self to God's will. The ideal circumstances for achieving good death were a drawn-out illness, such as consumption, whereby the dying undertook a spiritual test of faith, making explicit their humility and submission to the will of God in the face of painful and frequently premature death. The dying were not isolated in their trial but accompanied by family and friends who also prayed for fortitude and the abnegation of their desires to God's will. The importance attached to dying well was reflected in the proliferation of texts and visual tracts dedicated to advising the sick and those caring for them on how to achieve a good death. Most 'art of dying' texts ostensibly served a didactic purpose in providing guidelines for managing the dying process well, but they also served a pragmatic and psychological purpose in preparing families for the emotional trials of dying and outlining what dying might look, sound and feel like.

Although overwhelmingly tied to Christian precepts of salvation, the good death was also tied to placing domestic affairs in order to suggest the interplay of sacred and secular elements within the organization and understanding of a dying process. Medieval wills were often composed or altered on deathbeds indicating the attendance of legal men as well as clerics upon the dying (Horrox 1999). In the early modern period, the drawing up of a will embodied the merging of sacred and secular with the legal process frequently involving a priest and a testament of faith (Houlbrooke 1998).

The good death model depends partly upon its antithesis, crudely referred to as the 'bad death'. Bad deaths most commonly referred to deaths that were deliberately unchristian, such as the death of an atheist or an unrepentant sinner, or sudden death where no spiritual preparation for dying was possible. Violent and accidental deaths were thought to leave families uncertain of the salvation of the deceased, but these deaths also ruptured the catharsis of active engagement with the social and familial management of dying. Similarly, deaths from highly infectious disease often deviated from expectations of good dying experience, not least because some infections made carers vulnerable to death. Deaths from bubonic plague, for instance, were rapid and tended to condemn an entire household to death, leaving little time or inclination to make assiduous preparation. Deaths from some diseases, such as smallpox which covered the skin in pustules, rendered the dying contagious, unfamiliar and repellent to the senses and can hardly have been 'good' even within a Christian context. The worst death was suicide. As life was God-given, self-murder represented a heinous sin and left bereaved families riddled with self-recrimination.

As most historians acknowledge, the good/bad death model is flawed, not least because it rests overwhelmingly on notions of what dying *ought* to be like rather than the messiness of personal dying experience. Likewise, it is notable that much of the visual and textual literature associated with 'art of dying' models was written by purveyors of good deaths such as clerics or lawyers or mourners reimagining the dying process rather than the dying themselves. Nonetheless, the good death model reflects contemporary dominant depictions of dying across a vast swathe of Western history and, crucially, highlights key themes in the history of understanding the dying experience.

Religion

Despite the overlap between sacred and secular elements of good death, historical understandings of the art of dying rest overwhelmingly on Christianity and the spiritual preparation of the dying for death and an afterlife. In emphasizing the impact of shifts in religious belief and practice on the organization and understanding of dying, historians have situated Christianity at the kernel of a history of dying. Moreover, religion has provided a useful chronological spine for histories of dying because most deaths, especially interments, have involved the Church or some form of organized religion. Within British culture, the formalization of a doctrine of Purgatory, the apocalyptic meanings imposed onto the Black Death, Protestant Reformation, the Enlightenment, Evangelical revival, the perceived clash between religion and science post-Darwin and the steady march of secularization have provided hooks for assessing change and continuities in attitudes towards dying. Likewise, religion was the focus of most didactic literature on how to die well. In these texts, the dying process was framed within a concern for an afterlife, and most of the activities and organization of the deathbed were conducted with a spiritual destiny in view. Thus, the dying were expected to take responsibility for their soul in negotiating confessional obligations, such as taking the Sacrament, seeking atonement for sins and accepting death without fear. Despite placing the onus on the dying, this perception of the organization of dying also emphasized the deathbed as a place for worship where loved ones joined with the dying in a spiritual quest for humility, faith and fortitude, often underpinned by the involvement of clergy.

Most historians acknowledge that the good death was an ideal. In practice, the religious obligations on the dying and those caring for them could be difficult to negotiate. For instance, the Evangelical Victorian idealization of terminal illness as providing opportunity for preparation of the soul was compromised by the lived experience of death. As Jalland notes, death at home in bed was valued because it allowed intimacy between the dying and their loved ones and enabled the constant surveillance of the deathbed. Yet submission to God's will and fortitude were in many cases ruptured by searing pain and loss of consciousness. Notions of the good death provided guidelines for managing the process of dying, offering a raison d'être for suffering and providing a language of comfort and reunion in the afterlife. However, the centrality of Christian belief in contemporary approaches to managing dying also created problems. To begin, the deaths of children precipitated self-recrimination in some parents who mused on whether they and their offspring were being punished for sins committed by the parents. Others struggled to reconcile a loving God with the suffering of the dying and located the deathbed not as a space for the confirmation and strengthening of faith but, rather, as a locus for doubt and anger.

Likewise, the emphasis on religion could render dying a space of hostility and guilt. Jalland gives the example of Ada, Lady Lovelace, who died from cancer in her late thirties. A freethinker, Ada's prolonged death was characterized by the battle between her Evangelical mother and her husband for control of the deathbed and Ada's beliefs. The vehement determination of Ada's mother to save her soul and trump her son-in-law exposed how conceptions of good death, one rooted in Christianity and another in self-determination, competed for domination with the sick situated at the centre of a power struggle. The organization, management and meaning of dying was, potentially, a locus for competing claims to authority: intimate, religious, legal and medical.

Finally, the location of religion at the centre of a model of dying raises difficulties when approaching social groups for whom Christianity was irrelevant or whose religious beliefs are unknown because, within an orthodox good/bad binary, non-Christian deaths cannot be good. It is noticeable that the few analyses of the responses to dying of non-believers in the Victorian period, for instance, have highlighted the 'absences' (of consolation and hope chiefly) in the management of dying and grieving and the chasm created by an assumed normative Christian approach and atheist or agnostic responses to death (Garland 1989; Jalland 1996). This may well reflect contemporary anxieties, but it also potentially limits the questions asked of alternative responses to dying.

Domesticity, activity and agency

Pivotal to good death models was an assumption that dying would take place in a domestic context. In addition to the religious significance of time to prepare for death, domestic settings enabled a degree of observation, communication and management of the dying. Despite depictions of dying as a prolonged and uncertain process, good death-beds were also represented as managed spaces with clearly defined roles and tasks assigned to participants. Pivotal to the organization of dying was the lucidity of those in decline coupled with knowledge that illness was terminal. On a secular level, the good death model was underpinned by a desire to put domestic affairs in order. As noted above, for those with estates to bequeath, this involved the drawing up of a legal will and last testament. A burgeoning business and professional class from the early modern period also meant that increasing numbers of dying people, usually but not exclusively men, had financial and administrative tasks to complete and order. Kellehear points to the shift from a religious-oriented dying experience focused on preparation of the soul to one that rested on a notion of 'service' whereby the dying summoned the assistance of lawyers, medics and clerics to undertake specific tasks (2007). On a less formal level, the organization of domestic affairs usually involved the negotiation of personal and affective relations. Integral to the good death model was making time to say final goodbyes and to inscribe one's death with individual significance, making gifts of personal possessions, seeking assurance of future obligations and giving thanks or making amends for things past.

Most historians of dying note the attendance at some point of a cleric or religious emissary. Even among poor households in a supposedly godless urban industrial context, the dying were often welcoming to priests, prayers and words of heavenly reunion (Strange 2005). For many, belief was amorphous, and, even in the absence of clear understandings of doctrine and scripture, a Christian language of hope and resurrection provided a loose script for comforting the dying and their loved ones (Williams 1999). From the Middle Ages, the presence of medical men at the deathbed could prove contentious as practitioners sought to conceal impending death from the sick and to alleviate suffering, practices at odds with Christian emphasis on the necessity of knowing when death was imminent in order to prepare for it (Horrox 1999). It was not until the Victorian period that the medical man's will began to hold sway over that of the cleric, especially as medicine increasingly moved from a palliative to a curative function (Jalland 1996; Porter 2001).

Amongst the affluent, medical care and pragmatic chores (such as washing the sick, turning them over, changing bedding, cleaning vomit) were often administered by paid employees, medical men and, by the later Victorian period, trained nurses. For many poorer families, medical attention was unaffordable necessitating an informal, home-based care as the key source of ameliorating pain and discomfort. Formalized and familial care were not, however, mutually exclusive. Attempts to provide some physical relief to the dying, such as moistening the lips with water, wiping a brow, attempting to feed the sick, cleaning vomit and simply touching or holding, also operated on an emotive level to provide reassurance for the dying and those caring for them. Small gestures were frequently rooted in intimacy and enabled a form of non-verbal communication, for instance, acknowledging the presence of deathbed participants. The activity of striving to alleviate pain also enabled those close to the dying to create a sense of purpose in an often helpless situation whilst organized surveillance of the sick provided an element of control against the unknowable timescales of death.

For those who were very ill but conscious, dying could be boring. Accounts of deathbeds across socio-economic class and period relate the efforts of relatives and friends to stimulate the dying by reading to them, praying with them or relating news. Among the affluent, deathbeds were frequently situated within a bedroom or private chamber, which was policed by close relatives and, in later periods, medical attendants (Jalland 1996; Houlbrooke 1998). Whilst hope for recovery remained, deathbeds were understood as sickbeds. The physical separation of the very ill from everyday life was often rooted in pragmatic concerns: fear of contagion and a desire to maintain a tranquil and policed environment for the comfort of the sick. Yet the tangible separation of the terminally sick had abstract meanings too, investing the dying with a definite identity and apparently locating the dying process as something removed from everyday life. Notions of 'social death' tend to be used in social-science approaches to the withdrawal of the dying in the twentieth and twenty-first centuries, but physical removal and loss of consciousness could also facilitate a form of social death as the dying's status shifted from 'sick' to proto-corpse. In poorer households, the dying were rarely separate from the living, and the process of dying was, perhaps, less clearly defined, a factor that has been invested with moral value. In the Victorian period, middle-class observers frequently lamented the location of the dying in the midst of homes often depicted as thoroughfares of neighbours and associates. Similarly, although the continuity of life around the terminally sick was directed by circumstance, it tended to be interpreted as fatalism or apathy towards the dying. Yet evidence suggests that when poor families were given the chance of separating the dying from the living through admission to hospital, families were resistant to separation. In this context, the presence of the dying at home could facilitate the inclusion of the dying in everyday life and enable relatives and friends to undertake surveillance and care without disruption to other pragmatic tasks (Strange 2005).

Likewise, despite efforts to separate the dying from the hurly-burly of everyday life, historians have emphasized how good deathbeds across socio-economic groups had an element of public spectacle, not least because the social organization of dying required extra-familial resources. The deathbed process became common knowledge whereby a stream of medical staff, clergy, relatives and friends visited the dying and communities engaged with the deathbed from a distance, for example, with church congregations praying for the dying and neighbours relaying news and sending messages of sympathy.

It is notable that the forms of dying that were explicitly public, such as death through violence or accidents, were usually classed as bad deaths, partly because they were sudden but also because they lacked the intimacy and domesticity of 'good' modes of dying. Capital punishment was the most unambiguous spectacle until 1868 when it stopped taking place as a public event. As V. A. C. Gatrell notes, public executions were typified by a carnival atmosphere tempered by the crowd's interpretation of moral justice. Crowds anticipated a degree of performance from the felon whilst the state and church authorities hoped for public contrition. For those about to hang, a final speech provided an opportunity to invest their death with independent meaning. Notably, there was a long history of publishing the final speeches of repentant felons sent to the gallows (Gatrell 1994).

Even the most intimate deathbed could be made public by the documentation and dissemination in print of an individual's demise, through funeral sermons, religious tracts or the publication of exemplary deathbed narratives. Houlbrooke suggests that the 'art of dying well had never been so closely observed and analysed as it was during the 150 years following the Reformation' (1999: 179–90). That was until the Victorians. Evangelical accounts outlining how to die well burgeoned from the late eighteenth century, reaching a peak in the high Victorian period with the boom in print culture rendering reading materials available to all but the poorest (Dixon 1989; Jalland 1996; Davin 2001).

The publication of deathbed narratives recreated dying in a different context and, potentially, divested the agency of the dying. Historical emphasis on the memoirs of the bereaved risk depicting the dying as a passive recipient of solace, but historians point to the ways in which the dying were active participants in the management of and meanings attached to their demise. Both Jalland and Houlbrooke note the efforts of terminally sick adults and children to reassure loved ones of their acceptance and preparedness for death. Studies of Victorian Evangelical texts suggest that the dying visualized Heaven, sometimes proclaiming that they could see Jesus or deceased relations. Dying children promised to reunite with parents and siblings in a heavily domesticated Heaven (Dixon 1989; Jalland 1996). Such accounts indicate the extent to which the attainment of a 'good' death was fundamental to shaping the grief of the mourner, but they also suggest that depictions of 'good deaths', overwhelmingly derived from those left behind, were vulnerable to manipulation and reinterpretation.

Preparations for good death conferred an obligation upon the dying to remain lucid for as long as possible and to comply with religious and social expectations. The extreme discomfort of prolonged illness and loss of consciousness or coherence compromised the full participation of the dying in the deathbed drama, however. Likewise, whilst deathbeds were often the locus for expressions of love and longing, they could also become spaces of recrimination and oppression. Examples of individuals who resisted the missionary fervour of relatives highlight not only the agency of the dying in giving meaning to their demise but also how vulnerable they were to the zeal of relatives or friends. Once the dying expired, they surrendered control of the meanings ascribed to their deaths. As Jalland notes, shared conceptions of the good death provided a cultural script for dying, but they also enabled the bereaved to reimagine deathbeds in idealized terms.

Most contemporary writers acknowledged that achievement of the good death was difficult and created room for manoeuvre in their advice, enabling onlookers to discount or reinterpret behaviour or sentiments that contradicted an ideal type, thereby compromising the agency of the dying in post-death commemorative texts (Houlbrooke 1999). Thus, distressing deathbeds were recreated in terms of repose and dignity, conversions to Christianity obtained whilst the dying were insensible or under duress were glossed over, and the family disputes that sometimes erupted at a deathbed could be renegotiated and explained. Similarly, dying experiences presumed to be intimate and domestic took on different meanings when circulated in a public domain and for didactic purposes.

Nonetheless, the imagined deathbed could offer solace to the bereaved when dying took place away from a domestic and managed environment. Analysis of commemorative ritual to mark the fallen of the First World War threw into sharp relief the emotive and psychological significance of the deathbed, saying final words and possession of a corpse. For many bereaved during war, the importance they attached to obtaining information concerning the demise of a loved one also indicates the way in which the pursuit and retrieval of knowledge to create an imagined deathbed could operate as a way of regaining a sense of control and comfort when dying happened at a distance (Winter 1995).

The emotion of dying

Attention to the tasks of death highlights the multiple obligations on the dying to put their spiritual and temporal house in order prior to expiration. But dying is an emotional experience too. One of the principal difficulties in achieving a good death was that it required the cooperation of the dying and their loved ones in accepting death as the inevitable outcome of illness or accident. Historians of death and grief have turned to bereavement studies' theories of non-linear 'stages' of reaching reconciliation to death and restitution from loss to depict emotional responses to dying. Indeed, studying early modern responses to death and dying, Ralph Houlbrooke remarks on the familiarity of symptoms of loss to modern readers, noting that there was 'no obvious contrast between the sensibility of the late seventeenth century and that of the late twentieth' (1999: 187). The relatively abundant survival of personal papers from the 'much biographied elite' from the early modern period on has facilitated close readings of affective responses to dying, notably Houlbrooke's analysis of post-Reformation elite families' management of dying (1998), Pat Jalland's moving and sensitive account of the complex emotions of Evangelical Christians to deaths they were supposed to accept as God's will (1996) and David Cannadine's pioneering analysis of the devastation occasioned by deaths in the First World War whereby any notion of management or organization was ruptured by the violent, distant and, in some cases, uncertain, demise of male relations (1981).

Accounts of deathbed scenes, largely by the bereaved, have been used to good effect to extrapolate love and loss during final illnesses, the trauma of sudden deaths and the importance of reimagining deathbed scenes after the event. For Jalland's subjects, affective ties also problematized the smooth course of Evangelical notions of good death. Narrating the experience of Archbishop Tait and his wife Catherine in the mid-nineteenth century as one after another of their children died from fever, Jalland demonstrates the sheer range of emotion centred on the sickbeds and deathbeds of the children: the Taits moved between expressions of rage, incomprehension at God, fear, hope, submission, acceptance, disbelief, despair and love. As Jalland notes, neither parent moved seamlessly from one stage of loss to another, nor did their feelings necessarily coincide. What united their experience was the attempt to control their emotions at the bedside of the dying and in front of their living children (Jalland 1996: 129–39). This suggests that emotion might be seen as cluttering the deathbed, rendering the task of reconciliation more difficult. This is not to suggest that emotion was absent from the dying experience but that it was expressed in ways that avoided displays deemed excessive, self-indulgent or disruptive.

Curiously, the apparent absence of emotion in poorer households has caused consternation among historians inclined to read silence less as the management of feeling than as evidence of a limited capacity to feel. This is encapsulated in the presumed causal relationship between the rise of capitalism and the supposed rise in affective relations described in Lawrence Stone's *Family, Sex and Marriage in England, 1500–1800* (1977). David Vincent's essay on love and death in working-class autobiography (1980) marked a pioneering attempt to grapple with the perception that emotion and, in particular, grief were 'luxuries'. For Vincent, the ability to contain feeling in working-class culture was underpinned by the material impact of death on the financially insecure and the sheer frequency of mortality, especially among infants, within the average working-class family. Yet Vincent's conclusions are tentative, qualified by the complexities of interpreting personal testimony as evidence of an emotional self, especially when those narratives were composed for dissemination in the public domain. Similarly, many authors' grasp of language was limited, encouraging the use of religious and secular clichés. Vincent's concern that women's voices were largely absent from the story indicates an awareness that emotion was mediated through gender whilst the assertion that family experience differentiates 'otherwise homogeneous social, economic and occupational sections of the population' suggests Vincent's underlying discomfort with generalizations that appeared to place sensibility on a class-based sliding scale.

Vincent highlights many of the difficulties in writing about emotion. Jalland is more confident, expressing a commitment to 'experiential history' and asserting that historical actors 'must first speak to us in their own words' to reveal 'their innermost lives' (Jalland 1996: 2). Drawing on the 'rich experiential source material' of an articulate Victorian elite, Jalland moves between reading her archives as evidence of innermost feeling and acknowledging that her sources were representations of emotion. Further, Jalland is reticent about the historian's involvement with the subject. As Sarah Tarlow observes, the historical analysis of dying and death always represents an implicit analysis of the author's own response to loss (1999: 21). Similarly, there is a danger, as Vincent readily admits, of seeking to impose sentiment where none is evident (1980) and to identify affective cultures as part of a broader valorization of particular social groups. This is not to suggest that we cannot write about emotion but, rather, to note that the words and deeds of those in the past are not inevitably a reflection of an innermost life. Depictions of affective ties indicate a linguistic and symbolic representation of feeling whose expression is situational (Pollock 2004) and the historical analysis of which is also potentially biographical (Steedman 1986).

Since Vincent's hesitant conclusions about the apparent absence of emotion in working-class testimony, other histories have suggested that silence can be pregnant with meaning. Ellen Ross's analysis (1993) of the silent but unwavering presence of mothers at the bedsides of sick children in Victorian London suggests that the simple attendance of a parent could signify emotional investment. More recently, research into the domestic strategies of the urban poor and working classes in managing dying experiences has contended that the absence of emotive displays or expressions was not at odds with profound affective investment in the careful management of deathbeds. For instance, the frustration of health officials at parents' and spouses' reluctance to be separated from extremely sick family members suggests, of course, not only a degree of lower-class prejudice against institutionalized medicine but also a desire for familial intimacy, domestic familiarity, communication and small comforts in the face of death. Similarly, whilst middle-class observers emphasized the apparent apathy or fatalism of the lower classes towards dying relatives, reports of resignation were at odds with acknowledgement of the sacrifices made for the comfort of the dying, the capacity to adapt living arrangements to accommodate the sick and the importance attached to watching over the dying. Crucially, a candid acceptance of death, the thing that was so important but frequently difficult for Jalland's Evangelical families to attain, did not necessarily denote fatalism in a working-class context. Rather, candour enabled the dying to participate in decision-making processes regarding the management of dying and its subsequent impact on domestic and kinship arrangements (Strange 2005).

The 'good death': afterlives

As purveyors of the good death model acknowledge, the art-of-dying literature is based overwhelmingly on the history of elites. Notably, there is relatively little historiography that engages at length with the dying experiences of diverse ethnic and confessional groups, notably the significant populations of Jewish and Irish Catholic migrants, or the poor. There is an implicit suggestion in the good death model, relying as it does on the practices of the well-to-do, that one form of dying is somehow better than another. This is related to the tendency for a good death model to depend upon and perpetuate a bifurcated view of dying where an 'art' of dying is held up as an ideal and deviations from it are somehow identified as 'bad'. To a point, this reflects the tendency to invest dying experiences and diseases with moral value. Indeed, recent sociological literature on competing and multiple languages of death and grief suggest that dichotomies between 'good' and 'bad' deaths are misguided, implying a narrow vocabulary of affective response and a limited experience that rarely reflects the messiness of responses to dying or loss (Hockey 1993).

Researching categories such as the good death may reflect contemporary discursive practice, but it also limits the questions historians ask of the past. Notably, where an elite 'good death' model has appeared inappropriate and irrelevant to dying experiences, for instance with socially excluded groups such as paupers, it has been possible to identify alternative approaches to dying that whilst not 'good' in an orthodox 'art-of-dying' context have enabled the dying and those around them to invest the process with positive meaning and a sense of active and strategic participation (Strange 2005). Indeed, a recent overview of the social history of dying contests that the model of 'good death' might be better understood as 'managed' death, with the dying and those around them participating in processes that deliberately shape and give meaning to the dying experience (Kellehear 2007).

There is a danger, however, of replacing notions of an art of dying with conceptions of deaths that are 'well' managed and those that are not. This may be motivated by a desire for all social groups to have access to dying processes that are dignified and empowering, but links between particular dying modes and values risk promoting assumptions that some forms of managing death are better than others or that everyone is viewing dying through the same lens. It is notable that histories of dying in the twentieth century are frequently driven by debates as to whether death in this period became 'bad' for a broader constituency of people or whether it was managed in different ways that were, nonetheless, alienating and less satisfactory (Ariès 1981; Walter 1994; Kellehear 2007). Dying in the twentieth century might look different largely because the voices of the dying are more accessible than ever before. Histories of dying for marginal or excluded groups must, of course, engage with issues of disenfranchisement and critically assess depictions of dying that were rooted in value judgements, but there is much to be gained from recognizing that meanings attached to dying are not fixed in particular periods nor even in specific dying experiences and resisting imposing paradigms that evaluate those experiences.

References

Ariès, P. (1976) *Western Attitudes Towards Death: From the Middle Ages to the Present*, London: Marion Boyars.

(1981) *The Hour of Our Death*, New York: Knopf.

Binski, P. (1996) *Medieval Death: Ritual and Representation*, London: British Museum Press.

Braddon, M. (2008) *The Doctor's Wife*, Oxford: Oxford World Classics. First published 1864.

Brooks, C. (ed.) (1989) *Mortal Remains: The History and Present State of the Victorian and Edwardian Cemetery*, Exeter: Wheaton.

Cannadine, D. (1981) 'War and Death, Grief and Mourning in Modern Britain', in J. Whaley (ed.), *Mirrors of Mortality: Studies in the Social History of Death*, London: Europa, pp. 187–242.

Charmaz, K., Howarth, H. and Kellehear, A. (eds.) (1997) *The Unknown Country: Death in Australia, Britain and the USA*, London: Macmillan.

Curl, J.S. (1972) *The Victorian Celebration of Death*, Newton Abbot: David & Charles.

Davin, A. (2001) 'Waif Stories in Late Nineteenth-Century England', *History Workshop Journal*, 52: 67–98.

Dixon, D. (1989) 'The Two Faces of Death: Children's Magazines and Their Treatment of Death in the Nineteenth Century', in R. Houlbrooke (ed.), *Death, Ritual and Bereavement*, London: Routledge, pp. 136–50.

Dollimore, J. (1998) *Death, Desire and Loss in Western Culture*, London: Routledge.

Drakeford, M. (1998) 'Last Rights? Funerals, Poverty and Social Exclusion', *Journal of Social Policy*, 27 (4): 507–24.

Epstein Nord, D. (1995) *Walking the Victorian Streets: Women, Representation, and the City*, London and Ithaca, NY: Cornell University Press.

Garland, M.M. (1989) 'Victorian Unbelief and Bereavement', in R. Houlbrooke (ed.), *Death, Ritual and Bereavement*, London and New York: Routledge, pp. 151–70.

Gatrell, V.A.C. (1994) *The Hanging Tree: Execution and the English People, 1770–1868*, Oxford: Oxford University Press.

Gittings, C. (1984) *Death, Burial and the Individual in Early Modern England*, London: Croom Helm.

Gorer, G. (1965) *Death, Grief and Mourning in Contemporary Britain*, London: Cresset Press.

Guthke, K. (1999) *The Gender of Death: A Cultural History in Art and Literature*, Cambridge: Cambridge University Press.

Harding, V. (2002) *The Dead and the Living in London and Paris, 1500–1670*, Cambridge: Cambridge University Press.

Hockey, J. (1993) 'The Acceptable Face of Human Grieving? The Clergy's Role in Managing Emotional Expression During Funerals', in D. Clark (ed.), *The Sociology of Death: Theory, Culture, Practice*, Oxford: Blackwell, pp. 129–48.

Horrox, R. (ed.) (1994) *The Black Death*, Manchester: Manchester University Press.

(1999) 'Purgatory, Prayer and Plague: 1150–1380', in P. Jupp and C. Gittings (eds.), *Death in England: An Illustrated History*, Manchester: Manchester University Press, pp. 90–118.

Houlbrooke, R. (1998) *Death, Religion and the Family in England, 1480–1750*, Oxford: Oxford University Press.

(1999) 'The Age of Decency, 1660–1760', in P. Jupp and C. Gittings (eds.), *Death in England: An Illustrated History*, Manchester: Manchester University Press, pp. 174–201.

Howarth, G. (1997) 'Professionalising the Funeral Industry in England 1700–1960', in P. Jupp and G. Howarth (eds.), *The Changing Face of Death: Historical Accounts of Death and Disposal*, Basingstoke: Macmillan, pp. 120–34.

Jalland, P. (1996) *Death in the Victorian Family*, Oxford: Oxford University Press.

Jupp, P. (2006) *From Dust to Ashes: Cremation and the British Way of Death*, Basingstoke: Palgrave.

Kellehear, A. (2007) *A Social History of Dying*, Cambridge: Cambridge University Press.

Laqueur, T. (1993) 'Cemeteries, Religion and the Culture of Capitalism', in J. Garnett and C. Matthew (eds.), *Revival and Religion Since 1700*, London: Hambledon, pp. 183–200.

Litten, J. (1991) *The English Way of Death: The Common Funeral Since 1450*, London: Hale.

Lewis, J. (1980) *The Politics of Motherhood: Child and Maternal Welfare in England, 1900–1939*, London: Croom Helm.

Marks, L. (1996) *Metropolitan Maternity: Maternal and Infant Welfare Services in Early Twentieth Century London*, Amsterdam: Rodopi.

Morgan, N. (2002) 'Infant Mortality, Flies and Horses in Later 19th Century Towns: A Case Study of Preston', *Continuity and Change*, 17 (1): 97–132.

Morgan, P. (1999) 'Of Worms and War, 1380–1558', in P. Jupp and C. Gittings (eds.), *Death in England: An Illustrated History*, Manchester: Manchester University Press, pp. 119–46.

Morley, J. (1971) *Death, Heaven and the Victorians*, London: Studio Vista.

Pollock, L. (2004) 'Anger and the Negotiation of Relationships in Early Modern England', *Historical Journal*, 47 (3): 567–90.

Porter, R. (2001) *Bodies Politic: Disease, Death and Doctors in Britain, 1650–1900*, London: Reaktion.

Prior, L. (1989) *The Social Organisation of Death*, Basingstoke: Palgrave.

Razzell, P. E. and C. Spence (2007) 'The History of Infant, Child and Adult Mortality in London, 1550–1850', *London Journal*, 32 (3): 271–92.

Richardson, R. (1987) *Death, Dissection and the Destitute*, London: Routledge & Kegan Paul.

Rose, L. (1986) *The Massacre of the Innocents: Infanticide in Britain 1800–1939*, London: Routledge & Kegan Paul.

Ross, E. (1993) *Love and Toil: Motherhood in Outcast London, 1870–1918*, Oxford: Oxford University Press.

Shuttleton, D. E. (2007) *Smallpox and the Literary Imagination, 1660–1820*, Cambridge: Cambridge University Press.

Snell, K. D. M. (2003) 'Gravestones, Belonging and Local Attachment in England, 1700–2000', *Past and Present*, 179: 97–134.

Sontag, S. (1978) *Illness as Metaphor*, New York: Farrar, Straus & Giroux.

(1989) *AIDS and Its Metaphors*, New York: Farrar, Straus & Giroux.

Steedman, C. (1986) *Landscape for a Good Woman: A Story of Two Lives*, London: Virago.

Stone, L. (1977) *Family, Sex and Marriage in England, 1500–1800*, New York: Weidenfeld & Nicholson.

Strange, J.-M. (2005) *Death, Grief and Poverty in Britain, 1870–1914*, Cambridge: Cambridge University Press.

Tarlow, S. (1999) *Bereavement and Commemoration: An Archaeology of Mortality*, Oxford: Oxford University Press.

Vincent, D. (1980) 'Love and Death and the Nineteenth-Century Working Classes', *Social History*, 5: 223–47.

Walter, T. (1994) *Revival of Death*, London: Routledge.

Williams, S. (1999) *Religious Belief and Popular Culture in Southwark, c. 1880–1939*, Oxford: Oxford University Press.

Winter, J. (1995) *Sites of Memory, Sites of Mourning: The Great War in European Cultural History*, Cambridge: Cambridge University Press.

7 | *Dying and philosophy*

GEOFFREY SCARRE

Philosophers, who have written much about facing death, have had notably little to say about dying. Perhaps this is because while facing death is a matter of attitudes, and thus a subject for normative judgements, dying has tended to be seen as a mere matter of physical and mental decay, a process that need engage little philosophical attention. But this is a purblind view, since, as Allan Kellehear reminds us on the first page of his introduction to this volume, dying is also 'a particular form of social life and experience', and philosophers are traditionally concerned with what pertains to the existence of Aristotle's 'social animal' (Aristotle 1905: 28; 1253a). While it is true, as Heidegger emphasized, that no one else can die my death, there is a sense in which others can share in my dying (Heidegger 1962: 303). Indeed, the renegotiation and adjustments of social relationships that are involved in dying might plausibly be held to be not merely concomitants of dying but partly constitutive of it. In dying we frequently have to learn new ways of living with others – a fact perhaps forgotten, or not sufficiently minded, by those philosophers who have focused on the individual's confrontation with the Grim Reaper or the King of Terrors. If dying is the anteroom to death, it is not a space that we occupy quite alone.

Some occasional philosophical deliverances on dying have been of questionable helpfulness. For example, the rather feeble witticism that life is a fatal condition is echoed in Montaigne's contention that 'You are in death while you are in life ... Or if you prefer it thus: after death you are dead, but during life you are dying' (1987: 103). But it is just false that, as it is sometimes put, 'you're dying from the day you're born.' Nature dictates that we do some growing up first, and though Montaigne is right that '[f]rom the day you were born your path leads to death as well as life' (1987: 103), that is *not* equivalent to saying that dying is a lifelong process. Nor should we confuse senescence with dying, though sooner or later it leads to death. In physiological

147

terms, senescence – literally, growing older – occurs when, in the natural process of replacement of bodily cells, old cells are replaced by slightly poorer, less efficient, copies of themselves. Whilst senescence involves physical decline, a person may be declining for a very long time before it would be appropriate to speak of him or her as dying. Mortal creatures may be destined to die, but to be mortal is not to be dying.

Even though we are not forever dying, there is often no clear beginning to a person's dying. Consider, for instance, someone in whom a malignant and ultimately fatal tumour is working its damage for a period before any symptoms are apparent. Should we say that the subject is dying from the onset of the cancerous condition, or from the point when the symptoms begin to show, or from the time when those symptoms become very severe or the doctors declare the condition incurable, or when the final catastrophic breakdown of physiological functioning sets in? None of these answers is clearly right or wrong. (Similarly there is no evidently correct answer to the question of when someone who survives with HIV for ten years before dying of AIDS begins dying.) This is not because of any epistemological difficulties about *determining* when exactly dying starts; the point is not that we have sharply defined but hard-to-apply clear criteria to govern the use of the term 'dying'; rather, there are no such criteria. This is not the result of conceptual muddle or linguistic laziness but reflects the status of dying as a social and existential condition as well as a medical one, with multiple significances. Tracing those significances is unlikely to issue in a precise definition of the kind beloved by dictionary-makers. In practice, our use of the word 'dying' is guided not by a crisp set of necessary and sufficient conditions but by a range of paradigms, models and striking examples, some of them open to dispute.

Dying: some modest paradoxes

It may seem scarcely controversial to describe dying as a prelude to death. Yet the relations between death and dying are more complex than we might first think, and even this apparently uncontentious statement needs to be treated with some caution. When we look at dying closely, it turns out to have a number of potentially surprising aspects. I shall term these 'modest paradoxes' of dying and briefly outline three of them.

As a preliminary, note one feature of dying which, whilst it would be an exaggeration to call it even a modest paradox, may just stir an eyebrow. Montaigne may have claimed that living was dying but, in reality, the reverse is true: *dying is a form or phase of living.* Dying is not the opposite of living, as death is the opposite of life. We need to be alive to be dying, and only when we are dead are we finished with dying. A dying person may still have many things to do, some of which could not have been done, or done so well, before. So she may seek to make her peace with herself, her neighbours, or God. She may also regard her progressive disengagement from her accustomed activities and commitments not in negative terms, as a reluctant and tragic 'bowing out' of life, but as a chance to bring closure and completeness to her affairs. Of course, not all the dying have such opportunities: an Alzheimer's sufferer or a heavily sedated dying patient may have lost most or all of their standing as autonomous agents. Yet even if they have lost all authorship of their own biographies, those biographies continue.

The first modest paradox of dying is that, while death is universal, *dying is not universal.* Admittedly, read one way, this may seem a straight falsehood. How, it might fairly be asked, could one die without dying? To which the answer is that, in one obvious sense, one couldn't. Understood as 'shuffling off our mortal coil', dying is something we all must do. But now think of dying in the sense which is chiefly of interest to the writers of this volume: not as the event that closes life but as an extended phase of life during which subjects exhibit what the editor refers to as 'dying behaviour'. Not everyone's life ends with a phase of this kind. Where a previously healthy person dies instantaneously from a cardiac arrest or in an accident or bomb blast, her or she never undergoes dying in this sense.

Is such a person fortunate or unfortunate in omitting this phase of common human experience? Might the suddenness of death be some compensation for its premature occurrence? Dying, after all, can be a painful, frightening, even horrifying experience, and it is natural to recoil from experiences of that sort. In Cardinal Newman's poem *The Dream of Gerontius*, the dying man movingly expresses the shocking sense of impending loss of self, 'this strange innermost abandonment ... This emptying out of each constituent / And natural force, by

which I come to be' (Newman 1866: ll. 9, 11–12). For Gerontius, the
existential suffering surpasses the physical; hardest to bear is

> That sense of ruin, which is worse than pain,
> That masterful negation and collapse
> Of all that makes me man; as though I bent
> Over the dizzy brink
> Of some sheer infinite descent[.]
>   (Newman 1866: ll. 94–8)

No wonder that Gerontius is 'wild with horror and dismay' (Newman
1866: l. 110). Would it have been better for Gerontius to have arrived
at a goodly age in a reasonable state of health and then expired of
a sudden and unexpected cerebral haemorrhage? Death without the
dying may seem a better mode of exit, shorn of the existential chill at
heart that beset poor Gerontius. Yet sudden, unanticipated death has
its downside too, depriving the subject of the chance to reflect on and
weigh up his life, and rudely and abruptly rupturing his social relationships. Many people would therefore prefer to have the chance to die,
like Gerontius, in their beds, bringing their lives to a gradual rather
than a drastic close, whatever the associated pains, fears and sadness.
Interestingly, personifications of death as a reaper are most common in
connection with deaths that are sudden or at any rate not protracted,
where the element of personal control over how we die is nil or minimal
(suicides might almost be said to reap themselves). Death without dying
may have the merit of sparing us a lot of mental and emotional anguish
but it has the arguably outweighing disadvantages of being more shocking to the survivors and of preventing us from making our own moral,
spiritual and social adaptations to our changing condition.

Besides, dying is not always as terrible as it was for Gerontius (though
Newman probably thought of him as Everyman). As Kellehear notes,
'[d]ying can be traumatic and frightening, but [other people] have
reported transcendence, insightfulness and peace' (Chapter 1 of this
volume, p. 18). Seneca thought that many dying people felt tranquil
because they had 'outworn [their] desires and left them behind' (1969:
58). This may seem a rather negative source of satisfaction, a *pis aller*
for having desires that could still be fulfilled (moreover, it is not very
likely that a dying person would outrun *all* desires, if only the desire
for a reasonably painless death). But Seneca was rightly pointing to
the restful sense of relief from demands, both internal and external,

that can be a genuine compensation for having arrived (like a runner at the finish of a race) at the end of one's course.

The second paradox of dying is that *dying need not end in death*. By this I do not intend the obvious and trivial point that someone who is dying from some fatal condition may in the end die of something else (as the terminal-cancer patient may be killed by a brick falling on his head). The more interesting observation is that dying is not only sometimes characterized by 'oscillation' (where the subject does not deteriorate in a simple linear fashion but experiences 'cycles of health and illness, decline and improvement' (Chapter 1 of this volume, p. 6)), but may even be discontinued altogether. Imagine that Jim, a non-swimmer, is drowning in the lake into which he has tumbled, when athletic John comes successfully to his aid. Drowning, we should allow, is a mode of dying. So it follows that Jim was dying even though he did not die. It might be objected to this description that Jim, although his vital processes were becoming seriously compromised before his rescue, could not have been literally *dying* since, with John's help, he managed to survive; so we should rather say that he was in acute danger of drowning rather than actually drowning. But this is incorrect, for while Jim did not *complete* his drowning, his dying-by-drowning was well on the way when John intervened. (Had John not been on the scene, we would have no temptation to say that Jim was merely in danger of drowning rather than actually drowning.)[1] Or think of a woman, Sue, who is dying from cancer when a newly discovered wonder drug is administered that saves her life. We can compare her case with that of another cancer-sufferer, Sid, whose illness has taken exactly the same course as Sue's but who does not receive the drug and who dies shortly after. To say that only Sid, but not Sue, was dying during that stage of their illness before Sue received the drug is implausible in view of their identical conditions and prognoses up till that time.[2]

---

[1] The controversial US practice of 'waterboarding' prisoners to extract information has sometimes been described as 'simulated drowning'. But critics have rightly pointed out that the drowning is not simulated: it is *actual* drowning which is discontinued before death can occur.

[2] It has been suggested to me that a person can never say with justified certainty 'I am dying', because this assumes an outcome that may not occur. So, ironically, we could never be sure that we were right to assert that we were dying, since the earliest point at which this could be known is the point at which we cease to be a conscious subject. But this must be wrong, if the second paradox is correct. Before Sue receives the life-saving drug, it is

The third and last paradox of dying I shall note is that *dying can happen to a person more than once*. This paradox is really a corollary of the second. For Jim and Sue, dying is not merely suspended, to be resumed on a subsequent occasion (which would be a kind of 'oscillation'), but is cancelled altogether. Suppose that, years later, Jim succumbs to incurable cancer and Sue to a fatal heart condition. Each, therefore, experiences two discrete and non-identical episodes of dying. It does not follow that because one can die only once, one cannot be dying more than once; an unfortunate individual might undergo multiple experiences of dying, though only the last one issues in death. (It is only in a figurative sense that cowards, as Shakespeare's Brutus remarks, 'die many times before their deaths'; yet it is not just cowards who may find themselves dying many times before their deaths.) Note that were Sue's cancerous condition to return after several years and this time prove fatal, it may still be more apt to describe this as the repetition of a dying condition than as the resumption of a suspended process of dying.

To sum up these 'modest paradoxes' of dying in a few words, dying is a form or phase of living that does not, however, occur within everyone's life story though it can happen more than once to some people and, while death is the end, dying is not always the prelude to the end.

The many faces of dying

One moral that we can draw from the 'modest paradoxes' is that dying is a more significant experiential phase in some lives than in others. Someone without previous experience of a life-threatening condition, who dies instantaneously of a stroke or in a car accident or bomb blast has no experience of dying at all. Here, one might say, there is no dying, only death. A person who spends his last days in a coma may be dying during that time even if he has no awareness of it; in this case, dying is not part of his first-personal story as it plays no part in any autobiographical account he could ever have given of

---

true of her (a) that, if she knows the facts of her condition, she has impeccable warrant for believing herself to be dying, and (b) that she actually is dying. This, I contend, is sufficient to permit our saying not only that she has justified certainty that she is dying but that she *knows* that she is dying – even though she doesn't die.

himself.[3] There can also, of course, be people who are dying and conscious, but not conscious that they are dying.

Sometimes a person knows beforehand she is about to pass into the state of dying. In Ian McEwan's novel *Atonement*, seventy-seven-year-old Briony Tallis is told by her doctor that she is in the early stages of vascular dementia. Rather to her own surprise, Briony is elated rather than devastated by the news, excited by the momentousness of moving into a stage of her life which will be quite different from any that has gone before. But objectively she realizes that the prognosis is grim. Her brain will slowly close down until she will remember nothing and recognize no one, even herself, and her past will be a blank: 'My phone number, my address, my name and what I did with my life will be gone.' Aware that she has started to die, Briony realizes that her dying will take the form of a 'fading into unknowing' (McEwan 2002: 354, 355).

For Briony Tallis, dying will be both journey and transformation, a transition from living person to dead person, but, more importantly, a gradual extinction of the self. Where, as in her case, the self disappears before the body dies, dying may be thought more terrible, or at least a more significant termination, than death itself. At a recent funeral I attended, the son of the deceased Alzheimer's patient remarked to me, 'We weren't really so very sorry when she died, since we lost the Mum we knew a long time ago.' Yet for those who supply the day-to-day care of the dying, the story isn't over until it's over – even when whatever made the self distinctive has disappeared, the physical frame still needs to be fed, cleaned, clothed and kept as far as possible in a state of comfort. Ironically, by taking over the functions that a dying person has previously exercised for herself, those who care for her themselves contribute to the annihilation of the self as agent (albeit with the best of intentions), emphasizing her personal incompetence to manage her own affairs. A dying person aware of the substitution of others' agency for her own may respond with a complex of emotions: gratitude and relief may mingle with frustration and resentment while there may also be shame at her own resentment ('how awful of me to feel like this when people are so kind').

---

[3] Some coma patients may, however, have some consciousness of what is happening to them that includes awareness that they are dying. See Chapter 12 of this volume for further discussion of the pertinent clinical literature.

If forms of dying are many and various, so too, as Kellehear points out, are the theoretical models implied or suggested in the empirical literature. The seven themes isolated for discussion in this volume – dying as personal control, as a journey, as a state of oscillation between life and death, as disengagement, as collapse, as a form of social disenfranchisement and as transformation/transcendence – collectively indicate both the complexity of the phenomena and the richness of the currently available attempts at understanding them. Not only do people die in many different ways but perspectives on dying are likewise various, representing a wide range of cultural, theoretical, philosophical, religious, literary and practical perspectives. Obvious though it may be, it is worth emphasizing that no one academic discipline, be it medicine or psychology or sociology or nursing studies, has a monopoly of insights into dying, with other studies adding merely footnotes. Dying is, par excellence, a topic for multidisciplinary treatment.

But how can unity be brought into so potentially confusing a mass of themes and paradigms, empirical data from medicine, psychology, sociology, anthropology and other studies, plus personal or private experiences, reflections, fears and hopes? Can there be a genuine conversation about dying, or will there always be multiple voices speaking past one another? One notion that can help to facilitate discourse across the disciplinary boundaries, and induce some sense of a common subject, is that of dying as a stage in the *narrative* of a life. When Briony Tallis contemplates her dying, she reflects on the relations between her past, present and future, considering how the diagnosed dementia will change her from what she has been to something – even someone – else (or perhaps no one at all), 'just a dim old biddy in a chair, knowing nothing, expecting nothing' (McEwan 2002: 354). Dying, for Briony, is not an isolated, discrete phase of existence but the final chapter of a lengthy story, drawing its meaning from the way in which it caps or cancels, completes or negates, the themes of earlier chapters.

It may seem evident that dying should be understood in relation to the life that precedes it, but I suspect that this does not always occur. Where, for instance, dying is thought of in purely clinical or physiological terms, or as a 'problem' for carers, or as a health-service delivery issue with economic implications, there is a danger that sight will be lost of the 'biographical context' of dying. To be sure, a surgeon who is fighting to save the life of a dying patient needs at that juncture to understand the patient's physiology, not his life story. But when he is outside the operating room he may care to reflect on why human lives are worth saving and why a later death is (usually) better than an earlier. Thinking about life in structural, narrative terms is a valuable counterpoise to the inevitable professional abstractions that represent the dying as failing physical mechanisms, or occupiers of beds, or economically non-productive units, or Alzheimer's cases, or objects of social responsibility. 'Bon voyage!' Briony ironically wishes herself. A mutually enlightening conversation between groups of professionals concerned with dying could profitably pool insights into dying conceived of as a stage in life's journey, with multiple medical, psychological, social, existential and religious aspects.

Dying: the narrative perspective

Narrative has plausibly been characterized as a genre of explanation (Velleman 2003: 1). If someone asks us, 'Why did you resign your job/ kick the dog/go to London/insult Smith?' we will typically respond by relating the act to a context: 'I got tired of my boss's bullying/the dog stole the sausages/I wanted to see the latest show/Smith insulted me first'. We can then elaborate on this context as much as need or interest dictates. A narrative is always more than a mere chronicle of events ('first X happened, and then Y'); it is usually more, too, than a bare record of causal sequence ('X happened, so consequently Y'). Narratives normally comprise optative and teleological elements: they refer to the desires and purposes that generate and guide our actions. Asked why I raised my arm, I reply that I wished to brush away a fly or shade my eyes from the sun; in Aristotelian language, I specify the 'final' rather than the 'efficient' cause of my action (the various muscle movements that caused my arm to go up).

The teleological aspect of narrative merits special emphasis when we think of whole lives in narrative terms. Our actions are directed on ends and are not mere random bodily movements; and, as self-conscious, rational agents, we seek to organize our projects and commitments into a coherent whole (cf. MacIntyre 1984: 209). In Jeff Malpas's words, '[t]he organization and unity of a life is essentially a matter of the organization and unity of the projects that make up that life and the integration of those projects as part of a larger project that may be understood as the life itself' (1998: 126–7). Alasdair MacIntyre, who has been one of the chief exponents of the idea that '[n]arrative history of a certain kind turns out to be the basic and essential genre for the characterization of human actions', notes that our outlook on our lives is essentially forward-looking, 'informed by some image of some future and an image of the future which always presents itself in the form of a *telos* – or of a variety of ends or goals – towards which we are either moving or failing to move in the present' (MacIntyre 1984: 208, 215–16). Thus, on a natural conception, one sees oneself as 'the subject of a narrative that runs from one's birth to one's death' (MacIntyre 1984: 217). (One might even see the narrative as extending *beyond* one's death, as Gerontius does.)

It might be objected to the comparison of lives with narratives that we do not have full authorial control over our own lives in the way that novelists and storytellers do over the destinies of their characters. In the non-fictional world, we have to live with the given and start from where we are, not from where we might wish to be. While our biographies may include an aspirational element, they should not, like Walter Mitty's, be rooted in fantasy. We also have to cope with the fact that reality is notoriously unpredictable and that, as Burns warns us, even the best-laid plans 'gang aft agley'. A major source of uncertainty is that our personal narratives are intricately interlocking structures, forcing us constantly to adjust our ends and means in order to reach the best accommodation with other people; the authorship of our own lives is something we share with others (though in compensation we also share in the authorship of *their* lives). These reflections do not undermine the claim of 'narrative history' to be the proper genre for understanding human lives, but they bring home that life narratives are necessarily complex constructions, requiring continual updating and revision in the light of circumstances. They also emphasize the social dimension of our individual stories, and their inevitable, mutually enriching combination of the public and the private. Not only do we live in community and not as hermits, but who we are, and who we take ourselves to be, are heavily dependent on the expectations that society lays on us: what MacIntyre calls 'the roles into which we have been drafted' (1984: 216).

My suggestion – to repeat – is that it helps to bring out the nature and significance of dying and to impart some unity to the various professional perspectives from which dying is commonly viewed, to consider it as a stage in a life, where the stages of life are conceived as connected in the manner of parts or chapters of a narrative. This approach can serve to counteract two different kinds of tunnel vision that can afflict those who study dying or who are concerned with the treatment or care of the dying. First, there is the narrowed vision that might be labelled 'professional lensing' – the habit of seeing the subject of one's theoretical or practical concern only in the familiar terms of one's own discipline, sometimes accompanied by scepticism as to whether anyone outside that discipline could possibly have anything interesting to say about it. (The slogan of such professional prejudice at its worst might be 'Abandon hope, all ye who do *not* enter here.') Recognizing that other angles on the story are possible, and that one's own professional perspective is only one of a number of valid viewpoints on the nature of dying, is a vital restorer of sight and insight.

If the first narrowing of vision involves divorcing one's particular professional perspective from those of others, the second divorces dying from the rest of a human life, ignoring its essential temporal relatedness, its status as a stage-in-a-life. This error is the more fundamental of the two, since someone who commits it has not so much an unsatisfactorily straitened view of dying as – to put it bluntly – no grasp of it at all. A person may be dying in the present, but we cannot begin to comprehend what that means for the subject herself or for her family, friends and associates, without some consideration of the past. (We may be able, without knowing the antecedents, to describe the overt features of her physical condition, but that is all.) Our cognitive and emotional responses to a person's dying are a function of the links we make between past and present and, in particular, our own involvement in that person's history. (This is why – to state the obvious – we are more painfully affected by the dying of a loved relative or friend than we are by that of a stranger.) Such temporal contextualization of dying is by no means unique to the third-person viewpoint. A person's experience of her own dying is likewise conditioned by the narrative connections she draws with her past. Whether she feels happy or sad, relieved or anxious, fulfilled or unfulfilled, content ('I've done what I set out to do') or distraught ('Whatever will happen to my children now?') is largely dependent on how well she feels she has brought her story to a close.

Dying has different significances in different lives. As we saw earlier, dying (as a time-extended phase) does not feature in some lives at all, while in others it can occur more than once. There are very few true generalizations about dying. In *As You Like It*, the melancholy Jaques enumerates the seven ages of man, beginning with 'mewling and puking' infancy and ending with the 'second childishness and mere oblivion' of the aged, 'sans teeth, sans eyes, sans taste, sans every thing'.[4] Yet, as Jaques and all of us know, there are plenty of departures from this default narrative. Many lives end long before second childhood has been reached. And even lives that extend a full span can have very different existential characters. Some lives seem to be lived predominantly in a minor key. So dying may well have a quite different feel to sad, pessimistic Jaques than it does to happy, positive Rosalind.

Dying and retrospect

Knowing that one is soon to die can, as Dr Johnson famously observed, concentrate the mind wonderfully. But people who are dying are not always in good enough mental shape to frame profound thoughts about life and death, or even any thoughts at all. A dying person may be comatose, or suffering from a degree of dementia, or heavily sedated as a result of pain-relieving drugs. Even if she is fully conscious and aware of her condition, she may be too distracted by the immediate exigencies and the routines of her treatment to focus on searching self-examination. It is sometimes imagined that the dying are in a particularly privileged position to grasp truths that are obscure to others. But, as Robert Kastenbaum remarks, though 'wise people may have wise things to say as they near the end of their lives, it is possible that foolish, boring, and neurotic people stay in character by saying foolish, boring, and neurotic things' (1993: 281–2). Last words are not necessarily wise words, nor is it clear that there are any notable insights into the human condition that are uniquely accessible to the dying.

Yet, while dying may not in itself bring wisdom, it is a condition that encourages retrospect. Like any project that is coming to an end, a life that is near its close is ripe for review. The final chapter of many people's life narratives is short on action but strong on reflection. Human beings are not only the lead characters in the narratives of their lives, the referents of the perpendicular pronoun, but they can simultaneously play their own critics, stepping temporarily out of the protagonist's role and examining their own motives, acts, achievements and failures with more or less objectivity. We like to pause and

---

[4]   William Shakespeare, *As You Like It*, Act II, Scene 7, ll. 139–66.

take stock when individual projects come to a close and also when we believe life itself to be approaching its end.

The motive for reviewing the narrative of a life may be partly aesthetic: the dying person is curious to know what sort of tale he has told: he hopes to find it distinctive and interesting, coherent, consecutive and unified. But a still more powerful motive stems from the characteristic human concern with meaning. The dying subject seeks to reassure himself that he has lived to some purpose, achieved worthwhile ends, made a difference for the better. If he fails, then his self-respect is in danger of expiring before he does. It is important not just to have pursued worthy ends but to have brought some narrative closure to one's projects; to be forced to leave significant unfinished business is a kind of failure, however little one may be responsible for its non-completion. (Where one has participated in an ongoing, multi-agent project, the crucial thing is to have completed one's own part in it.) Sadly, the results of such self-examination are not always very palatable, and they have added poignancy for the dying subject who has run out of time to put things right.

Note that the critical retrospect on past life that I am referring to here is different from mere random reminiscence, the 'dwelling in the past' that elderly people commonly indulge in (and which often seems peculiarly irritating and irrelevant to the young). Since critical review is a particularly appropriate exercise for those of the dying who are consciously living out the final chapter of their life story, it could reasonably be considered as an eighth basic theme in terms of which dying can be understood and studied. What shape a review takes, and what its conclusions are, evidently depends on the values and beliefs of the person conducting it. A dying person may be well satisfied with a life that others, with different ideals, might judge less favourably; or he may be dissatisfied with achievements that others would rate highly. Sometimes a subject may judge his life to have been seriously misdirected, though it would be an unusually grim retrospect that concluded that a life had been *totally* misspent.

But do the retrospects of the dying carry any special authority? Suppose that in the course of a dying review, a person concludes that her life has been wanting in important respects. Why, if these thoughts had not struck her before, should she trust them now? Popular lore has it that people on their deathbeds can now afford to be honest with themselves, having no further need for self-deception.

This seems to me quite untrue: if we wish to die with untroubled souls, then the safest thing is to keep the wool pulled firmly over our eyes. Yet it may be hard for a person who is confined to a bed of sickness to shut her ears anymore to the little nagging doubts and troubling suspicions which she could earlier dismiss as so much white noise. Dying people may be no more honest or enlightened than other people or their earlier selves, but there may be less now to distract them from the recognition of uncomfortable facts. Physical incapacity and limited opportunity for action may also leave them with more time on their hands to contemplate their pasts. The knowledge that the sands of life are running out may encourage, too, a more focused effort to determine 'the things that really matter' than had been attempted hitherto.

The cathartic role which retrospection can play in the experience of the dying is movingly illustrated in the greatest literary portrayal of dying, Tolstoy's *The Death of Ivan Ilych*. Ivan Ilych Golovin, a middle-aged judge in the Court of Justice, is dying slowly and painfully from an internal injury caused by falling against a piece of furniture while hanging some curtains. Forced to give up his work and busy social round, the bedridden Ivan Ilych reflects on his past life with an increasing sense of distaste and dismay. Most disconcerting to him are his revised valuations of what had previously seemed to him good and worthwhile:

the further he departed from childhood, and the nearer he came to the present, the more worthless and doubtful were the joys ... Then during the first years of his official career ... some pleasant moments again occurred: they were the memories of love for a woman. Then all became confused and there was still less that was good ...

Afterwards came his marriage, 'a mere accident', followed by years of 'that deadly official life and those preoccupations about money':

And the longer it lasted, the more deadly it became. 'It is as if I had been going downhill while I imagined I was going up. And that is really what it was. I was going up in public opinion, but to the same extent life was ebbing away from me.' (Tolstoy 1960: 147–8)

Ivan Ilych's increasingly agonized reflections closely mirror Tolstoy's own midlife doubts as to whether anything in human life was really valuable *sub specie aeternitatis*. We need not follow him in his cosmic pessimism. There is no fundamental reason why a last-chapter review of a life should not reveal much to be proud and happy about. (If our lives don't seem very important from the point of view of the universe, why should this bother us, since ours is not the perspective of the universe? Almost all that happens in the universe has no bearing on our own lives.) Most such reviews, if honestly conducted, probably reveal a mixed bag of good and bad. Like Ivan Ilych, however, we may well receive a few surprises, though these need not all be unpleasant ones. Our latest evaluations may revise our earlier ones in unexpected ways, with a consequent reappraisal of priorities. Some things we once thought important may now seem to be relatively trivial, while others may appear to have been formerly underrated.

How can the dying be sure that any revised valuations they make are themselves correct? Might the dying condition itself breed a despondency that causes things in general to take on too dark a hue? Are the dying not liable to represent their past pleasures and achievements in an unwarrantedly sombre light (if not generally as bleakly as Ivan Ilych does)? Maybe life is easier to leave behind if it can be portrayed as nothing very special. Such distortions of vision are real dangers, and dying people in reviewing their lives should be careful not to suppose themselves infallible in their terminal condition. They must allow for the possibility of a negative bias induced by the sadness natural to their state. Yet they should not desist from retrospection by the fear of making mistakes. To fail to put themselves under their own spotlight is to miss the final opportunity for objective self-appraisal and thus to leave the narrative of their lives essentially uncompleted.

Acknowledgement

I am grateful to Anthony Bash and Allan Kellehear for very valuable comments on an earlier draft of this chapter.

References

Aristotle (1905) *Politics*, trans. B. Jowett, Oxford: Clarendon Press.
Heidegger, M. (1962) *Being and Time*, trans. J. Macquarrie and E. Robinson, Oxford: Blackwell.
Kastenbaum, R. (1993) 'Last Words', *The Monist*, **76**(2): 270–90.

MacIntyre, A. (1984) *After Virtue*, 2nd edn, Notre Dame, Ind.: University of Notre-Dame Press.

McEwan, I. (2002) *Atonement*, London: Vintage Books.

Malpas, J. (1998) 'Death and the Unity of a Life', in J. Malpas and R. Solomon (eds.), *Death and Philosophy*, London and New York: Routledge, pp. 120–34.

Montaigne, M. de (1987) *The Complete Essays*, trans. M.A. Screech, Harmondsworth: Penguin.

Newman, J.H. (1866) *The Dream of Gerontius*, available online at www. ccel.org/n/newman/gerontius/gerontius/htm (accessed 20 July 2008).

Seneca, L.A. (1969) *Letters from a Stoic*, trans. R. Campbell, Harmondsworth: Penguin.

Tolstoy, L. (1960) *The Death of Ivan Ilych and Other Stories*, New York: Signet Classics.

Velleman, D. (2003) 'Narrative Explanation', *The Philosophical Review*, **112**(1): 1–26.

8 | *The art of dying*

CLARE GITTINGS

Death has not been as extensively studied by art historians as it has by historians, despite a handful of ground-breaking exhibitions held in the past decade or two (Llewellyn 1991; McTavish 2002). In art-historical literature, the aspect that has received the most attention is funerary sculpture (Curl 1993; Penny 1977; Llewellyn 2000). Although the dying sometimes appear on such monuments, much more frequently the deceased are shown as they were in life, or the soul is represented, newly released from the body. More recently, cultural theorists, when considering illness, have discussed artworks that include dying people, sometimes from a gender perspective, but without differentiating dying as a distinctive state (Herndl 1993; Komninou 2006; Skelly 2007).

While individual artworks discussed in this chapter have been studied by art historians in the context of their artist's oeuvre or of particular art-historical movements or, indeed, may even have been the subject of an entire book, they have not before been brought together to illuminate what art can tell us about dying in the Western world over past centuries (Thomas 1972; Spector 1974; Cohen 1997). The study that has previously come closest to doing so is Ariès's *Images of Man and Death* (1985) although it treats dying rather less thoroughly than some other aspects of death. There have also been studies of death in art in particular countries or periods, which include references to dying (Llewellyn 1991; Binion 1993; Binski 1996).

In response to the dearth of existing studies, this chapter sets out to survey what would be the bedrock of any such project – potential key artworks for studying dying in Western art. The chapter also sketches some possible lines of analysis that might be explored. Reproductions of almost all of the works can be accessed on the Internet by typing title and artist into a search engine that can retrieve images. The range of media surveyed includes painting, sculpture, drawing, textiles, engraving, photography and video, and encompasses some sequences of work as well as individual pieces. Thought-provoking depictions of dying are not confined to the greatest artworks, and some lesser-known artists appear here among their more illustrious contemporaries. As there is no established canon of artworks for this subject, the choice of images inevitably may seem idiosyncratic. In this chapter, one individual painting or small group of works has to stand for a whole genre or artistic movement. However, this initial, extremely broad-brush survey might encourage others to delve more deeply and to reveal greater subtleties in studying dying in art.

Art historians have reacted in very different ways to dying as the subject matter of artworks, from virtually ignoring it to accusing artists of exploiting the dying through their art. In traditional formal art-historical narrative, the subject matter is generally subordinated to concerns of composition and style. At the other extreme, the literary scholar Elizabeth Bronfen, in an essay provocatively entitled 'Violence of Representation – Representation of Violence', asks 'whether every representation of dying is not violent precisely because it implies the safe position of a spectator ("voyeur") and because ... a severing of the body from its real materiality and its historical context ("fetishism") is always built into such images' (Bronfen 1992: 44). This present chapter falls somewhere between these two positions in neither ignoring nor condemning the subject matter of these works but rather attempting to place them in the context of changing ideas about dying over the centuries. There rightly remains, however, the dilemma that seeing beauty in representations of human dying raises uncomfortable moral issues, a view first expressed in the eighteenth century, initially in response to the *Laocoön*, the famous sculpture in which a man and his sons are slowly crushed to death by huge, coiling snakes (Beard and Henderson 2001: 65–74).

Art and death have long been bedfellows; the study of anatomy was, for several centuries, part of an artist's training. Direct observation of the dead has inspired some of the most searing and powerful artworks ever created, including the early sixteenth-century Isenheim crucifixion by Grünewald and Holbein's *Dead Christ* (1531), or, in a domestic setting, Monet's portrait of his dead wife, Camille (1879). However, despite Bronfen's concerns, comparatively few artworks depicting the dying were created 'from life'; most images of dying are imaginative compositions. There were obvious practical reasons for this in the past, when dying was often a less extended process than today (Kellehear 2007). One looks to artworks, therefore, more for idealized or dramatized versions of dying than for everyday reality. One feature of a number of these images, particularly those of Catholic origin, is that they go beyond the merely human to make visible the supernatural forces surrounding the dying person. This cosmic drama around the deathbed can turn the artificiality of the image into its positive strength.

Artists of all eras have relished depicting dying from causes other than illness, ranging from the crucifixion and the deaths of saints, through suicides, battle scenes, executions, accidents and disasters. So, which of the seven theories of dying discussed in the introduction to this book – agency, linearity, fluctuation, disengagement, disintegration, indeterminacy and transcendence – resonate most clearly with dying as reflected in Western art?

The most useful concept appears to be that of **agency**, which occurs repeatedly in this chapter. It provides a valuable tool that can equally be applied to different aspects of the creation of these artworks, including to artists and viewers as well as to subjects. The most obvious question is whether the dying are shown as the playthings of fate or whether they exhibit agency in their dying, either alone or with others, such as family or professionals. In permitting deathbed portraiture, the dying person exerts agency, not least in giving consent. The ultimate agency in artworks rests with the artists themselves, while the viewer also possesses agency, which artists can exploit in very different ways, as shown, for example, in the comparison between Rubens and Poussin below.

The notion of dying as a journey (**linearity**) sometimes appears in art, as in the sculpture by William Theed the Younger of Queen Victoria and Prince Albert in Saxon dress (1863–7). The couple stand lovingly together on the seashore, Albert gesturing upwards, having dropped his sword on the sand, capturing the shattering moment when Albert told Victoria that he was dying. **Disengagement** is sometimes rendered pictorially, particularly in funerary sculpture, by the drawing of a veil or by the dying subject turning away. **Disintegration** is one of the themes in the work of Expressionists such as Munch and Schiele, who employ it in their self-portraits. Oscillation (**fluctuation**) is essentially time-based, unlike much visual art across the centuries, although several works, including Luke Fildes' *The Doctor* (1891) depict a moment in the balance between life or death, where the outcome is still uncertain.

Whereas dying had been a reasonably consistent subject for artists across most of Western art history, it disappears more from sight (**indeterminacy**) in the twentieth century, possibly reflecting denial, although death itself remains obliquely referenced. Finally, while there are many portrayals from different periods of the joys of Heaven or pains of Hell awaiting the soul on its release from the body, particular visionary artists have produced images not dissimilar to those described in the near-death-experience research (**transcendence**). These include Blake's depictions at the turn of the nineteenth century of souls hovering above their bodies or Bosch in the late fifteenth century in his *Ascent of Souls to Heaven*, where angels guide them to the mouth of a long circular tunnel from the far end of which emanates a brilliant light.

Classical: dying bravely

This account draws on the more usually agreed interpretations of the images discussed here, although classicists are far from unanimous about dates, whether surviving artworks are copies or originals or how Classical viewers would have reacted to them, dissentions that reflect a lack of real evidence (Beard and Henderson 2001). Scenes of domestic dying are not part of the iconography of Classical art, though the rituals following a death and dying in combat are both represented. However, the sculptural gravestones of Classical Greece from the fifth and fourth centuries BC give a sense of how dying was interpreted, through the imagery of parting as if for a journey or through veiling the face as if withdrawing from the world. Many of the gravestones excavated from the Kerameikos in Athens show figures with clasped hands in the customary gesture of parting – a girl from her parents; a young man named Bion from his father and paternal aunt, while a small dog watches from under his chair (Figure 8.1). On other gravestones, women pluck at their veils, in the action of drawing them across their faces (Knigge 1991).

In contrast to these indirect allusions to dying, direct representations of dying warriors form part of the corpus of Greek sculpture, not least, perhaps, because a near supine figure fills the lower extremity of

Figure 8.1. *Gravestone with relief panel showing Euphrosyne, Eubios and Bion.* Marble, mid 4th Century BC (replica). Keram-eikos, Athens (replica). Photograph © Reserved, 2008.

a Classical pediment, fitting neatly into the sharply acute angle of the triangle's base. A pair of examples from the late fifth century BC, from the Temple of Aphaia on Aegina, Greece, show the smitten warriors oblivious to the battle against the Trojans still raging in the centre of the pediment. The better-preserved figure uses his circular shield to support his failing body as his face droops towards the ground (Spivey 1997: 112–14).

The most famous of all Classical dying figures sculpted in the round is not a battling armed warrior but is already vanquished – the so-called *Dying Gaul*. This life-size marble figure, and the related sculpture of a Gaul killing himself and his wife rather than fall into enemy hands, both exist now as Roman works. However, they have generally been held to be copies of Greek originals in bronze, made in about 220 BC in Pergamum, now in Turkey (Spivey 1997: 363–5), though the evidence for this is uncertain (Beard and Henderson 2001: 160–4). The *Dying Gaul* clearly represents a Celt, naked, with a Celtic torque around his neck; if the sculpture is Greek he is from Galatia in Asia Minor, if Roman, from Gallia (France). These powerfully emotional sculptures reveal a feature of Classical attitudes towards their dying enemies that is found in other works discussed below: a genuine respect for bravery even in a 'barbarian' people. This was not unadulterated altruism, however, as victory over a worthy enemy carried greater kudos. In the Classical world, suicide, far from being the sinful act of Christian theology, was the honourable action of last resort, to be praised, not vilified.

For a full-scale battle scene, it is necessary to turn to a superb mosaic from Pompeii, made in about 120–100 BC, showing Alexander routing the Persians, under their commander, Darius. It is usually, but not universally, believed that the original was a Greek painting of *c.* 330–10 BC; the mosaic is made with such minute tesserae that it may be able to replicate the lost original in considerable detail (Beard and Henderson 2001: 13–18; Cohen 1997). Despite its damaged state, various dying Persians can be made out, shown with much humanity by the artist (in contrast to many Renaissance and later battle scenes where the fallen become merely anonymous bodies). Among the forest of lances, Alexander's pierces a Persian cavalier as the man's dying horse falls beneath him; the man bravely seizes the fatal weapon, trying to wrench it from his side. A trampled man does not cower but looks up through the many flailing hooves that will shortly destroy him. Even more striking is the representation of a fallen man about to be sliced in two by the wheels of Darius's fleeing chariot. Seen from behind, the reflection of his face appears inside the burnished shield which he clutches to the last.

A Roman work, *Trajan's Column* of AD 113, which rehearses several of the themes already encountered, completes this brief survey of dying in Classical art. The scenes carved on the column, read from the bottom, form a sophisticated strip cartoon spiralling upwards, telling the story of Trajan's successful wars against the Dacians (people from

Romania). They, too, proved an admirable enemy, though some of the scenes are disputed (for instance, do they commit mass suicide with poison or are they merely drinking?). Certainly, they are treated with respect by the artist, particularly the Dacian king, Decebalus, who slit his own throat rather than be paraded in triumph by Trajan. He appears in a favoured position near the top of the column and is shown with the curved knife at his throat as the Roman soldiers arrive to attempt his capture; Trajan had to be content with his head and right hand (Kleiner 1992: 212–20).

Medieval and Renaissance: dying well

The ultimate model for dying well throughout the Christian era is Christ's own death on the cross, which is probably the most frequently represented scene of all time in Western art. Although often shown already dead, Christ's final agony and the patience and humility with which he bore his crucifixion are also frequently depicted. In all the early Anglo-Saxon crucifixions, Christ is shown alive; it is not until the ninth century that the dead Christ first appears, and even then this does not predominate (Raw 1990: 109 and 135). Specific events in the crucifixion story appear in art; Rubens, for example, more than once painted the raising of the cross, employing vertiginous diagonals as Christ's body is swung upright. Various scenes from the crucifixion narrative formed a common compositional language on which artists in later centuries drew when wishing to infuse depictions of secular dying with a pseudo-religious significance. The deaths of saints provided further examples of how a Christian should die. King Edward the Confessor, still wearing his crown, is shown dying well in the *Bayeux Tapestry* (after 1066) with his wife Edith weeping, his kinsman Harold and a priest beside him; the Latin inscription reads 'Here King Edward in his bed addresses his faithful servants.' His end is in direct contrast to Harold's on the battlefield, depicted vainly trying to pull the fatal arrow from his eye.

The mid-fifteenth-century *Triumph of Death,* originally painted for a Palermo hospital, makes a powerful didactic statement about the attitudes of both rich and poor towards dying. Death gallops wildly across the fresco on a chillingly skeletal horse, a quiver of arrows at his bony waist. Beneath the horse's hooves lie clergy, already greying in death, while to the left the poor, mindful of imminent dying, pray devoutly. To the right, however, the rich continue heedless in their pleasures – hunting, idling by a fountain, listening to music and admiring each other's jewellery; it is at them that Death aims his bow. One woman, struck in the neck, reacts with an expression of surprise and distaste, as though merely stung by an annoying insect. *The Triumph of Death* in Pisa, from the previous century, presents a similarly critical view of the rich, although there the scythe-wielding Death swooping in to destroy them is a woman with flowing hair and bat-like wings (Guthke 1999: 71–5).

With the advent of printed books in the fifteenth century, the importance of dying well was promoted by illustrated instruction manuals, the *Ars Moriendi,* originally in Latin but translated into many different European languages. They provided a step-by-step guide for Catholic laypeople when no priest was present to direct the dying person (O'Connor 1966; Ariès 1985: 147–60; Binski 1996: 39–41). The woodcuts show the many temptations to which the dying could succumb, representing aspects of dying badly in this period, egged on by hideous, winged demons. These temptations included impatience, causing the dying man to kick out at those tending him, despair, lack of faith and spiritual pride, in which the demons lay crowns on his bed. Hieronymus Bosch, painting in about 1510, portrays the fifth temptation, avarice, in his *Death of a Miser* (Binski 1996: 43). The miser sits up in his bed while an angel draws his attention to the figure of Death entering the room and to a small crucifix in the window high above. The demons do their best to distract him back to his worldly wealth; one peers down at him over his bedhead, another waves an important financial document at him, and a third sneakily appears under his bed curtain, pushing a large bag of money towards the miser's right hand. Which path he will take hangs in the balance; the dying man, through his choices, can be the agent of his soul's fate.

The *Ars Moriendi* ends with a representation of dying well. A lighted candle is placed in the dying man's hands, his soul is saved by angels, the crucifixion appears with the Virgin Mary among those at the foot of the cross, and the demons are put to flight. During the fifteenth century in northern Europe, representations of the dormition (literally, 'falling asleep') of the Virgin Mary show similar scenes, though frequently omitting any supernatural participants. This is a new departure in Marian iconography; previously she had usually been depicted as already dead, while artists in later centuries often show her direct Assumption to Heaven (Duclow 2007). Many of these deathbed scenes take place in luxuriously furnished bedrooms filled with people, often including a priest with rosary, holy oil and prayer book, the Roman Catholic trappings of dying. The viewer is placed either at the foot, or to one side, of Mary's bed as she contemplates the candle placed in her hands. Several artists, including Albrecht Dürer (Figure 8.2), created engravings of the scene, encouraging the spread of this design. However, Peter Bruegel, in 1564, while still showing

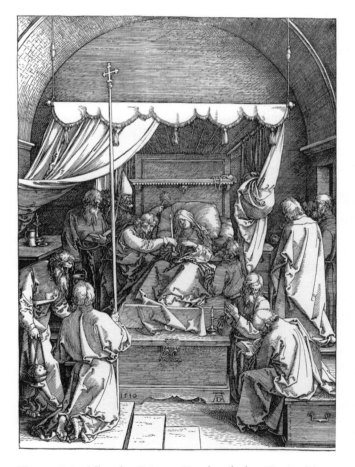

Figure 8.2. Albrecht Dürer, *Death of the Virgin Mary.* Woodcut, 1510. British Museum, Prints and Drawings, E.2.188. 288 x 205mm. © Trustees of the British Museum.

the Virgin in bed, creates a totally different atmosphere, heightening the drama by setting his painting in a darkened room while Mary alone is flooded with brilliant light.

The Protestant good death, shorn of Roman Catholic rituals, appears in a few undistinguished English portraits, all by unknown artists. In each case, although other people are present, the dying man is shown as being in control at the centre of the action, supported and assisted by those around him (Kellehear 2007: 114). In two paintings, the emphasis is on will-making. Thomas Braithwaite, in 1607, sits in bed writing his own will with his friend holding the document, while, in an Elizabethan picture, King Henry VIII, wearing elaborate nightclothes, gestures towards his son Edward, indicating that he will inherit the throne (Aston 1993; Sumner 1995). In the case of Sir Henry Unton, dying in France in 1596, his attendants weep or pray while a doctor takes the sick man's pulse (Strong 1965) (Figure 8.3). The Unton portrait depicts living and dying as a symbolic journey, with the river of life running across the picture from sunshine in the east out into the moonlit sea of eternity in the west; Unton's corpse crosses the river without disturbing its flow when his body is brought back from France for burial.

Figure 8.3. Unknown Artist, *Sir Henry Unton with scenes of his life*. Oil on panel, c.1596 (detail showing deathbed). National Portrait Gallery, London, NPG 710. 740x1632 mm. © National Portrait Gallery, London.

Baroque to neoclassical: the dying hero

The seventeenth and eighteenth centuries were the heyday of the dying being represented as having agency; artists depicted heroes as moral exemplars. Dying heroes feature in many major paintings by the Antwerp painter Peter Paul Rubens, whether Christian or Classical in subject matter. Particularly striking are the enormous oils, commissioned in about 1616, as tapestry designs, which make up the Decius Mus cycle. Decius Mus was a Roman consul chosen by the gods to lead the army to a great victory against the Latins in the battle of Veseris, but at the cost of his own life. Throughout, from the omens singling him out to his consecration by the Roman high priest, Decius Mus knows he will die, bowing his head in acceptance of his duty. In the spectacularly dramatic battle scene, he slides from his rearing horse, which Rubens based on a now-lost battle scene by Leonardo (Jaffé 2005: 41). At the blow of an enemy lance, Decius Mus sees the sky above him open in recognition of his sacrifice.

Equally dramatic, though utterly different in composition, feel and colouring, is Rubens' *Death of Seneca* (1615). Seneca's death has been ordered by his former pupil, now emperor, Nero. The elderly philosopher stands in his bath, his veins already opened by his companions, awaiting his death in duty to his emperor. Rubens based his figure on a highly imaginary Renaissance reconstruction of a severely damaged Classical figure (Beard and Henderson 2001: 1–3). Rubens brings the viewer remarkably – almost devotionally – close to his dying subjects; in both paintings, the heavenward looks, rapt expressions and submission to duty make these Classical characters resemble Christian martyrs.

The contrast between Rubens' compositions and the Classical approach of Poussin is revealed in the French artist's great images of dying, *The Death of Germanicus* (*c.*1627) and *The Testament of Eudamidas* (1643–4). The scenes are not lacking in heroic drama but emotion and gesture are severely restrained, with the viewer held deliberately at a distance (Carrier 1993: 197–203). At Germanicus' deathbed, the expiring Roman consul asks his assembled friends to avenge his death; Eudamidas, in a story by Lucian retold in Montaigne's essay 'On Friendship', dictates his will, requesting that his two closest friends care for his wife and daughter (Bätschmann 1990: 51). In each case, the dying man receives support from others around him in the painting. Both images are elegantly composed scenes which the viewer is permitted to glimpse from afar rather than being drawn into as a participant.

A similar contrast between the immediate and visceral Baroque and the elegantly distant neoclassical can be seen in the changing representations of death itself, in two papal tombs in St Peter's, Rome: those of Alexander VII by Bernini (completed in 1678) and Canova's Clement XIII (1792). Each pope awaits death on his knees, in prayer. Death comes to Alexander VII as a hideous skeleton, clambering up from the depths below brandishing an hourglass – the epitome of dying as horror story. In Clement XIII's monument, dying is akin to falling asleep, death and sleep being brothers in Classical mythology. A sorrowful winged youth, beautiful and almost naked, languishes in a melancholy pose, holding a down-turned torch whose flames are gently extinguished, a symbol taken from Roman monuments (Honour 1968: 147–50).

Rejecting both Baroque and neoclassical conventions, the British artist William Hogarth deliberately set out to depict 'modern subjects' with a moral purpose, creating images of dying completely at odds with the prevailing heroic models. Dying horribly, in several of Hogarth's series of paintings and engravings, is the punishment for the wickedness of his anti-heroes. The unfaithful earl in *Marriage à la Mode* (*c.*1743) is stabbed by his wife's lover. His countess, having swallowed laudanum, is kissed farewell by her syphilitic infant while her father removes the rings from her fingers: as a suicide they would be forfeit on her death. Hogarth chooses to close his sequence of drawings for *Industry and Idleness* (1747) at a morally equivocal point, as the idle apprentice, sitting with his back against his coffin, is taken by cart to be publicly hung at Tyburn, the ultimate dying journey (Figure 8.4). Will Tom Idle summon up sufficient agency to heed the exhortations of the Wesleyan preacher (faintly sketched by Hogarth in the cart) to repent and save his soul? Will Tom muster the requisite bravura on the scaffold to achieve the traditional 'good death' at the gallows (the three-legged structure in the drawing)? Or will he fail on both counts? Hogarth leaves the viewer to decide (Linebaugh 1975).

A domestic depiction of dying of *c.*1725, previously ascribed to Hogarth but now attributed to a Dutch painter working in London, Egbert van Heemskerk III, provides contemporary comment on the increasing professionalization of dying (Kellehear 2007: 132–4). Among those assembled are the doctor, examining the patient's urine,

Figure 8.4. William Hogarth, Finished drawing for Plate 11 of
© Trustees of the British Museum Pen and black ink with grey
wash, over graphite, 1747. British Museum, Prints and Drawings,
1896, 0710.25. 227x388 mm © Trustees of the British Museum

the lawyer, busy with documents, and the clergyman, prayerbook in
hand; all three are clearly far wealthier than the dying person. While
the family, weeping, gaze on the patient's face, the three professionals
turn away from the bed, intent on their own activities – agency clearly
has passed to them from the dying man. Many versions of this painting exist, one inscribed 1674, so it clearly remained topical for at least
fifty years, simply by updating the costumes.

For neoclassical painters in the later decades of the eighteenth century, the death of Socrates was a popular subject. The heroic self-
control which Socrates exerted over his suicide when condemned to
death appealed not just for its Classical setting but through its mix-
ture of heightened emotion and intense moral seriousness. Most famous is the depiction by Jacques-Louis David (1787); the raised arm of
Socrates, as he reaches for the goblet of poison, recalls the raised arm
of the oath-swearer in Poussin's *Germanicus* (Lindsay 1960: 55–7;
Carrier 1993).

Neoclassical painters did not, however, restrict themselves to classical scenes but also depicted the dying heroes of their own day. In
1770, the American artist Benjamin West showed James Wolfe, the
hero of Quebec, dying on the battlefield surrounded by companions.
West took considerable care over the accuracy of Wolfe's uniform but
received criticism for not adopting a Classical setting and dress. The
painting, however, is far from historically accurate (McNairn 1997:

125–43); it enhances the heroic, even sacred nature of Wolfe's sacrifice by employing a composition similar to that often used in depicting the descent from the cross. The same visual reference is used by West's compatriot John Singleton Copley in portraying the death of Lord Chatham while addressing the House of Lords (exhibited 1781) although in fact Chatham did not actually expire for a further month (Prown 1966: 278). In both paintings, people are shown for the sake of completeness who were not actually present at the event; it has even been suggested, probably inaccurately, that West sold the right to appear with Wolfe (McNairn 1997: 137–41). In his *Death of Nelson* of 1806, West transfers the whole scene up onto the main deck of the *Victory* to add grandeur, though two years later he produced a slightly more realistic version set below decks (Von Erffa and Staley 1986: 222–3). Whether Classical or contemporary, the moral lesson of the hero's sacrifice was paramount, and all aspects of the image had to work to that end.

Romantics and realists: dying less heroically

Choosing contemporary subjects, however, particularly highlighted the falsification inherent in the neoclassical approach to heroism and the deliberately limited range of human emotion it evoked. Romantic representations of dying encompassed a far wider emotional range. This is seen in Paul Delaroche's *Execution of Lady Jane Grey* (1833) where those present respond with pity, despair and shock at the imminent decapitation of an innocent young girl; even the executioner shows some concern (Figure 8.5).

In Spain, early in the nineteenth century, Goya lived through a series of atrocities as the Spanish resisted French attempts at domination. In Valencia Cathedral in 1788 he had already explored the theme of dying in an extraordinary work, the complete antithesis of neoclassical heroism: *St Francis Borgia at the Deathbed of an Impenitent*. The sinner, his face contorted, shares his bed with four evil supernatural creatures worthy of a bad death in the most gruesomely imaginative medieval *Ars Moriendi*. The crucifix in St Francis's hand spouts blood over this hideous depravity, damning him for eternity (Schulz 1998).

Among the scenes which Goya himself witnessed was the savage revenge taken by the French in Madrid, following Spanish rioting the previous day. In his painting *3 May 1808*, those already executed

Figure 8.5. Paul Delaroche, *The Execution of Lady Jane Grey*. Oil on canvas, 1833. National Gallery London, NG 1909. 246x297 cm © The National Gallery, London.

lie to the left, while those about to be shot file in from the right. No French faces are seen as they take aim at the central figure – a man in a white shirt with a look of wide-eyed terror on his face, lit up by a large lantern (Vaughan 2006: 95–6). He stands, with bravely outstretched arms and an indentation on his right palm, as if crucified, but, like Christ, no pity will save him from his executioners (Thomas 1972). His is a very different kind of heroism from that of the neoclassicists – both the victims and their dehumanized executioners have little or no agency. This painting has challenged all artists depicting dying in conflict ever since 1814, when Goya created it, influencing, in particular, Édouard Manet in his *Execution of the Emperor Maximilian* in 1867.

Géricault's famous *Raft of the Medusa* (1818–19) presents further extremes of dying, again with contemporary victims as its subjects. In 1816, the *Medusa*, poorly equipped by the French Government, had run aground on its way to Senegal and, with insufficient lifeboats, 150 people had been set loose on a makeshift raft to experience mutiny,

cannibalism, madness and death (Eitner 1972). Only fifteen still
remained alive when, after two weeks, a ship was spotted in the distance; despite frantic waving, it disappeared from sight, and the possibility of life faded again into the near-certainty of death – a ghastly
rapid oscillation between living and dying. This was the moment
Géricault selected for depiction; although the ship returned two hours
later, only ten men were to survive the whole ordeal (Vaughan 2006:
240–1). In the foreground, Géricault placed lifeless bodies, based
partly on his drawings in the morgue but also heavily influenced by
Michelangelo, creating images of Classical perfection, free from signs
of starvation. An elderly man cradles his dead son, oblivious to all
else; these figures have a timeless, intense beauty of precisely the kind
that raises conflicting responses between subject matter and aesthetics. Géricault shows other survivors from behind as they desperately
try to signal their distress – their straining bodies draw the viewer
into the scene, scanning the horizon with them.

Géricault's model for the dead youth lying facedown beside the
grieving father was the painter Eugène Delacroix (Eitner 1972: 158–9).
Delacroix's depictions of dying were far more sensual and exotic,
particularly in his Orientalist fantasy, *The Death of Sardanapalus*,
painted 1827–8 (Spector 1974). Sardanapalus, a legendary Assyrian
king facing defeat by his rebellious subjects, chooses to destroy himself and all his possessions, both material and human. Byron had
published his play *Sardanapalus* in 1821, and the excesses of this tyrant's final act appealed to a certain kind of Romantic sensibility. In
Delacroix's depiction, the King reclines on a massive bed loaded with
treasure, watching an orgy of stabbing as his eunuchs and guards kill
the naked women of his harem, except for one who chooses to hang
herself. A black slave dispatches the King's horse, and the flames
that will finally consume everything can be seen in the background.
This disturbingly violent subject matter is matched by equally violent
colours, with a strong preponderance of reds and a strangely distorted pictorial space (Vaughan 2006: 249–50). The massacre over
which the tyrant gloats does not appear in Byron's play but seems
to have been the product of Delacroix's own imagination, revealing
a view of dying heavily entwined with pain, eroticism and sadism.
Although the King clearly has agency over his own and many others'
dying, he could not be further from the heroic ideal (Spector 1974:
67, 90–105).

The Pre-Raphaelites were attracted to death and dying in literature of a more high-minded kind, bringing closely observed realistic details to their subject matter. Two paintings with literary connections explore, in different ways, awareness of dying in both their subjects and viewers. In Millais' *Ophelia* (1851–2), the viewer knows that 'muddy death' shortly awaits her, but she herself is oblivious as she floats downstream with her flowers; it is said that Millais' model, Elizabeth Siddal, was herself in danger of catching fatal pneumonia by posing in a rapidly chilling bath. William Lindsay Windus's *Too Late* (1858), based on a poem by Tennyson, takes the subjects' recognition of dying as its theme. An errant lover returns to find his hoped-for bride dying of consumption (tuberculosis). Pale and thin, she supports herself with a stick as she walks with a female companion, whose obvious health makes her illness even more apparent; her despairing lover covers his face. Tuberculosis, with its propensity to attack the young with slow wasting away, was the Romantic disease of choice in many art forms, including novels and operas, as well as painting. However, *Too Late* aroused severe criticism, including for its subject matter, perhaps because the ghastly ravages of the disease are here revealed all too clearly as his heroine feebly totters along. Windus, devastated by this failure and by the death of his own wife shortly afterwards, gave up painting (Wood 1976: 97–8).

The mid-nineteenth century saw the birth of photography, in itself a potentially highly realist technology. Its introduction led to the production of countless post-mortem images, particularly of dead children. The British photographer Henry Peach Robinson, however, wanted to claim a higher status for this new technology, as an art form in its own right. He therefore constructed elaborately composed images, using multiple negatives, posed by models, basing his choice of subjects on contemporary painting. His *Fading Away* of 1858 shows a young woman dying of tuberculosis with her family around her, captioned with lines from Shelley, just as a painting might have been. Critics were mixed in their responses to both image and technique, but copies of the photograph sold well, suggesting it touched a popular chord (Harker 1988: 26–7).

In France and Britain, realist painters looked to the poor for their subjects, but, by often including children, created some distinctly sentimental effects. Luke Fildes was moved to paint his extremely popular picture *The Doctor* (1891) after his own young son had died in

1877, despite the care of a conscientious doctor. Fildes first did careful research, even having a reconstruction of a fisherman's cottage erected in his studio, while rejecting, in favour of a model, approaches from doctors clamouring to appear in it (Wood 1976: 100–2). The painting has received different interpretations. It remains an open question whether the young girl sleeping in the makeshift bed on two chairs, watched over by the thoughtful but – before antibiotics – powerless doctor, will live or die. What is clear is that the doctor's presence would in reality have generally been unaffordable to poor people such as the girl's parents, relegated to shadows in the background (Jalland 1999: 240–1).

The dying poor were not just the preserve of realist painters, however. A totally different approach, though with equally carefully observed details, is taken by the German symbolist painter working in Switzerland, Carlos Schwabe, in his turn-of-the-century masterpiece, *Death and the Gravedigger* (Figure 8.6). Death comes for the white-bearded gravedigger while he is at work in a snowy cemetery beneath the bare branches of a weeping tree, redolent of the ending of life; only the snowdrops in the foreground give hope of renewal. As the old man stands in the newly made grave, he looks up at the kneeling Angel of Death – modelled by Schwabe's wife – with her enormous, curved, black wings encircling his shoulders. She holds a candle giving off an eerie green light; her other hand points heavenwards (Guthke 1999: 196). This type of image, in which each detail has a symbolic, but often fairly obscure, meaning, was to influence the way dying was to be represented in the first decades of the following century.

Expressionism and beyond: dying and time

In the past 100 years, the art of dying has quite frequently explored notions of time, not least through the creation of time-based works, especially, in recent decades, using video. However, other aspects of time influenced earlier works, too. The Norwegian painter, Edvard Munch, declared 'I was born dying'; as a child he developed tuberculosis, which had already killed his mother, and thought that he, too, would die (Heller 1984: 11). In fact, in 1877, it was his elder sister Sophie who died of it, begging her helpless doctor father to save her, when Munch was fourteen, an event that scarred him for

Figure 8.6. Carlos Schwabe, *Death and the Gravedigger.* Gouache and watercolour, c.1900. Louvre, Prints and Drawings, RF 40162.BIS, Recto. 760x560 mm. © The Bridgeman Art Library.

life with sorrow and guilt (Heller 1984: 19). His *Sick Child* of 1885 took a year to complete: an ashen-faced, red-haired girl sitting in bed turns towards a female figure doubled up in grief. Returning again and again to Sophie's awful dying, Munch created five more painted versions during his life and several graphic ones too, saying that his sister's death was 'of such significance' to him (Heller 1984: 21). The painting, for all its nineteenth-century feel, shows, in its flattening of space and form and heightened colouring, the Expressionism Munch was later to develop further (Heller 1984: 31). The Expressionist painter Egon Schiele declared that for him 'everything is living death' (Short 1997: 15). Death permeates his anguished images as the limbs of the living become skeletal, seemingly dying before the viewer's eyes. His *Death and the Maiden* (1915) is a self-portrait with his lover model; three years later he was dead in the influenza epidemic, aged only twenty-eight.

One influence on Schiele was the Swiss painter Ferdinand Hodler. In 1915, as Hodler's mistress, Valentine Godé-Darel, was dying slowly of cancer, he made a series of images that documented her dying months (the subject of Bronfen's essay referred to earlier, in which she argues that these images do violence to Godé-Darel by inevitably failing to transmit her pain to the spectator). As Godé-Darel comes closer to dying, Hodler draws her prone body in profile as if kneeling by her bed, reminiscent of Holbein's *Dead Christ*. The effect has been likened by various art historians to Hodler's Expressionist landscapes reduced to their bare elements, suggesting that, in her dying, she, too, is gradually becoming elemental and timeless. This is an interpretation which Bronfen argues 'de-individualizes' and diminishes Godé-Darel's own experience of dying (1992: 49). Certainly these immensely private images, although made with their subject's consent, raise uncomfortable questions of intrusion by the viewer. Hodler himself permitted some to be exhibited; later artists making equally personal final drawings of those close to them have also chosen to show their works publicly (Hambling 2001a and 2001b).

Photography has been a major tool for artists in the past 100 years, as well as an art form in its own right, capturing frozen moments of time. Picasso was deeply affected by newspaper photographs of the horrific aftermath of the bombing of Guernica in 1937, creating his great anti-war masterpiece in response. In it he exposes the barbarity of a new twentieth-century form of dying – that of civilians under aerial bombardment (Fisch 1988). The woman on the right is flung upwards by the force; above and below her flames burn, like medieval jaws of Hell.

The American artist Andy Warhol also used newspaper photographs in his work, but in a very different manner, reflecting, in his screen prints on canvas, a culture desensitized to death and dying by the ubiquity of such images. He presents the same one captured moment over and over again, such as a horrific car wreck strewn with the dead and dying, washed in an attractive colour. Warhol's *Disaster* series, begun in the 1960s, exposes how easily the single shocking moment is reduced to banality when repeated like wallpaper. As he himself put it, the more repetitions you see, 'the more the meaning goes away' (Foster 2001: 72). For his car wrecks, Warhol chose photographs so harrowing that even local newspapers had baulked at publishing them. He also relished the poor quality of the newspaper image; in the *Suicide* series, tiny, anonymous figures are seen falling from very tall buildings. In the *Electric Chair* series, dying is conjured up by absence – 'the tension of allusion' – a technique already exploited in the nineteenth century in various images of the empty cradle (Bastian 2001: 30). In Warhol's work, the horror of the execution is supplied by the viewer of this apparatus of judicial death but then rendered commonplace by its endless repetition.

When Bill Viola videoed his mother dying in 1991, it was not to create an artwork but because, faced with her lying unconscious following a brain haemorrhage, he 'had to do something' and because video 'had become [his] own lifeline to the world' (Viola 2001). However, in the following year, he incorporated some of the footage into two artworks, *The Passing* and the *Nantes Triptych*. The three screens of the triptych, the outer two in colour, the central one in black and white, show a woman giving birth, a body suspended in water (a frequent Viola image, partly based on a near-drowning experience when he was ten) and his mother's face as she lies dying. The soundtrack moves through crying, watery noises and breathing (Viola 2001). More recently, the French conceptual artist Sophie Calle videoed her dying mother deliberately to create an artwork: *Pas pu saisir la mort* (*The Last Breath, Impossible to Capture*). In 2006, Calle heard simultaneously that she had been invited to exhibit at the Venice Biennale and that her mother had a month left to live. 'She was so horrified about not being there, I thought the only way I can make her be there is if she's the subject' (Chrisafis 2007).

The dying artist has long been the subject of artworks, such as Ingres' *François I at the Deathbed of Leonardo* (1818), while self-portraits painted during illness go back at least to Goya's self-portrait with his doctor (1820). In the later twentieth century, artists have used photography to present their dying selves. Robert Mapplethorpe, in his powerful, black and white *Self-Portrait* of 1988, grasps a walking stick topped by a carved skull and looks unflinchingly into the camera, mirroring his awareness of his own impending death from AIDS.

His hand and stick are in focus, his face less so, while, by wearing black, Mapplethorpe reduces his body to near invisibility (Morrisoe 1995: 335).

Another American, Hannah Wilke, a performance artist and photographer, chose to document, with her husband's assistance, the whole course of her dying of cancer between 1991 and 1992, to create *Intra-Venus,* exhibited posthumously. She produced over-life-size photographs with an intensity of colour and an unwavering eye for every detail of her bodily disintegration, mounting them as diptychs. A performer to the last, she pairs portraits exploring different roles for dying women. One showing her bald-headed with her hands clapped to her face is coupled with another referencing the Virgin Mary, draped in a bright-blue hospital blanket, with eyes serenely closed (Skelly 2007). In such works, the agency of artist and subject merge so that art and dying become one.

A chapter of this short length can do little more than outline some of the wealth of images of dying in Western art and hint at some possible themes to explore. So what appears to be the future for the academic study of dying in art? Museums and art galleries have a critical role to play in presenting dying as a topic for consideration by the general public. This is abundantly clear, to give but two contrasting examples from London at the time of writing, early in 2008. For some time now, the National Gallery has hung Paul Delaroche's *Execution of Lady Jane Grey* (Figure 8.5) between Manet's *Execution of the Emperor Maximilian* (1867) and Puvis de Chavannes's *Beheading of St John the Baptist* (c.1869) – three stylistically very different paintings linked by subject matter. The Wellcome Collection is currently showing a much-visited exhibition by the German photographer Walter Schels and journalist Beate Lakotta, called *Life before Death,* which pairs portraits of sitters taken when they were dying, with images of them after their deaths; the captions use the subjects' own words. Interestingly, several of the subjects said, unprompted, how being photographed while dying, far from being exploitative as Bronfen suggested, had increased their sense of self-worth. One woman added that no longer being photographed by her family since developing cancer made her feel she was treated as if she were already dead (Beate Lakotta, personal communication).

Art galleries and museums have additionally brought the art of dying to academic attention as an aspect of death in art (Llewellyn

1991). Academics have also focused on the public presentation of images of dying by museums and galleries, although subsuming them within the representation of illness (Komninou 2006). It is hoped that in future the art of dying will be recognized as a worthwhile academic topic for study in its own right, unlocking the rich possibilities in Western art using concepts developed by those social scientists who research death and dying.

References

Ariès, P. (1985) *Images of Man and Death*, trans. J. Lloyd, Cambridge, Mass.: Harvard University Press.

Aston, M. (1993) *The King's Bedpost: Reformation and Iconography in a Tudor Group Portrait*, Cambridge: Cambridge University Press.

Bastian, H. (2001) *Andy Warhol Retrospective*, London: Tate Publishing.

Bätschmann, O. (1990) *Nicholas Poussin: Dialectics of Painting*, London: Reaktion Books.

Beard, M. and Henderson, J. (2001) *Classical Art from Greece to Rome*, Oxford: Oxford University Press.

Binion, R. (1993) *Love Beyond Death: The Anatomy of a Myth in the Arts*, New York: New York University Press.

Binski, P. (1996) *Medieval Death: Ritual and Representation*, London: British Museum Press.

Bronfen, E. (1992) *Over Her Dead Body: Death, Femininity and the Aesthetic*, Manchester: Manchester University Press.

Carrier, D. (1993) *Poussin's Paintings: A Study in Art-Historical Methodology*, University Park, Pa.: Pennsylvania State University Press.

Chrisafis, A. (2007) 'He Loves Me Not', *The Guardian*, 16 June, available online at www.guardian.co.uk/world/2007/jun/16/artnews.art (accessed 9 May 2008).

Cohen, A. (1997) *The Alexander Mosaic: Stories of Victory and Defeat*, Cambridge: Cambridge University Press.

Curl, J. (1993) *A Celebration of Death: Funerary Architecture in the Western European Tradition*, London: Batsford.

Duclow, D. (2007) 'The Virgin Mary', in *Encyclopaedia of Death and Dying*, available online at www.deathreference.com/sy-vi/virgin-mary-the.html (accessed 13 May 2008).

Eitner, L. (1972) *Géricault's Raft of the Medusa*, London: Phaidon.

Fisch, E. (1988) *Guernica by Picasso: A Study of the Picture and Its Context*, trans. J. Hotchkiss, London: Associated University Presses.

Foster, H. (2001) 'Death in America', in A. Michelson (ed.), *October Files: Andy Warhol*, Cambridge, Mass.: MIT Press, pp. 67–88.

Guthke, K. (1999) *The Gender of Death: A Cultural History in Art and Literature*, Cambridge: Cambridge University Press.

Hambling, M. (2001a) *Father*, London: Morley Gallery.

   (2001b) *Maggi and Henrietta: Drawings of Henrietta Moraes by Maggi Hambling*, London: Bloomsbury.

Harker, M. (1988) *Henry Peach Robinson: Master of Photographic Art, 1830–1891*, Oxford: Basil Blackwell.

Heller, R. (1984) *Munch: His Life and Work*, London: John Murray.

Herndl, D. (1993) *Invalid Women: Figuring Feminine Illness in American Fiction and Culture, 1840–1940*, Chapel Hill, NC: University of North Carolina Press.

Honour, H. (1968) *Neoclassicism*, Harmondsworth: Penguin Books.

Jaffé, D. (2005) *Rubens: A Master in the Making*, London: National Gallery Company.

Jalland, P. (1999) 'Victorian Death and Its Decline: 1850–1918', in P. Jupp and C. Gittings (eds.), *Death in England: An Illustrated History*, Manchester: Manchester University Press, 230–55.

Kellehear, A. (2007) *A Social History of Dying*, Cambridge: Cambridge University Press.

Kleiner, D. (1992) *Roman Sculpture*, London and New Haven, Conn.: Yale University Press.

Knigge, U. (1991) *The Athenian Kerameikos: History; Monuments; Excavations*, trans. J. Binder, Athens: Krene Editions.

Komninou, E. (2006) 'Images of Illness on the Museum's Walls: Representations of Disease in Contemporary Visual Arts', available online at www.city.ac.uk/cpm/research/cpm_award_lecture.pdf (accessed 13 May 2008).

Lindsay, J. (1960) *Death of the Hero: French Painting from David to Delacroix*, London: Studio.

Linebaugh, P. (1975) 'The Tyburn Riot Against the Surgeons', in D. Hay (ed.), *Albion's Fatal Tree: Crime and Society in Eighteenth-Century England*, London: Allen Lane, 65–117.

Llewellyn, N. (1991) *The Art of Death: Visual Culture in the English Death Ritual*, London: Reaktion Books.

   (2000) *Funeral Monuments in Post-Reformation England*, Cambridge: Cambridge University Press.

McNairn, A. (1997) *Behold the Hero: General Wolfe and the Arts in the Eighteenth Century*, Liverpool: Liverpool University Press.

McTavish, L. (2002) 'Picturing the Dead', *Canadian Medical Association Journal*, **166** (13): 1700–1, available online at www.cmaj.ca/cgi/content/full/166/13/1700 (accessed on 14 May 2008).

Morrisoe, P. (1995) *Mapplethorpe: A Biography*, New York: Random House.

O'Connor, M. (1966) *The Art of Dying Well: The Development of the Ars Moriendi*, New York: AMS Press.

Penny, N. (1977) *Church Monuments in Romantic England*, New Haven, Conn.: Yale University Press.

Prown, J. (1966) *John Singleton Copley in England 1774–1815*, Cambridge, Mass.: Harvard University Press.

Raw, B. (1990) *Anglo-Saxon Crucifixion Iconography and the Art of Monastic Revival*, Cambridge: Cambridge University Press.

Schulz, A. (1998) 'The Expressive Body in Goya's Saint Francis Borgia at the Deathbed of an Impenitent', *Art Bulletin*, 12 January, available online at www.encylopedia.com/doc/1g1–54073965.html (accessed on 13 May 2008).

Skelly, J. (2007) 'Mas(k/t)ectomies: Losing a Breast (and Hair) in Hannah Wilke's Body Art', *Thirdspace: A Journal of Feminist Theory and Culture*, **7** (1): 3–16, available online at www.thirdspace.ca/journal/rt/printerfriendly/skelly/0 (accessed on 9 May 2008).

Short, C. (1997) *Schiele*, London: Phaidon Press.

Spector, J. (1974) *Delacroix: The Death of Sardanapalus*, London: Allen Lane.

Spivey, N. (1997) *Greek Art*, London: Phaidon.

Strong, R. (1965) 'Sir Henry Unton and His Portrait: An Elizabethan Memorial Picture and Its History', *Archaeologia*, **99**: 53–76.

Sumner, A. (ed.) (1995) *Death, Passion and Politics: Van Dyck's Portraits of Venetia Stanley and George Digby*, London: Dulwich Picture Gallery.

Thomas, H. (1972) *Goya: The Third of May 1808*, London: Allen Lane.

Vaughan, W. (2006) *Romanticism and Art*, London: Thames & Hudson.

Viola, B. (2001) 'The John Tusa Interview: Bill Viola'. Available online at www.bbc.co.uk/radio3/johntusainterview/viola_transcript.shtml (accessed on 9 May 2008).

Von Erffa, H. and Staley, A. (1986) *The Paintings of Benjamin West*, London and New Haven, Conn.: Yale University Press.

Wood, C. (1976) *Victorian Panorama: Paintings of Victorian Life*, London: Faber.

9 | *Dying in Western literature*

JOHN SKELTON

Kellehear's introduction to this volume gives us in essence a list of metaphors by which we can attempt to understand dying. He does so in an appropriately nuanced manner: as he stresses, there is a great deal of 'overlap' and 'social complexity' in the analysis. Metaphors are, however, an excellent place to start. They are embedded in all languages ('embedded' is a metaphor, for example) and – a claim made sometimes weakly, sometimes strongly (two more metaphors here) – can drive (metaphor) how we reflect on (metaphor) the world. Thus, in English, 'illness' is perceived in an essentially allopathic manner: people *fight battles* with disease, and so on (Skelton et al. 2002). Similarly, the idea that life is a journey towards an inevitable end, a metaphor which Kellehear picks up with respect to dying, is a widely quoted example (Lakoff 1993): thus, one's life can *lack direction* or *hit the buffers,* or one can *know where one is going,* and so on.

The journey metaphor underpins a great deal of world literature, from *The Epic of Gilgamesh* (Anon. 2003) to *The Odyssey* (Homer 2003) or *The Pilgrim's Progress* (Bunyan 1973). Within a specifically English context, there is the wonderful image Bede gives to a nobleman while King Edwin and his court debate whether to accept Christianity:

Your Majesty, when we compare the present life of man on earth with that time of which we have no knowledge, it seems to me like the swift flight of a single sparrow through the banqueting-hall where you are sitting at dinner on a winter's day with your thanes and counsellors. In the midst there is a comforting fire to warm the hall; outside, the storms of winter rain or snow are raging. This sparrow flies swiftly in through one door of the hall, and out through another. While he is inside, he is safe from the winter storms; but after a few moments of comfort, he vanishes from sight into the wintry world from which he came. Even so, man appears on earth for but a little while; but of what came before this life or of what follows, we know nothing. (Bede 1990: 129–30)

Such metaphors are known as 'conceptual metaphors' (or 'cognitive metaphors'), and many of these are listed on Lakoff's website, where they are set out, as is the convention, in the form 'A is B' ('Life is a journey'), where A is the *source* and B is the *target*. Lakoff and Turner (1989), in fact, look at English conceptual metaphors for death (rather than dying, that is), suggesting for example:

Death is departure.
A lifetime is a day/year (and death is night/winter).
Death is sleep.
Death is silence.
Death is a final destination.
Life is bondage (and death is deliverance).

I have dealt principally with literature of outstanding rather than dubious quality. I take it that the themes of both outstanding and dubious literature are similar and draw on the same cultural heritage. They offer the same kinds of meaning, too, in some sense. And they also draw on the same stock of metaphor.

Great literature partly works because great writers are capable of dealing with the basic stuff of life and of the metaphors through which we tackle it, with a richness and subtlety that gives new meanings. Much of what follows is designed simply to be an illustration of this point. I don't intend to pick up all Kellehear's metaphors by rote, but even where I don't, the relevance of these in literature, and the resonance literature can give them, will, I hope, be clear enough.

There are two caveats I should enter, however. First, writers use themes – 'dying' in this case – for their own purposes. More formally, *dying* is not necessarily the source ('Dying is like X') but the target ('X is like dying') – for example, in a book such as Camus's *The Plague* (2002), something like 'Existence is like a plague.' Second, I suppose if literature has any single overriding goal it is to explore the question 'What is life like?' and, by extension, to explore whether we see life clearly, whether life is perhaps a dream of some kind, whether therefore death rather than life is more meaningful, and so on. The question of how dying is represented in Western literature is in this way perilously close to the rather vacuous question, 'What do writers write about?'

Dying is a journey

'Dying is a journey', then, is a metaphor familiar for thousands of years
in the West, at least since the myth of the ferry across the Styx. It is, of
course, the nature of myths that their meaning deepens with time, as
peoples and cultures reflect on and retell them. Similarly, the metaphor
of the journey, in the hands of the outstanding writer, has a resonance
which has partly some profound general mythic provenance or springs
from an ages-old conceptual metaphor. But most of the resonance – the
creative bit, as it were – springs from the writer. Emily Dickinson gives
a strange, rather eerie example of the dying journey (Poem 712):

> Because I could not stop for Death –
> He kindly stopped for me –
> The Carriage held but just Ourselves –
> And Immortality.
>
> We slowly drove – He knew no haste
> And I had put away
> My labor and my leisure too,
> For His Civility –
>
> We passed the School, where Children strove
> At Recess – in the Ring –
> We passed the Fields of Gazing Grain –
> We passed the Setting Sun –
>
> Or rather – He passed Us –
> The Dews drew quivering and chill –
> For only Gossamer, my Gown –
> My Tippet – only Tulle –
>
> We paused before a House that seemed
> A Swelling of the Ground –
> The Roof was scarcely visible –
> The Cornice – in the Ground –
>
> Since then – 'tis Centuries – and yet
> Feels shorter than the Day
> I first surmised the Horses' Heads
> Were towards Eternity –
>
>   (Dickinson 1970: 350)

Dickinson is the poet of dying (''Tis dying – I am doing – but / I'm not
afraid to know' (Poem 692)), in the same way as one might say Sylvia

Plath ('Dying / Is an art, like everything else. / I do it exceptionally well') is the poet of suicide ('Lady Lazarus', Plath 1965).

The familiarity of dying – it's a matter of 'Civility', it's like a carriage ride – and the collapse of the distinction between great themes (Immortality) and commonplaces (I should have worn something warmer) turn the protagonist into a fairly detached spectator of events – of the children playing, the chill in the air, her own dying, so that the poem also echoes the idea of death as disengagement/withdrawal, in Kellehear's terms. The general sense of disorientation and yet naturalness is echoed in the rhyme scheme. Lines 2 and 4 in each stanza are rhymed, sort of, but the closeness of the rhyme ranges from slight ('Ring' and 'Sun') to identical ('Ground' and 'Ground'). The collapse of time in the last stanza, incidentally, illustrates Dickinson's familiarity with Christian idiom ('each day to him is like a thousand years'), and the way in which Western writers use Christian iconography to contextualize their work.

Compare this with Dickens' *Dombey and Son,* a substantial part of which is concerned with one of the most haunting of all portrayals of a parent and a child – the young Paul Dombey – who is always sickly, and eventually dies.

Dombey Senior is head of a great company, a businessman whose passion is money, leaving him little time for ordinary emotions. Except that, with the arrival of his son, whom he at first sees as an heir, he struggles inarticulately towards human feeling. Thus, when for the first time he takes the young Paul to the school where he will board, he says on the threshold 'Now, Paul ... This is the way indeed to be Dombey and Son, and have money. You are almost a man already' (Dickens 2002: 171). Yet at the moment of parting, 'He bent down, over his boy, and kissed him. If his sight were dimmed as he did so, by something that for a moment blurred the little face, and made it indistinct to him, his mental vision may have been, for that short time, the clearer perhaps' (Dickens 2002: 170). The reader's last glimpse of Paul in this scene (a Dickensian moment, quasi-cinematic as he often was, and with a sadly witty image): 'And there, with an aching void in his young heart, and all outside so cold, and bare, and strange, Paul sat as if he had taken life unfurnished, and the upholsterer were never coming' (Dickens 2002: 171).

In the end, Paul becomes more and more unwell:

> Paul had never risen from his little bed. He lay there, listening to the noises in the street, quite tranquilly; not caring much how the time went, but watching it and watching everything about him with observing eyes.
>
> When the sunbeams struck into his room through the rustling blinds, and quivered on the opposite wall like golden water, he knew that evening was coming on, and that the sky was red and beautiful. As the reflection died away, and a gloom went creeping up the wall, he watched it deepen, deepen, deepen, into night. Then he thought how the long streets were dotted with lamps, and how the peaceful stars were shining overhead. His fancy had a strange tendency to wander to the river, which he knew was flowing through the great city; and now he thought how black it was, and how deep it would look, reflecting the hosts of stars – and more than all, how steadily it rolled away to meet the sea. (Dickens 2002: 248)

Life itself is a river along which we journey towards the unknown seas beyond. But at the same time, this river is the Thames, the centre of the world's trade, and at the heart of the great London trading empires that were being created. What Paul is watching, as he too drifts into a dreamlike state of disengagement in which his narrative point of view is briefly identical to that of the omniscient narrator, is the source of London's wealth drifting away. Beautiful and foul, a symbol of meretricious riches, of greed, poverty, life and death. (In Dickens' great novel of the Thames, *Our Mutual Friend* (1997), boatmen scavenge from the corpses found floating in it.)

This is the subtlety of great art: to take a familiar metaphor, reuse it with such emotional power, and in doing so give it further meanings. Poor literature is at the other end of the scale. Thus, for example, though dying is a journey, we might seek to reassure by claiming that it doesn't take one very far. The other side of the Styx is not too distant:

> Death is nothing at all,
> I have only slipped into the next room
> I am I and you are you
> Whatever we were to each other, that we are still.

This immensely popular consolatory piece of writing (googling the first line yields 41,000 hits) is in fact a passage from a sermon (Holland

1919), invariably quoted these days as if it was verse (it isn't), and taken irritatingly out of context, as if Holland were stating a personal belief (he isn't, he's expressing the wish that we actually could treat death like this).

This is a piece of writing which is probably taken seriously because it has the ponderous cadences of the sermon. As a poem it fails pretty miserably – hardly the author's fault – because it gives no subtlety to the metaphor.

Genuinely amateur efforts, as opposed to those of someone like Holland, who was a gifted creator of sermons (some of them still in print and admired), and in that sense a professional writer, will of course typically lack aesthetic merit. Heartfelt, and to be honoured for that reason, but as poetic statements rather than personal expressions they don't work. Unlike Holland, who appears bathetic only when a poetic structure is superimposed, they will often relapse into the clichés of the greetings-card industry. This difference is well illustrated by, for example, Wall (no date), who echoes Holland. Here it is the demonstration of human contact rather than the poetic achievement which is touching.

The clichés themselves will draw on the same metaphorical stock, however. Thus, writers will play with questions such as: 'What does it mean to say dying is a journey?' or, for that matter, to insist on such notions as 'dying is control' (a thousand variations on the theme of 'Granddad's gone to be with Grandma', implying a choice about the process), and many others.

But, after all, this is what literature is for, to pick up such questions, such ideas, and explore them.

One of the great writers on dying is Thomas Mann, and Mann's elaborate artistry takes us right to the opposite end of the scale of subtlety, as metaphor, myth and the general cultural tradition are interwoven.

Mann's *Death in Venice* (1991) deals with the last days of Gustav von Aschenbach, a famous writer. He becomes a musician in the Visconti film, partly no doubt to provide a richer context for the soundtrack of Mahler's music but partly also because Mann gives his Aschenbach a physical resemblance to the great musician. Exhausted by work, Aschenbach visits Venice for a change of scene and approaches the city in a gondola ('That singular conveyance ... black as nothing else on earth except a coffin') rowed by a man with an 'unpleasing, even brutish face': rowed well, so that Aschenbach concedes 'even if you hit me in the back with your oar and send me down to the kingdom of Hades, even then you will have rowed me well' (Mann 1991: 21–4). This, clearly, is the journey over the Styx.

In Venice, Aschenbach becomes obsessed with a beautiful Polish youth called Tadzio. He is aware of fatigue and physical decay, of the difference in age and learning between himself and the youth – he imagines a relationship such as that between Socrates and Phaedo for themselves. He cannot settle: the weather does not agree with him, he makes a half-hearted attempt to leave then willingly abandons it. There are hints of sickness in the city: '[Aschenbach] noticed in the first place that though the season was approaching its height, yet the number of guests declined and, in particular, that the German tongue had suffered a rout, being scarcely or never heard in the land' (Mann 1991: 55). The 'rout' of the language which is the foundation of Aschenbach's life is typical of Mann's layered approach. The sense of heat, the crumbling beauty of Venice, the rumours of disease – all combine to provide a sense of foreboding and collapse. Aschenbach seeks to forestall his personal decay cosmetically, and visits the barber:

Aschenbach ... watched [the process] in the mirror and saw his eyebrows grow more even and arching, the eyes gain in size and brilliance, by dint of a little application below the lids. A delicate carmine glowed on his cheeks where the skin had been so brown and leathery ... it was a young man who looked back at him ... the [barber] at last professed himself satisfied ... 'Now the signore can fall in love as soon as he likes.' (Mann 1991: 74)

'The heat', we are told, 'took away [Aschenbach's] appetite and ... he was haunted with the idea that his food was infected'. Then, 'One afternoon he pursued his charmer deep into the stricken city's huddled heart ... He slunk under walls, he lurked behind buildings or people's backs: and the sustained tension of his senses and emotions exhausted him more and more' (Mann 1991: 74–5). Finally Aschenbach is once more on the beach, covertly gazing at the young boy, who is standing in the sea in front of him:

with a sudden recollection, or by an impulse, [Tadzio] turned from the waist up, in an exquisite movement, one hand resting on his hip, and looked over his shoulder at the shore ... It seemed to [Aschenbach] the pale and lovely Summoner out there smiled at him and beckoned; as though with the hand he lifted from his hip he pointed outward as he hovered on before into an immensity of richest expectation.

Some minutes passed before anyone hastened to the aid of the elderly man sitting there collapsed in his chair. They bore him to his room. And before nightfall a shocked and respectful world received the news of his decease.

(Mann 1991: 79)

In a very Thomas Mann touch, there is a camera on a black tripod overlooking the scene, 'apparently abandoned'.

Throughout the novella, Mann has suggested a link between Tadzio and Hermes, the Greek god who travels between this world and the other. Strangely, Lowe-Porter, in the standard English translation, simply omits a sentence at the end of the penultimate paragraph quoted above: 'And as so often, he set out to follow him.' (See Heilbut 1997, whose translation this is, for a brief discussion). Aschenbach's trajectory in *Death in Venice*, in other words, shows him on a journey from the public life of fame and honours he has enjoyed, towards his death.

Aschenbach dies under the spell of an obsession which at once gives him clarity and deludes him. He is bereft of willpower, deluded by love and the presence of cholera. Does he collude in his death? Is he – to pick up another of Kellehear's metaphors – in control of his dying? Mann denies us an easy answer.

Dying as control

In journey narratives, old age represents at best a happy ending. Indeed, there are occasional stories in the press about people separated in childhood and miraculously reunited in old age. This is always told as a happy story, with the fifty years of separation less important than, say, five years together at last. This counts as 'living happily ever after', with the fairytale formula erasing time as it does and allowing us to finish with a tableau rather than the harsh fact of impending demise.

The sentiment is well caught by James Boswell, the great biographer of Dr Johnson. Here he reflects on one Mr Cambridge, who has supplied him with some memories of Johnson:

I gratefully acknowledge this and other communications from Mr. Cambridge, whom, if a beautiful villa on the banks of the Thames, a few miles distant from London, a numerous and excellent library, which he accurately knows and reads, a choice collection of pictures, which he understands and relishes, an easy fortune, an amiable family, an extensive circle of friends and acquaintance, distinguished by rank, fashion and genius, a literary fame, various, elegant and still increasing, colloquial talents rarely to be found, and with all these means of happiness, enjoying, when well advanced in years, health and vigour of body, serenity and animation of mind, do not entitle to be addressed fortunate senex! I know not to whom, in any age, that expression could with propriety have been used. Long may he live to hear and to feel it! (Boswell 2008: 871)

And at the very end of life, in the Western tradition, are texts on the *Ars Moriendi,* the art of dying. Homilies offering advice on how to make a good Christian end begin in the fifteenth century, and continue for generations thereafter (see O'Connor 1942). Sylvia Plath's reference to dying as an 'art', quoted above, carries an ironic echo of this tradition, consciously or not.

The death of Socrates is often taken as the exemplar of the good death – foolishly condemned to death by the state, he died surrounded by his peers, drinking hemlock at a moment of his own choosing and talking philosophy. A death controlled, in other words: indeed, Socrates died only because he chose to accept the death penalty rather than negotiate it into something trivial, as everyone had expected him to do. (Compare Socrates' death with the ambiguous collusion in dying of Mann's Aschenbach, who, it will be recalled, had wished to be like Socrates in other respects.)

The great French essayist Montaigne is one of those who mentions Socrates in this respect. And in fact, as Heitsch (2000) suggests, Montaigne is one of the first to distinguish in detail 'dying' as being something different from death itself (and from living, for that matter). Death is 'the end but not the aim of life' and, 'Among the many duties included under the general and principal head of knowing how to live, is this article of knowing how to die' (Montaigne 1963: 329).

A more modern *Ars Moriendi* is Yeats's graceful tribute – seven short poems, of which I shall give the first – to his friend Mabel Beardsley (sister of Aubrey), who died of cancer in 1916 (Petronius Arbiter was the author of *The Satyricon,* a famously scandalous Roman work).

Upon a Dying Lady
I
Her Courtesy

With the old kindness, the old distinguished grace,
She lies, her lovely piteous head amid dull red hair
Propped upon pillows, rouge on the pallor of her face.
She would not have us sad because she is lying there,
And when she meets our gaze her eyes are laughter-lit,
Her speech a wicked tale that we may vie with her,
Matching our broken-hearted wit against her wit,
Thinking of saints and of Petronius Arbiter.
                                               (Yeats 1994: 132–4)

She made, as the phrase is, a good end. The well-rounded narrative is the last gift we can give ourselves.

Dying is transformation

Kellehear's 'transformation' metaphor is concerned with 'arriv[ing] at another social place where both consciousness and social interaction are altered in substantial ways' (p. 15), and he has specifically in mind near-death experiences and deathbed visions. This is both the hardest concept to pin literature to and the easiest. The fact is that there is hardly a literary text which doesn't deal with transformation of some kind or another, or which doesn't in effect ask, 'what state is real?'. There is a famous Chinese story of an emperor who dreams he is a butterfly and on waking wonders if he is a butterfly dreaming he is an emperor. (The story is mentioned in Li Shang-Yin's exquisite poem 'The Patterned Lute' (1965)).

The classic Western source for narratives of transformation is Ovid's *Metamorphoses* (2004), a series of stories in which people find themselves in altered states (the hunter Actaeon, stumbling on the goddess Diana naked, is turned into a stag and torn to pieces by his hounds – that kind of thing). Behind the urbanity which is Ovid's hallmark is the deeper question, 'what is it to change?'. Through hundreds of writers, most recently Ted Hughes (1997), echoes of these stories, and the idea of literary transformation itself, has come down to us.

Wordsworth provides an example. This is one of the so-called 'Lucy poems', meditations on the death of a real, or more likely imagined, lover:

A slumber did my spirit seal;
I had no human fears:

She seemed a thing that could not feel
The touch of earthly years.

No motion has she now, no force;
She neither hears nor sees;
Rolled round in earth's diurnal course,
With rocks and stones, and trees.
                    (Wordsworth 2000: 218)

The poem seeks – well, how would you describe it? – to merge, to dis-solve, our notions of life, death, memory, sleep, imagination. Behind the conscious simplicity of metre and – with the exception of that 'diur-nal' – vocabulary, the ideas are extraordinarily complex. The first line, for example, can mean no more than 'I was asleep' but allow a more religious meaning to 'spirit', and it can look as if the poet is making some kind of reference to a darker, more disillusioned state of mind. We might if we choose find supporting evidence for this conjecture in the way that Lucy is dehumanized, first into 'a thing' and second the appar-ent equivalent of 'rocks and stones and trees'. But this last line can in turn be taken as a reference either to a kind of animism or, as we might now express it, a sense that we are all of the earth and return to the earth ('dust to dust'), and this in turn we can interpret as being an affir-mation of the Christian message or a rejection of it, perhaps depending on whether we assume that Lucy is impervious to the 'touch of earthly years' because she is with her maker or because she is simply dead.

But then too, after all, the poet doesn't actually say how things are: he only says how they 'seem'. The actual state of things is too confused for us to grasp at anything. Living, dying, dreaming, death: all are aspects of the same thing – or at any rate, we can't tell the difference. The question, 'What is it to die?' in other words invites the question, 'What is it to be alive?'

Of course, faced with the death of a loved one, this kind of ques-tion can seem like a shallow, even a rather cruel, parlour game for the effete. But this is unfair: one of the points of literature is that much of the time it does indeed work through – to quote Wordsworth again, in a well-known phrase whose force is usually not explored – 'emotion recollected in tranquillity'. Because we live with death, bereavement and the knowledge that one day we too will go through the process of dying, we seek to make sense of it, and of the living that precedes it, by reflecting on it at moments of distance.

Tolstoy's brief masterpiece, *The Death of Ivan Ilyich,* takes us through the process of dying in detail and takes us into the heart of a dying man's (ambiguous, as I shall suggest) transformations: from shallow to profound, from a man too attached to the world to one who achieves detachment, and a state where the world as he understood it seems itself transformed, and perhaps – perhaps – transfigured by an awareness of God's presence.

Ivan Ilyich is a judge, but not particularly admirable: unimaginative, driven by small concerns, a man without inner complexity and, therefore, rather like most of us. He learns he is dying, and ultimately we see in him and his suffering a kind of dignity and spiritual depth which perhaps only dying could release in him.

Towards the end, his wife persuades him to take communion:

His wife came in to greet him after communion. She said the usual things, and then added: 'You really do feel better, don't you?'

'Yes,' he said, looking away.

Her clothes, her figure, the look on her face, the sound of her voice – all said the same thing to him: 'This is wrong. Everything you have lived by, and still do, is a lie, a deception that hides life and death away from you'. And the moment this thought occurred to him, his hatred welled up, and along with the hatred came physical suffering and agony, and along with the agony came awareness of the inevitable destruction that was now so close. There was something different about it: a twisting, shooting pain, and constricted breathing.

The look in his face as he said 'Yes' had been dreadful. When he had got the word out, looking straight at her, he wrenched himself over face down remarkably quickly for one so weak, and roared at her: 'Get out! Go away! Leave me alone!' (Tolstoy 2008: 214–15)

After this terrible episode, he begins screaming and continues non-stop for three days. Eventually he becomes aware of his young son standing beside him crying and feels sorry for him, and for his wife. This in turn makes him reflect on his own situation:

'What about death? Where is it?'

He was looking for his earlier, accustomed fear of death, but he couldn't find it. Where was death? What death? There was no fear whatsoever, because there was no death.

Instead of death there was light.

'So that's it!' he said suddenly, out loud. 'Oh, bliss!'

All of this happened to him in a single moment, and the meaning of that moment was not going to change. For those present his agony went on for another two hours. There was a rattling in his chest. His wasted body shook. Then the rattling and the wheezing dwindled away.

'He's gone!' said someone over him.

He caught these words and repeated them in spirit. 'Death has gone,' he told himself.

'It's gone.'

He took in some air, stopped halfway through a deep breath, stretched out, and died. (Tolstoy 2008: 217)

This is one of the great climaxes in Western art, as the transition from living to dying to death itself is made. The reader knows the climax is inevitable, but at the same time it has an extraordinary suddenness, linked to the swiftness of the change from living to dying and the rapid alteration in Ivan's perception of the world.

Tolstoy underwent a conversion to Christianity at around the time he wrote *The Death of Ivan Ilyich,* and the novella is sometimes assumed to be straightforwardly Christian, with Ivan's death full of echoes of Christ's. However, the situation is far more complex.

Consider the phrase rendered here as 'He's gone', from a recent translation (by Briggs et al., Tolstoy 2008). Other translations (e.g. by Duff and Maude, Tolstoy 2003, with the translation itself dating from the 1930s), have gone for the equally possible: 'It is finished!' with an echo of the normal English translation of Christ's words on the cross, rendered in Vulgate Latin as *'consummatum est'*. The English has an ambiguity to it, with 'finished' able to mean either 'completed' or simply 'over' with the possible connotation of disillusion. The Russian translation of St John does not preserve this ambiguity. The word used, *sovershilos'* has the sense of something achieved. But this is not the word Tolstoy uses; rather, he employs the word *koncheno* – hence the alternative, neutral translation. Yet *koncheno* is the word Tolstoy also uses in his strange retelling of the gospel stories, written at around the same time and published a few years earlier in 1883 (Tolstoy 1997). I should stress that I don't read Russian and am reliant on Rice (2003) for this point. Rice concludes, 'Therefore nearly every reader of Tolstoy in the Russian spiritual tradition has been oblivious to the biblical reference ... Tolstoy's translation effectively disembowels the Russian Gospel texts, purposefully robbing them of all rhetorical power and poetry' (Rice 2003: 89).

It's hard to tell, in other words, how much religious consolation there is at the end of the story. This is how literature is, of course: essentially a vessel for presenting life's complexity, and one way in which this complexity is achieved is through the manipulation of the iconography (religious and secular) which surrounds us.

Dying as target metaphor

'Dying' in literature, like any of the great literary themes, exists to serve the purposes of literature. More formally, for our purposes, it often exists as a target metaphor, not a source metaphor.

Ibsen's *Ghosts* (1964) is a good example. The plot revolves around the return of Osvald Alving to his family home. His mother, Mrs Alving, is building an orphanage in memory of her husband, who was much admired in the community for his good works. Mrs Alving knows, however, that her husband was in fact a thoroughly unpleasant man but is not aware that her son has inherited syphilis from his father and that he has no expectation of living much longer. Osvald thus represents a sick society.

The ending of the play is overwhelmingly moving. Osvald tells his mother the truth and talks of his own dread at the 'loathsome' death that awaits him, with the possibility that he will linger, unable to look after himself. He wants an escape from Lawton's 'dirty dying' (2000), in effect, and asks his mother to promise she will help him to die when the time comes. As dawn is on the point of breaking, she at last agrees, but at once pushes things back to the superficial:

MRS. ALVING [*bending over him.*] This was just a terrible delusion of yours, Osvald – only a delusion. All this excitement has been too much for you, but now you shall have a rest – at home with your mother, my dearest boy. You shall have everything you want, the way you did when you were a little boy. There! It's all over now. You see how simple it was – I knew it would be. And look, Osvald, we're going to have a lovely day – bright sunshine. Now you'll really be able to see your home.

[*She goes to the table and puts out the lamp. The sun rises; the glacier and the peaks in the distance glow in the morning light.*]

OSVALD [*sitting in the arm-chair with his back to the view, suddenly speaks without moving*] Mother, give me the sun.

MRS. ALVING [*at the table, looking at him with a start*] What did you say?

OSVALD [*again, dully and without expression*] The sun ... the sun ...

MRS. ALVING [*going to him*] Osvald – what's the matter?

[OSVALD *seems to shrink in the chair; all his muscles go slack, his face is without expression, and his eyes stare vacantly.*]

MRS. ALVING [*shaking with fear*] What is it? [*With a loud scream*] Osvald – what's wrong? [*Falling on her knees beside him and shaking him*] Osvald! Osvald, look at me – don't you know me?

OSVALD [*still tonelessly*] The sun, the sun …

MRS. ALVING [*springing up in despair, grasping her hair in both hands, screams*] I cannot bear it! [*Whispering, as though paralysed*]; I can't bear it … never! [*Suddenly*] Where did he put them? [*Hurriedly feeling in his coat*] Here! [*She shrinks back a few paces and cries*] No no no … Yes! – No no …

   [*She stands a step or two away from him, with her hands twisted in her hair, staring at him in speechless horror.*]

OSVALD [*sitting motionless as before, says.*] The sun … the sun.

(Ibsen 1964: 101–2)

This is at one level a tragedy centred on the dying of one young man, and the power of the play to engage the audience is undeniable. Beyond that, if one wants to look at it this way, *Ghosts* is also a play about the stigma of syphilis (since the AIDS crisis it has become commonplace to remark on its contemporary relevance for just this reason), about assisted suicide, and so on. But to reduce a work of literature to the application of a set of themes generated in other fields is limiting, and rather lazy. Osvald's disease and dying trajectory are a means for Ibsen to remind us all that we have dark places hidden beneath the surface of our lives, and are a way of letting him express his disgust at the hypocrisy and secrecy of society. The difference between Mrs Alving and her son is that Osvald has reached a point of disengagement with life: and, with no further stake in the world, he has no need of illusions. No need, unlike his mother, to hide his dying.

The dying artist and the art of dying

What of the artist's own death? In this concluding section, I look at work written by two great artists when they were themselves dying.

First, Rainer Maria Rilke. The poem below was found after his death from leukaemia as an entry in his notebook, and it is not clear whether he regarded it as complete, or whether it was truly designed to be a public statement. The fact that Rilke's *Elegies* (1989), for example, are well described as a 'collection of fragments' makes this judgement doubly hard (Ryan 1999: 120).

Rilke, it should be said, is extremely resistant to translation. This (my translation) is moderately literal, at the risk of losing a lot of the rhythmic power which is part of Rilke's essence:

> Come you, the last I recognize,
> Pain beyond help inside the web of flesh:
> As once I burned in spirit, see, I burn
> In you: the wood that long rebels against
> The flame you kindle comes of age.
> My earthly mildness in your rage becomes
> A rage from hell, and not from here.
> Quite pure, quite planless, from the future free
> I climb upon the tangled stake of suffering
> So sure of never filling full again
> This heart whose hoard is silent.
> Is that me, past recognition burning?
> I drag no memories along.
> Oh life, life: this being outside.
> And I in flames. No one who knows me ...

The poem is raw, brutal and at the same time, as the work of a mature and brilliant artist, comfortable in his own style, extraordinarily sophisticated. (There is an interesting comparison with his earlier, more formal 'The Poet's Death' (1992), written twenty years previously.) The 'you' here is pain, death and, perhaps more precisely, the Angel of Death, an image Rilke had summoned in other poems (it's probably an Islamic angel in fact, a creature of light with no will of its own). But at this last point of his career, Rilke's words, his images and themes, the way he sets about the task of understanding, are his own. The achievement of the great artist is, in the end, to mean what all his previous work has enabled him to mean.

The extent to which Rilke knew how close to death he was is open to some dispute, though it is particularly interesting (death as control) that he was quoted by a friend as saying 'My dear, please help me to my death, I don't want the death of doctors – I want my freedom' (see Freedman 1996: 618).

For Rilke, then – and for us approaching his work – an understanding even of one's own death is mediated through an art developed over a lifetime.

I want to conclude by looking at John Keats. He, like Rilke, wrote a poem about his own imminent death, at just twenty-five, a sad and beautiful sonnet:

> Bright star, would I were stedfast as thou art –
> Not in lone splendour hung aloft the night
> And watching, with eternal lids apart,
> Like nature's patient, sleepless Eremite,
> The moving waters at their priestlike task
> Of pure ablution round earth's human shores,
> Or gazing on the new soft-fallen mask
> Of snow upon the mountains and the moors –
> No – yet still stedfast, still unchangeable,
> Pillowed upon my fair love's ripening breast,
> To feel for ever its soft fall and swell,
> Awake for ever in a sweet unrest,
> Still, still to hear her tender-taken breath,
> And so live ever – or else swoon in death.
> (Keats 2001: 461)

It is, however, the great Keatsian *Odes* I would like to draw attention to, written just a few months earlier, and on the same theme: steadfastness.

There are five of these *Odes: Ode to Psyche, Ode on a Grecian Urn, Ode on Melancholy, Ode to a Nightingale* and *To Autumn. Psyche* sets the scene. The poet laments the passing of the Classical world and sees his poetical task as bringing it into being again through his imagination – 'I see, and sing, by my own eyes inspired.' So he imagines he sees two lovers:

> They lay calm-breathing on the bedded grass;
> Their arms embraced, and their pinions too;
> Their lips touch'd not, but had not bid adieu ...
> (Keats 2001: 223)

That last line, of the lovers together yet not together, of a transient moment which is yet frozen in time for our contemplation is at the heart of the odes. In *Ode on a Grecian Urn* the urn itself is decorated with pastoral scenes, of lovers, musicians and a priest coming to the sacrifice. They are not subject to life's flow and life's decay. Art captures transience, and makes it permanent.

> Fair youth, beneath the trees, thou canst not leave
> Thy song, nor ever can those trees be bare;
> Bold lover, never, never canst thou kiss,
> Though winning near the goal – yet, do not grieve:
> She cannot fade, though thou hast not thy bliss,
> For ever wilt thou love, and she be fair!
> Ah, happy, happy boughs! that cannot shed
> Your leaves, nor ever bid the Spring adieu ...
> (Keats 2001: 221)

(Compare – another image of kissing which ends with the word 'adieu', you will observe, this from *Ode on Melancholy*: 'And Joy, whose hand is ever at his lips / Bidding adieu'.)

This is an imaginary world, a dream world in which Keats tries to conjure another reality into life. And, in the *Ode to a Nightingale*, there is a wholehearted attempt to bring reality and imagination together as the poet listens to the nightingale's song and seeks an illusion mediated through – a variety of suggestions in the poem – hemlock, opiates or wine. Why?

> That I might drink, and leave the world unseen,
> And with thee fade away into the forest dim –
> Fade far away, dissolve, and quite forget
> What thou among the leaves hast never known,
> The weariness, the fever, and the fret
> Here, where men sit and hear each other groan;
> Where palsy shakes a few, sad, last gray hairs,
> Where youth grows pale, and spectre-thin, and dies ...
> (Keats 2001: 218)

Perhaps, the argument is, we can transcend through the nightingale's song our dissolution and the fear of it. The poem ends with, it appears, the possibility of reality being changed: 'Was it a vision, or a waking dream? / Fled is that music – Do I wake or sleep?'

Keats at this stage was in the latter stages of consumption: it's easy to see him as the 'youth' who 'grows pale and spectre-thin'.

To Autumn deals with the same themes, but this time through a consideration of the changing seasons and life's transience evidenced through the coming of winter and the close of the year. Here too Keats is looking for ways to give life a 'steadfastness' it doesn't have. So he tries to see autumn as something which never ends, which merely produces more and more fruitfulness. It can:

> set budding more,
> And still more, later flowers for the bees,
> Until they think warm days will never cease ...
>   (Keats 2001: 232)

The slightly odd, and not quite ungrammatical, combination of two comparatives ('more' with 'later') tinges with hysteria this indefinitely prolonged piling up of bounty. But in the end, autumn will make way for winter:

> full-grown lambs loud bleat from hilly bourn,
> Hedge-crickets sing, and now with treble soft
> The red-breast whistles from a garden-croft,
> And gathering swallows twitter in the skies.
>   (Keats 2001: 233)

Personal decease as a theme in these poems is subsumed into something very different and much richer, and it can help us to understand our human condition all the better for that.

Conclusion

The study of dying in literature takes us a long way from the study of dying in isolation, and I have dealt at some length with Keats to attempt to illustrate just this point, that writers transmute their themes and give them a novelty which may strike us as novel indeed, or which may even mean that we no longer see the starting point of the artist's journey. Yet, for example, the burgeoning field of medical humanities often provides a reductionist shorthand in the interests of making texts accessible. To return to *Ghosts*, the excellent New York University website lists as its themes:

Dementia, Disease and Health, Euthanasia, Family Relationships, Human Worth, Illness and the Family, Infectious Disease, Mother–Son Relationship, Sexuality, Society, Suicide

Is this helpful? Yes and no.

The complexity of a great piece of literature reaches out into the world, because everything in life reaches out and touches everything else. The shallow sentiments of the greetings card or soap opera tap into this wider universe too and have the power to move for this reason.

Where does this leave the ordinary reader? At its least subtle, literature can provide a way of articulating feelings and ideas which are part of our metaphorical inheritance, sources we can easily tap into and which can therefore help us to make sense of events. At its most subtle, literature can change and deepen that understanding, but only if we know how to read it.

Acknowledgements

Extract from *Ecclesiastical History of the English People* by Bede. 'The History' translated by Leo Sherley-Price and revised by R. E. Latham, translation of the minor works, new Introduction and Notes by D. H. Farmer (Penguin Classics, 1955, Revised edition 1968, 1990). Translation copyright © Leo Sherley-Price, 1955, 1968. Translation of 'Ecclesiastical History of the English People' copyright © Leo Sherley –Price, 1955, 1968. Introduction copyright © D. H. Farmer, 1990. Translation of 'Bede's Letter to Egbert' and 'Cuthbert's Letter on the Illness and Death of the Venerable Bede' copyright © D. H. Farmer, 1990. Reproduced by permission of Penguin Books Ltd.

'Because I could not stop for death' and extract from 'The sun kept setting, setting still' by Emily Dickinson reprinted by permission of the publishers and the Trustees of Amherst College from *The Poems of Emily Dickinson*, Thomas H. Johnson, ed., Cambridge, Mass.: The Belknap Press of Harvard University Press, copyright © 1951, 1955, 1979, 1983 by the President and Fellows of Harvard College.

Extracts from *Death in Venice and Seven Other Stories* by Thomas Mann, translated by H. T. Lowe-Porter. In the UK, published by Secker & Warburg and reprinted by permission of The Random House Group Ltd. In the US, copyright © 1930, 1931, 1936 by Alfred A. Knopf, a division of Random House, Inc. and used by permission of Alfred A. Knopf, a division of Random House, Inc.

Extract from 'Upon a Dying Lady' by W. B. Yeats in *The Collected Poems of W. B. Yeats* (1994) Wordsworth Editions. Reprinted with the permission of A. P. Watt Ltd on behalf of Gráinne Yeats.

Extract from 'The Death of Ivan Ilyich' in *The Death of Ivan Ilyich and Other Stories* by Leo Tolstoy, translated by Ronald Wilks, Anthony Briggs and David McDuff (Penguin Classics, 2008). 'Death of Ivan Ilyich' translation copyright © Anthony Briggs 2006. Reproduced by permission of Penguin Books Ltd.

Extract from 'Ghosts' in *Ghosts and Other Plays* by Henrik Ibsen, translated by Peter Watts (Penguin Classics, 1964). Copyright © Peter Watts, 1964. Reproduced by permission of Penguin Books Ltd.

References

Works of literature referred to in the text

(Note: I have provided details of texts which are easily available rather than necessarily those which are canonical. I have also included dates of first publication, etc.)

Anon. (2003) *Epic of Gilgamesh*, A. George (ed.), Harmondsworth: Penguin.

Bede (1990) *Ecclesiastical History of the English People*, L. Sherley-Price and R.E. Latham (eds.), Harmondsworth: Penguin, Book 2, Chapter 13, pp. 129–30. (Written 731.)

Boswell, J. (2008) *The Life of Samuel Johnson*, D. Womersley (ed.), Harmondsworth: Penguin. (First published 1791.)

Bunyan, J. (1973) *The Pilgrim's Progress*, R. Sharrock (ed.), Harmondsworth: Penguin. (First published 1678.)

Camus, A. (2002) *The Plague*, R. Buss and T. Judt (eds.), Harmondsworth: Penguin. (First published 1947.)

Dickens, C. (2002) *Dombey and Son*, A. Sanders (ed.), Harmondsworth: Penguin. (First published 1846–8.)

 (1997) *Our Mutual Friend*, A. Poole (ed.), Harmondsworth: Penguin. (First published 1864–5.)

Dickinson, E. (1970) *Emily Dickinson: The Complete Poems*, T.H. Johnson (ed.), London: Faber & Faber.

Holland, H.S. (1919) 'King of Terrors', in C. Cheshire (ed.), *Facts of the Faith: Being a Collection of Sermons not hitherto Published in Book Form by Henry Scott Holland*, London: Longmans, Green & Co., pp. 125–34. (First preached 1910.)

Homer (2003) *Odyssey*, ed. and trans. E.V. Rieu, Harmondsworth: Penguin. (Written *c*. eighth century BC)

Hughes, T. (1997) *Tales from Ovid: Twenty-four Passages from the 'Metamorphoses'*, London: Faber & Faber.

Ibsen, H. (1964) 'Ghosts', in P. Watts (ed.), *Ghosts and Other Plays*, Harmondsworth: Penguin. (Written 1881.)

Keats, J. (2001) *The Complete Poems*, P. Wright (ed.), Ware: Wordsworth Editions.

Li Shang-Yin (1965) 'The Patterned Lute', in *Poems of the Late T'ang*, A.C. Graham (ed.), Harmondsworth: Penguin, pp. 141–74. (Written *c.* 850.)

Mann, T. (1969) *The Magic Mountain*, trans. H. Lowe-Porter, Harmondsworth: Penguin. (First published 1924.)

(1991) *Death in Venice*, trans. H. Lowe-Porter, Harmondsworth: Penguin. (First published 1912.)

Montaigne, M. (1963) 'On Physiognomy', in *Essays*, trans. J. Cohen, Harmondsworth: Penguin, pp. 311–42. (First published 1588.)

New York University: Medical Humanities. http://medhum.med.nyu.edu/ (accessed 24 June 2009).

Ovid (2004) *The Metamorphoses*, trans. D. Raeburn, Harmondsworth: Penguin. (Written *c.* 8 AD.)

Plath, S. (1965) 'Lady Lazarus', in *Ariel*, London: Faber & Faber, pp. 16–19.

Rilke, R.M. (1955) 'Komm du …', in *Sämtliche Werke, Rilke Archiv* (*Complete Works, Rilke Archive*), E. Zinn (ed.), Frankfurt: Insel Verlag, Vol. II, p. 511.

(1989) *Duino Elegies*, trans. S. Cohn, Manchester: Carcanet Press.

(1992) 'The Poet's Death', in *Neue Gedichte*, trans. S. Cohn, Manchester: Carcanet Press, p. 47. (First published 1907.)

Tolstoy, L. (1997) *The Gospel in Brief*, F.A. Flowers III (ed.), trans. I. Hapgood, Lincoln, Nebr.: University of Nebraska Press. (First published 1883.)

(2003) 'The Death of Ivan Ilyich', in *The Death of Ivan Ilyich and Other Stories*, trans. J.D. Duff and A. Maude, New York: Signet Classics, pp. 93–152. (First published 1886.)

(2008) 'The Death of Ivan Ilyich', in *The Death of Ivan Ilyich and Other Stories*, trans. A. Briggs, D. McDuff and R. Wilks, Harmondsworth: Penguin, pp. 155–218. (First published 1886.)

Wall, A. (n.d.) 'Don't Give Up', available online at www.familyfriendpoems. com/family/poetry.asp?poem=393 (accessed 25 February 2009).

Wordsworth, W. (2000) *William Wordsworth: The Major Works*, S. Gill (ed.), Oxford: Oxford World's Classics.

Yeats, W.B. (1994) 'Upon a Dying Lady', in *The Collected Poems of W. B. Yeats*, Ware: Wordsworth Editions, pp. 132–4. (First published 1919.)

References

Freedman, R. (1996) *Life of a Poet: Rainer Maria Rilke*, Evanston, Ill.: Northwestern University Press.

Heilbut, A. (1997) *Thomas Mann: Eros and Literature*, London: Macmillan, pp. 258–9.

Heitsch, D.B. (2000) 'Approaching Death by Writing: Montaigne's Essays and the Literature of Consolation', *Literature and Medicine*, **19** (1): 96–106.

Lakoff, G. (1993) 'The Contemporary Theory of Metaphor', in A. Ortony (ed.), *Metaphor and Thought*, Cambridge: Cambridge University Press, pp. 202–51.

Lakoff, G. and Turner, M. (1989) *More than Cool Reason: A Field Guide to Poetic Metaphor*, Chicago, Ill.: Chicago University Press.

Lawton, J. (2000) *The Dying Process: Patient's Experiences of Palliative Care*, London: Routledge.

O'Connor, M.C. (1942) *The Art of Dying Well: The Development of the Ars Moriendi*, New York: Columbia University Press.

Rice, J.L. (2003) 'Comic Devices in "The Death of Ivan Ilyich"', *Slavic and East European Journal*, **47** (1): 77–95.

Ryan, J. (1999) *Rilke, Modernism and the Poetic Tradition*, Cambridge: Cambridge University Press.

Skelton, J.R., Wearn, A.M. and Hobbs, F.D.R. (2002) 'A Concordance-Based Study of Metaphoric Expressions Used by General Practitioners and Patients in Consultation', *Family Practice*, **52** (February): 114–18.

10 | Cinematic visions of dying

FRAN MCINERNEY

The portrayal of dying in popular culture finds multiple outlets in late modernity. Televised news shows dramatic deaths resulting from accident, war and famine, with the press and Internet similarly preoccupied. Images include purported footage of a dying Princess Diana in the back of a Mercedes Benz in Paris and the hanging execution of former Iraqi President Saddam Hussein (Gibson 2007). Indeed, if it bleeds, it leads. hooks (1994: 10) contends that the leitmotif of the media generally and Hollywood in particular is 'the sensational heat of relentless dying ... with no time to mourn'.

Grisly dying also dominates overtly as entertainment; body counts in 'action' movies reflecting their excitement quotient (Gibson 2007). McIlwain (2005: 51) identifies television violence as 'hyperexaggerat[ed] ... representations of death', and 'brackets' such depictions to focus on the 'realistic' content he argues is contained in the television drama *Six Feet Under*. However, McIlwain's suggestion that exaggerated dyings reside at one end of the media spectrum and 'natural' representations the other ignores another dominant form. A significant arm of film in particular presents dying in a romantic light, depicting a soft-focused and wistful dying – a true 'fade to black'.

While violent and romantic portrayals of dying seem to be opposites, they arguably share an underpinning. Rather than an inevitable phenomenon, dying is presented as an extraordinary event in both genres. *Six Feet Under* notwithstanding, 'natural' dying is the exception in media depictions. Neither violent death nor the sentimental departures in what have been described as 'women's movies' or 'weepies' reflect the more 'mundane' dying that most in the developed West ultimately experience; both stereotypes ignore the lengthy periods of disability that typically characterize such dying.

The role of the media as a resource to construct meaning is particularly relevant in the case of social issues 'of which ... [people] ... have little or no personal experience' (Chapman and Lupton 1994: 94).

Durkin (2003: 43) observes that owing to social changes since the Second World War, resulting in a diminution in first-hand exposure, 'the mass media have become a primary source of information about death and dying'. Consideration of such media, which both reflects and shapes social understandings, can offer insights into dominant constructions of dying in the English-speaking world. As Ariès (1981: 389) writes, 'just as one can best measure the influence of psycho-analysis on the culture by studying women's magazines, similarly it is preferable ... to study the phenomenon of death in the bastard forms of vulgarization.'

Mahon (2000: 467) contends that popular media function as 'arenas in which social actors struggle over social meanings and as visible evidence of social processes and social relations'. Acknowledging cinema as a powerful medium for representations of dying, Knox (2006: 234) observes, 'Filmic duration incarnates simultaneously the concept of time, and of finitude ... [while its] ... mimetic capabilities ... make it a poignant medium for representing both the death of the individual subject and the technical/metaphysical problem of death.'

The media is fascinated with novel forms of dying and death (Pickering et al. 1997); 'conventional' dying in contrast makes poor copy. Violent, agonal moments occupy what might be called the 'harder', more masculine end of this spectrum, with 'softer' dying inhabiting the more 'feminized' end. Moreover, the highlighting of violence reflects a fascination with the moment of *death* itself, while the more muted emphasis allows exploration of the life of the characters prior to their death; ostensibly at least, their *dying* is the focus.

In this chapter I examine depictions of dying that look beyond the 'terminal moments' of a person and subsequent images of the corpse (Foltyn 2008) that dominate news broadcasts, action films and television series. Focusing on the 'softer' end of cinema, one of the most accessible and pervasive disseminators of cultural images in the English-speaking world (Mahon 2000), I explore dominant constructions around dying via a consideration of some thirty movies of this genre made over the past seventy years. I make no claim that these are the only films available or representations to be found but that they are a significant selection. My aim is not to assert any fundamental 'truth' but to explore the prominence of certain framings around dying within the ubiquitous medium of US film. Within the overarching romance genre of 'women's films/weepies', I identify six sub-genres, these addressing the dyings of young women, mothers, gay men, old people, death-row prisoners and celebrities.

Situating the representations of dying found in these sub-genres within Kellehear's social/behavioural research themes identified in the introductory chapter aids in foreshadowing some of their characteristics, to be explored below. In part owing to a surfeit of female characters, the dying are passive players; their agency is of the sacrificial endurance kind and the narrative focus is principally on survivors. The dying journeys depicted are largely linear; traversing a 'diagnosis-to-death' trajectory in a 100-minute span leaves little time for oscillation. The predominance of young, socially linked protagonists sees disengagement rarely acknowledged. Ceding to cinematic aesthetic requirements, overt bodily disintegration is seldom depicted; protagonists generally maintain their physical appeal throughout. Similarly, disenfranchised groups are avoided, and sanitized when they do appear. Transcendence is a dominant theme – not manifesting extra-corporeally but in finding meaning beyond existence (Williams 2006) – and often linked to sacrifice. Cinematic dying, enacting the narrative imperative for a 'happily ever after', promulgates passivity, linearity, beauty, resolution and salvation in the face of mortality.

Romantic dying

Death and the Maiden ...

The romance of the 'women's film' genre is an amalgamation of drama, fantasy and love story and often includes the dying of one or more characters. While women have been observed to dominate as receivers of violent death in film (Schultz and Huet 2000–1), a gender imbalance also applies in this genre; for a romantic portrayal of dying, nothing beats a woman. Preserving the visual appeal of these bright, young 'stars', their dying rarely manifests in outward physical signs, and, to add to the aesthetic fancy, their terminal course is painless and swift. There are a number of sub-genres within the 'weepie', with the first being the tragic love story.

Dark Victory (dir. Edmund Goulding, 1939) captures quintessential elements of this sub-genre. Feisty young heiress Judith Traherne's smoking, drinking and risk-taking challenges social boundaries. Experiencing headaches and double vision, she is diagnosed with a brain tumour, removed by the surgeon who falls in love with her, as romance holds sway. The surgery is not curative however; Judith will soon die, the only forewarning being a brief period of blindness. After a short interval of anger and denial, she finds her destiny as devoted wife (chiefly manifested in feeding her husband while he seeks the cure for cancer). However unlikely the medical scenario (clinical accuracy is rarely encountered in this genre; see Baxendale 2003; Wijdicks and Wijdicks 2006; Segers 2007), it eventuates precisely as foretold. Brave Judith hides her blindness, waving her husband off to a medical conference. In a famous final scene, she stoically ascends to her bedroom to die. Literally, the film, Judith's vision and her life fade to black.

Doomed heroine Jenny in *Love Story* (dir. Arthur Hiller, 1970) is another lively young woman, here a poor but talented music student. Jenny calls her father by his first name, profanes, is disparaging of American sports and is an atheist; she is a 'liberated' woman of the 1960s. However, in two important respects she is indistinguishable from her sister of 1939. Marrying Oliver and abandoning her own ambitions, she teaches music to support his studying law, finding joy in bringing him sustenance as he sits engrossed in legal tomes. More importantly, she contracts a fatal illness. Her journey from diagnosis to death involves the last ten minutes of the drama, as a glowing Jenny, following a last loving embrace, obligingly dies off stage. As hooks (1994: 10) observes in relation to this sub-genre, 'everyone knows that tears are in order, that the crying time will not last long'.

Shadowlands (dir. Richard Attenborough, 1993) depicts the relationship between the writers C. S. Lewis and Joy Greshem. Spirited, unconventional Greshem is diagnosed with bone cancer, marrying Lewis from her hospital bed. Radiotherapy provides a brief remission, during which their love blossoms, Lewis nurtured in intimacy by his loving bride. Their idyll is short-lived, however, as her cancer returns, and she dies the night she is discharged from hospital. While her dying is relatively realistically portrayed, with her joys and pains acknowledged, she is still depicted in soft focus, her death occurring swiftly and off-camera. Such 'prompt' deaths provide a conclusion to the narrative, maintain dramatic tension and allow the audience emotional release minus the discomforts potentially engendered by a more protracted dying.

Once a mother, always a mother

Unlike the dyads above, dying mothers inhabit another sub-genre. While childless women's dying serves as a point of 'romantic' tension and tragedy, here dying is the catalyst for dramatic tensions and interactions within families. This focus emerges from the ideology that a woman's identity is inextricable from her family; her death too has meaning principally in relationship to this unit as opposed to her existential journey or experience of community more broadly. *Terms of Endearment* (dir. James L. Brooks, 1983) recounts the tempestuous relationship between single mother Aurora and her daughter Emma. Emma's terminal-cancer diagnosis serves as a dramatic catalyst for the movie. Her connection with her older son, and, crucially, her and Aurora's embracing of their love, dominate.

Beaches (dir. Garry Marshall, 1988) tells of single mother Hillary, whose illness prompts a life review. The latter half of the narrative concerns Hillary's struggle with her premature dying and ensuring her child's care. While there are glimpses of anger, social withdrawal and physical collapse in this narrative, it is transcendence (here being enshrined in her daughter's memory through her friend CC's interventions) that predominate. Family issues resolved, Hillary fades into the sunset, dying reclined on a couch overlooking the ocean. *Fried Green Tomatoes* (dir. Jon Avnet, 1991) depicts an almost identical scenario, with single mother Ruth dying of cancer and her best friend Idgie assuming her son's care. Their lesbian relationship, overt in the book (Flagg 1987) on which the film is based, is obliterated here, reinforcing the ideologies of heterosexual romance and family that dominate such portrayals.

Stepmom (dir. Chris Columbus, 1998) concerns another dying mother's struggle to 'bequeath' her family, here to her ex-husband's young fiancée. Initially concealing her cancer, Jackie overcomes anger and denial and finally accepts her terminal diagnosis. In a cascade of events traversing the Kübler-Ross taxonomy ('You know how a caterpillar becomes something else?' Jackie poignantly asks her son), the final scene depicts a photo of the 'blended' family as all conflicts are resolved (with the presumably dead Jackie still in frame as testament to continuing bonds; see Klass et al. 1996). In *Steel Magnolias* (dir. Herbert Ross, 1989), young Shelby is heroically prepared to sacrifice her life for motherhood. Her unstable diabetes a known risk, she continues a pregnancy that destroys her health and leads to her death.

Her mother and friends continuing her 'legacy' with her child is a prominent feature of the narrative.

One True Thing (dir. Carl Franklin, 1998) sees forty-eight-year-old Kate suffering terminal cancer. Her daughter Ellen reluctantly returns home to nurse her, in the process resolving her relationship with her parents, as again the dying mother catalyses the subsequent action. Kate passionately declares, 'I'm still a mother! I'm still the mother here!', encapsulating the overpowering motherhood ethic in these films. The movie depicts her episodes of severe pain, exacerbated by her physician's failure to prescribe morphine until late in her illness. Despite being immobile, she ingests a fatal overdose; inexplicably autopsied, this is detected. Dying itself not being sufficient, no opportunity for dramatic effect is unturned as the writers search for the requisite 'adrenaline moments and conflict' (hooks 2001: 40) to sustain audience interest. Having not written a suicide note and thereby rendering her family suspects, reflecting dominant constructions around induced death (McInerney 2006), her actions are still depicted as heroic; her husband declares 'who else would've had the strength?' as he and Ellen plant symbolic spring bulbs on her grave. Such melodrama effectively deflects attention from her grieving loved ones; all must be resolved by the final frame.

Two Weeks (dir. Steve Stockman, 2006) presents a more realistic dying (at least in terms of Western demographic trends), focusing on a woman in her sixties. Dying mother Anita sits at the centre of a dysfunctional family, but greater attention is paid to her experiences than the melodramas of her offspring, as she grieves the ending of her life. Dying is still portrayed as involving the terminal phase – 'Two Weeks' referring to the span of the narrative – and the film realistically illustrates some of the physical manifestations of ovarian cancer, crediting the assistance of 'Alive Hospice' and the 'Kübler-Ross Foundation'. Nonetheless, the notion of contemporary hospice sits oddly with Anita receiving intravenous nutrition and her nurse's comment on the day she dies that her 'heart rate, pulse and breathing are steady and stable'; such activities ceding to the imperative to medicalize dying. However, in contrast to the genre, Anita's pain and more 'messy' symptoms – 'she's puking up shit' – are realistically portrayed until, in a scenario that would appal any hospice, her children are forced into a vigil involving administering her analgesia every ten minutes – a bizarre routine that results in another flirtation with euthanasia, seemingly for a dramatic 'twist' to the tale. In the more retrograde example *Evening* (dir. Lajos Koltai, 2007), elderly dying mother Ann undertakes a life review focused on a troubled romance. For much of the film her early dramas (played by a young and beautiful actress) dominate as she relives ancient romantic tangles, fantasy overriding more immediate considerations. Adhering to the tried and true romance formula, the film is concerned with a greater box office than reflective accounts of dying and loss might achieve.

Token fathers?

Two particular exceptions to the predominance of young dying mothers are found in *My Life* (dir. Bruce Joel Rubin, 1993) and *Life as a House* (dir. Irwin Winkler, 2001), where fathers drive the narrative. They are 'active' players, with George undertaking the symbolic task of house construction in the 2001 film and Bob making a video for his unborn child in *My Life*. In contrast to their more 'ladylike' counterparts, they both overtly express anger; however, there are other strong links to the dominant portrayals above. Both films focus on parents recently diagnosed with a terminal illness and their attempts to connect with their family. Both are typified by their protagonists' youth; like most of their female counterparts they continue in outwardly robust health for virtually the duration of the film. 'Family values' also prevail here; both see loose ends tied away as their families, having resolved their issues, achieve 'closure' and 'move on' in the best traditions of popular psychology.

The 'dying mother/father' plotline is a melodramatic frame for the ubiquitous contemporary notions of both 'family' and 'closure'. Redemption and renewal are the dominant outcomes of the central character's dying. Resolution of relationships is inevitably achieved, with dying principally serving as an impetus for this activity. The obligation to provide a 'happily ever after' via the message that 'life will go on', is central. How accurate a portrayal this is of family dynamics in the face of such loss is another question and one with which these films do not concern themselves (Meyer 2005).

'Wit': an honourable mention?

Wit (dir. Mike Nichols, 2001), a made-for-TV movie, is an exception here for its addressing difficult and painful issues and avoiding resolution. While forty-eight-year-old Vivian Bearing's death does mark the film's end, and she is a white, middle-class, articulate woman, there is none of the sense of 'completion' that preoccupies the above two sub-genres. Vivian is single, unattached and childless, already a radical departure from the norm. She reflects on her life prior to her diagnosis but not remotely in the neatly sanitized way that dominates elsewhere.

Raw and unresolved issues dominate here. Vivian is preoccupied with control, which she loses as her disease and the medical system overpower her. Her journey of disintegration contrasts painfully with the rigid restraint she has exercised throughout her life. The theme of disengagement is powerful, born not so much of her terminal illness but consistent with the life she has led. Vivian has few social connections and experiences her dying alone also; remarkably, no directorial attempt is made to 'redeem' her. The chaos of her dying and loneliness of her death, at odds with dominant Western discourse (Seale 2004), are simultaneously painful and a relief; the latter owing to this film's challenging the saccharine, contrived and fantastical within the 'weepie' genre.

Dying young men: the gay plague

An exception to the cinematic dominance of young dying women is found in the case of AIDS, where young homosexual men are prominent. This sub-genre appeared with the emergence of the AIDS pandemic in the West in the 1980s. While their gender enables them to exist outside of a couple or family relationship, and films in this category have been referred to as 'tragic and/or realistic melodrama' in an attempt to elevate them from the ranks of their cinematic sisters (Van Fuqua 1996: 31), in many respects their plotlines and characterizations fulfil many of the imperatives of the 'weepie'.

In the made-for-TV *An Early Frost* (dir. John Erman, 1985) Michael, a promising young lawyer recently promoted to partner, experiences various symptoms which he dismisses as 'just a bug'. 'There are a lot of bugs out there', his physician intones, and, indeed, Michael is hospitalized with *pneumocystis carinii pneumonia* (PCP) and diagnosed with AIDS. His life quickly unravels; he 'comes out' to his family as both deviant and dying, his lover confesses his infidelity, and his father and sister reject him. In hospital he meets other young men in varying stages of AIDS, with Kaposi's sarcoma (KS) lesions, wasting and debility prominent. His mother, who in true Hollywood tradition has been lovingly supportive throughout, encourages his former lover to visit, and they reconcile. Following a friend's death, Michael attempts suicide; his father intervenes, realizing his love for his son and urging him to 'fight' the disease. In an abrupt ending, Michael returns to the city but again conforming to the cinematic imperative for resolution, not before a last-minute, farewell embrace with his now pregnant sister.

Longtime Companion (dir. Norman René, 1990) focuses on the 'gay community', following nine friends who almost all succumb to AIDS over a nine-year period. The first of these is the beautiful John, who deteriorates rapidly; ostracized from his friends, disfigured by KS lesions, he dies frightened and alone on a ventilator (his alertness here another instance of 'therapeutic artistic licence'). The friends witness each others' illnesses and deaths; we witness their fear, self-surveillance, phobia, stigma and prejudice but also their mutual support, affection, humour and growing political activism. Shaun, soap-opera writer partner of wealthy David, experiences AIDS-related dementia. In a graphic depiction of his terminal phase, his partner changes his incontinence pad, loosening the shackles which his mental state obliges him to wear. 'Let's go', Shaun repeatedly utters during this scene. David responds 'You can go ... it's all right ... let go of everything. Don't hold on. That's OK.' The next scene shows Shaun dead in his bed, the inference being that having been given permission he 'chooses' to expire forthwith, in homage to the mythology that death can be summoned by will alone. David's own funeral is depicted in the following scene; the ultimate survivors from this group being a monogamous couple who witness the devastating litany.

In some respects *Philadelphia* (dir. Jonathan Demme, 1993) begins where *An Early Frost* ended. Young lawyer Andrew has been promoted to senior associate in his firm. Unlike his cinematic predecessor, Andrew's family is loving and supportive; however, he is not 'out' to his colleagues. The onset of symptoms, in particular stigmatic KS lesions, sees him discharged from his job. He struggles to find legal counsel to represent him in an unfair dismissal suit; Joe, an injury-claims lawyer and unrepentant homophobe, agrees. The movie depicts Andrew's decline; within seven months he is grey-haired and drawn. His facial lesions having resolved (a happy aesthetic coincidence), a key court scene involves him removing his shirt to expose his torso tumours, both demonstrating their vivid nature and allowing witnesses to look away in pity and horror. Michael experiences blindness

and collapses in court but lives to hear he has received a record compensation payout. Now actively dying, attached to medical apparatus, he bids farewell to his family and lawyer. Joe's fears resolve
as he tenderly readjusts Michael's oxygen mask in farewell. Michael
asserts 'I'm ready', and, in keeping with timely and oblique cinematic
demise and autonomy in death imperatives, Joe receives notification
of Michael's demise.

Dying in old age: beyond their use-by date

The average age of death for men and women in the developed world
approximates eighty years, with chronic disease contributing to lengthy
dying trajectories. However, the dying of older people is uncommon
in celluloid. Young individuals are the dominantly depicted dying
characters, their tragic situation compounded by the loss of romantic relationships and young families. Where older dying people are
involved in lead roles, they are frequently portrayed in terms of either
flashback or via the dramas of their children, thus maintaining the
dominance of youth.

In the unsubtle *The Bucket List* (dir. Rob Reiner, 2007), we are
aware that both ageing protagonists, billionaire Edward and erudite
mechanic Carter have less than twelve months to live. We witness
Edward's brain surgery (a dramatic, unlikely response to his haem-
optysis), and both men endure chemotherapy. Edward exploits comic
opportunities to enthusiastically vomit over the toilet bowl and rush
to this receptacle as diarrhoea threatens. There is a 'frat house' flavour
here that trivializes these events, and the film shortly degenerates into
travelogue, as the buddies (Edward's hair miraculously restored) ener-
getically traverse the globe on an ostensibly transcendent journey (the
'bucket list' of things to do before death). Carter returns to his loving
family, collapsing that night and dying during his own neurosurgery,
while Edward off-camera achieves miraculous remission and lives into
very old age, as this superficial tale comes to a merciful end.

There are notably fewer roles for older actors (Kessler et al. 2004), a
particular reality for older women (Bazzini et al. 1997). However, one
area of opportunity for this group is the portrayal of women dying
of dementia, a new sub-genre. Here, ageing is not portrayed as syn-
onymous with cognitive decline or something to be ridiculed (Combe
and Schmader 1999) but as subject to more considered dramatic

attention. In recognition of dominant cinematic values, Segers (2007: 55) observes that dementia is rarely focused on in film, 'probably because it affects mainly elderly people'. Further, Segers found two-thirds of demented characters depicted were women, another significant cinematic overrepresentation (Andersen et al. 1999).

Iris (dir. Richard Eyre, 2001) and *The Notebook* (dir. Nick Cassavetes, 2004) both use flashback or life review, which allows for lengthy periods of distraction from the older female leads. *Iris* tells of Iris Murdoch, the Anglo-Irish novelist. The film is taken up with her relationship with her partner John, in both their youth and later during her descent into dementia. Much of the focus is on John's struggles in caring for Iris, reflecting the carer-burden emphasis in much work around dementia (Gaugler et al. 2004). However, the profound loss and grief experienced by both John and Iris are convincingly represented. The lightweight *The Notebook* also focuses on a husband (Noah) and wife (Allie) relationship and on Noah's struggles to maintain their relationship via her journal, which he reads to her daily in the nursing home. This device allows the film to focus on the couple's early years, played by two young and beautiful actors. Like *Evening*, this narrative concerns the couple's early romantic dramas, with the life of the dying protagonist, however sympathetically portrayed, mere backdrop. Consistent with the film's romantic preoccupations, the conclusion is sheer fantasy; Noah enters her locked ward to spend the night, she miraculously regains lucidity, and they are found dead together in the morning.

Away From Her (dir. Sarah Polley, 2006) tells another older woman's journey with dementia. Fiona is an intelligent, educated woman, committed to her partner of fifty years, Grant. To spare him the burden of her care, she embarks on a particularly autonomous journey, admitting herself into a nursing home. The story depicts her disengagement from Grant (initiated by a 'rule' separating them for a month – another melodramatic plot device) as she simultaneously engages intimately with another resident and retreats further into her illness. While this couple's relationship is a point of tension in the film, as is Grant's subsequent affair, these are not romantic distractions but rather manifestations of loss and a search for meaning as the protagonists' worlds progressively fracture. This is a rare addition to filmic portrayals of dying, a gentle depiction all the more powerful for its understatement.

Another more thoughtful offering is *On Golden Pond* (dir. Mark Rydell, 1981), recounting a month in the lives of retired professor Norman and his wife Ethel. Norman at eighty shows unmistakable signs of dementia. Unlike media preoccupation with the latter and more fearful stages of the disease (Clarke 2006), Norman is in the early to moderate stage. He struggles with memory loss, disorientation and fear as he experiences cognitive decline and loss of self. Norman and Ethel are devoted to one another, and this film is as much their love story as a reflection on dying. While many films in this genre use a love or family relationship to deflect from the more unsettling implications of mortality, here the love between the leads and their family tensions serve as both a celebration of life and a reminder of the losses they face. The portrayal of a frail man is a refreshing addition here, albeit that the sufferer is highly educated, thereby conforming to another popular stereotype. Segers (2007: 58) suggests this is a dramatic device: 'just like it's probably worse for a piano player to loose [sic] his hand than to miss a leg'. The majority of individuals dying of whatever cause are portrayed as, if not educated, at least highly articulate, a product perhaps of a medium reliant on dialogue and an audience impatient of realism in their entertainment.

Dying on death row: God's waiting room

This sub-genre depicts unequivocal social outcasts in the persons of inmates on death row. They have the status (or lack thereof) of the disenfranchised dying; outcasts from the dominant culture, their dying goes largely unseen and unmourned. The protagonists are aware they are dying, their deaths having been predetermined by the State. Here more than elsewhere in the romantic dying genre, the characters represent lower socio-economic groups and are likely to be men. Hollywood has been fascinated with such characters and is preoccupied with their transcendence.

In *Angels with Dirty Faces* (dir. Michael Curtiz, 1938), gangster Rocky Sullivan finds himself lionized by a young street gang, and ultimately on death row. Awaiting execution, his former schoolmate, now Catholic priest Fr Connelly, urges him to feign cowardice so as not to die a hero to the impressionable youth. At first loathe to lose his tough-guy image, in a sentimental about-face Rocky complies, finding heroism in his last moments as his charade turns the boys from a life of crime. *The Postman Always Rings Twice* (dir. Tay Garnett, 1946) sees Frank the drifter sentenced to death for the murder of his lover Cora. Innocent of this crime, he and Cora had earlier escaped punishment for the killing of her husband Nick. Frank is tormented that Cora might think he intended her death and seeks solace from the attendant priest. In the face of new evidence that would now convict him of Nick's murder, Frank becomes reconciled to his dying for Nick's death and not Cora's. He now joyously accepts his fate, claiming 'Father, you were right, it all works out. I guess God knows more about these things than we do.'

I Want to Live! (dir. Robert Wise, 1958) tells the story of petty criminal and executed murderer Barbara Graham. Barbara, a young, attractive mother, is treated sympathetically in this film, which is a statement against capital punishment. Her torment while awaiting the gas chamber, her distress at saying farewell to her young son, the agonies of her various stays and delays of execution – 'Why do they torture me?' – all illustrate the cruelty of her dying process. Her refusal to plea for clemency, 'Don't beg for my life!', is consistent with her autonomy and dignity. The requisite visit from a priest sees Barbara assert her innocence and lack of fear. Considerable realist detail is devoted to the mechanics of the gas chamber, which is also captured in the depiction of her execution.

Dead Man Walking (dir. Tim Robbins, 1995) is based on Sr Helen Prejean's 1994 autobiography and recounts her relationship with Matthew, a convicted rapist and murderer. With a week until his execution, volunteer Helen becomes his 'spiritual advisor' – 'rid[ing] on into the sunset with me' Matthew quips. The prison chaplain declares Matthew 'in dire need of redemption', achievable by 'his receiving the sacraments'. Helen sees Matthew's redemption lying more in taking responsibility for his actions, but he resists, finally confessing his guilt when death is imminent. Helen rejoices, 'You have dignity now', to which he replies, 'It figures I'd have to die to find love.' In keeping with its anti-capital-punishment stance, the death scene is graphic. Matthew dies by lethal injection, the barbarity of his dying closely juxtaposed with that of his victims. His sudden intake of breath, eyes flying open and pinpoint pupils as the cardiac monitor signals asystole owe more to drama than accuracy; however, his journey to salvation in the face of state killing is powerfully portrayed.

The Green Mile (dir. Frank Darabont, 1999) is based on a novel by fantasy-horror author Stephen King (1996), depicting male inmates and wardens on death row. The electrocutions are portrayed horrifically; through the workings of malice and error we see smoke and flames, agonal paroxysms, screams and a witness stampede as violent death is showcased. The plight of John Coffey, a 'giant' African American with mystical powers wrongly convicted of murder, allows for a more considered approach to the dying experience, albeit one mired in fantasy and a confused salvation narrative. John's powers enable him to heal multiple ills (bizarrely transforming pain/evil into grey particles which he dramatically expectorates). It is his failed attempt to 'heal' two murdered children that sees him sentenced to die. He cures the Prison Governor's dying wife (and a mouse!) but remains doomed. Weary of the world's pain, he embraces his death, his executioners struggling with their grief but performing their task efficiently as their farewell gift to the 'gentle giant'.

Celebrity dyings: 'true to life'

Fowler (1991: 91) observes that individuals likely to achieve media prominence belong either to elites to whom anything happens or 'ordinary people to whom something unusual happens', an observation that holds true for dying in film. Film-makers have focused on dying via the 'biopic' sub-genre, with unusual celebrity dyings accentuating the dramatic tension. We have seen C. S. Lewis's wife Joy Greshem's dying portrayed in *Shadowlands*, along with the dementia journey of Iris Murdoch in *Iris*. *One True Thing* is based on the autobiography of the daughter depicted in the film (Quindlen 1994). *I Want to Live!* recounts the execution of convicted murderer Barbara Graham, while *Dead Man Walking* reflects Helen Prejean's experiences with death-row inmates. Celebrities are a point of identification in popular culture (Gibson 2007), and 'true' stories carry added potential impact as representative of contemporary dying, an instance of 'how it could be or once was for [the reader]' (Ellis 2005: 711).

Pride of the Yankees (dir. Sam Wood, 1942) tells of Lou Gehrig, famous for both his baseball career and contracting the fatal *amyotrophic lateral sclerosis* (ALS), which colloquially carries his name. The movie commences with a tribute to Gehrig: 'this is the story of a hero of the peaceful paths of everyday life.' That the Captain and games record-holder of the premier New York baseball team can be

equated with 'everyday life' is moot; however, the story depicts a simple, modest man. We see his humble immigrant beginnings, happy
marriage to Eleanor and rise to fame in an 'all-American dream' narrative frame. In the final third of the film, his insidious muscle weakness,
form slump and ultimate withdrawal from his sport ratchet up the
melodrama to be followed by confirmation of terminal ALS: 'It's three
strikes.' He conceals his fate from Eleanor: 'Doc, I don't want Mrs
Gehrig to know, ever', who has divined the dire situation: 'I'll never
let him know I know.' They 'bravely' engage in Glaser and Strauss's
(2005: 65) 'ritual drama of mutual pretense'; tragically echoing each
other's assertions of having 'all the time in the world'. Gehrig publicly
farewells the League, declaring himself 'the luckiest man on the face
of the earth', and symbolically exiting through the players' tunnel, as
the referee calls 'play ball' and life goes on. That he lived another two
years, seeking various experimental treatments and working as a parole
commissioner before his death at age thirty-seven (Lerner 2006) are
omitted here; in this genre, 'the end' means precisely that, and dying is
not about life but death, at which point the narrative concludes.

In like vein, the made-for-TV *Brian's Song* (dir. Buzz Kulik, 1971)
tells of the real-life relationship between US National Football League
(NFL) players Brian Piccolo and Gale Sayers. The film depicts the
friendly rivalry of the men, the first interracial NFL roommates
(Sayers is African American). We hear at the start of the movie that
someone will die; we await the doomed player's identity. As in *Pride
of the Yankees*, we witness training and action, high jinx in the locker
rooms, losses and victories, as the film pays homage to American
sports, athletic young men and the triumph of love and friendship.
The film embraces the romance of the buddy film and the sports film; a
'man's movie', it shares many components of the sentimental 'weepie'.

Piccolo develops weight loss, breathlessness, a cough and form slump
and is shortly after diagnosed with terminal lung cancer. We hear 'he
might never play football again ... or for a long time', but worse follows. After a partial pneumonectomy, we find our brave patient laugh-
ing, eating pizza and drinking beer, a hint of gauze under his pyjama
top the only indicator of major surgery. He declares 'it's just a detour ...
I'm not gonna let it stop me, I'm just not', and, indeed, like most dying
stars, he appears remarkably well. However, the tumour soon recurs,
and more radical surgery is scheduled. We next see Piccolo dying,
breathless and sweaty in his hospital bed (still handsome and with lux-
urious curly hair), receiving a blood transfusion (no oxygen however,

allowing for optimal close-ups), and experiencing a painful spasm. He farewells his friend, embraces his wife and dies off-screen. The film concludes with the sentimental declaration: 'It's not how he died that they remembered, but how he lived; how he *did* live.' Given that Piccolo's death was from disseminated cancer that included his lungs, breast, ribs, pericardium, mouth and jaw (Lerner 2006), certainly this film's audience will not accurately remember how he died, but nonetheless it is his early demise that assures him cinematic immortality.

Tuesdays with Morrie (dir. Mick Jackson, 1999), a made-for-TV movie by Oprah Winfrey's production arm from the book of the same name (Albom 1997), recounts the real-life relationship of seventy-seven-year-old sociology professor Morrie Schwartz and his former student, Mitch Albom. Morrie is dying of ALS, and Mitch reconnects with him after sixteen years. They meet each Tuesday, where Morrie imparts many life lessons, describing himself as 'a human textbook' on life's 'last great journey'. He regrets instances of pride, vanity and hardness of heart and advocates unconditional love. We see Morrie's courage in the face of his deteriorating health and his capacity to continue to embrace love, food, music and conversation. He does not deny his struggles, acknowledging sorrow, anger and bitterness at his lot, declaring 'I cry and rage and mourn and then ... I detach.' The film is replete with Morrie's prosaic aphorisms, which Mitch dutifully tape records, overcoming his own struggles with intimacy in the process. Morrie dies 'peacefully and simply with family around him' on a Saturday morning (and thus out of shot). Morrie wryly observes, 'now that I'm dying people are taking more of an interest in me', and certainly the book, movie and stage play of his dying story reflect his posthumous celebrity.

Morrie's 'successor' might well be Randy Pausch, a forty-seven-year-old computer-science professor achieving international fame after his diagnosis with terminal pancreatic cancer and delivery of a 'Last Lecture', where he shared homespun reflections on living life to the full. Pausch's story crossed the media genres of newspaper, radio, television, Internet and print – indeed, only film and stage have failed to present his story, an oversight it would be naive to believe will endure. His Internet homepage and 'update page' (Pausch 2008) ran from October 2006 until his death in July 2008. A book of his lecture was published (Pausch 2008); at the time of writing it is Number 1 on the *New York Times* list of 'advice books' (2008), Number 2 on Amazon (2008), and his lecture video has been viewed over 6 million times on YouTube (2008). Google's home page (2008) posted an *In Memoriam* link at his death, as testament to his widespread appeal.

Successful, handsome, articulate, father of three young children and with a rare fatal illness, Pausch embodied many of the dominant traits of the romance genre (indeed, his story closely parallels *My Life*). Without denigrating his experience, public interest in his plight is inevitably influenced by elements that fulfil our romantic notions about dying – the uncommon demises of attractive people more readily engaged with than the 'everyday' deaths of the old, the ugly, the poor, the outcast or the infirm. In the tradition of the lucrative *Tuesdays with Morrie* franchise – I suspect Pausch's story is even more attractive – a movie deal cannot be far away, in a circular case of life imitating art imitating life.

Dying projections

So, what cultural scripts (Seale 1998) dominate these cinematic depictions of dying? As earlier noted in relation to Kellehear's identified themes that open this volume, passive acceptance, linearity, resolution, aesthetics and salvation are the pre-eminent values portrayed. While dying children are off limits, protagonists are rarely out of their thirties. Dying overwhelmingly happens to white, middle-class, educated people, frequently in the prime of life. Women predominate, with mothers particularly evident. Terminal illness is almost always the proximate cause, most commonly cancer. Diagnosis occurs early in the melodrama, and the dying trajectory is very brief. Despite this, physical symptoms are rarely encountered, 'sufferers' sustaining physical vitality until their last moments. Such symptoms as are displayed are paradoxically overblown and generally linked to poor or late medical management. Similarly, the medical interventions that are depicted are dramatic and unlikely given the clinical scenarios. In contrast to contemporary realities in the West (Grunier et al. 2007; McNamara and Rosenwax 2007), death predominantly occurs at home (consistent with cinematic women's virtual incarceration there and associated demands for 'family' drama). Dying itself is almost never witnessed; with the exception of the 'death row' sub-genre, the camera coyly retreats to a discreet distance at the ultimate moment. It is rare for death not to eventuate, inevitably occurring in the final or second-last scene as the dramatic conclusion to the narrative.

The 'weepie' genre has been critiqued for sustaining the patriarchal image of women's social passivity; 'women initially strong and independent ... [are] ... reduced to different versions of the modality "sacrifice"' (Coliazzi 2004: 368). Certainly, the dying women portrayed across the opening two sub-genres fit this paradigm, conforming to what Waites (2006: 482) describes as the cinematic imperative: 'to cloak her and the disease in feminine claptrap that reduces her to a servant of masculinist ideology ... [which highlights] ... the collusion of popular culture in circumscribing women and negating their authentic identity'.

Their social role is primarily partner or mother, they rarely have a career, interests or even friendships outside of the family home, and they exhibit little or no agency in their dying. Initially independent women become nurturing partners before they succumb, and nurturing mothers maintain this role, with the narrative focus firmly on their spouses and children. In this respect, the sacrificial role of dying women is overt; while their situation is the initial impetus for the narrative, it becomes subsumed within the maintenance of 'family'. Dying fathers, in contrast, exhibit more agency, still family-centred but exercising a greater emotional range and leaving more tangible and individual memorials.

A cinematic search for salvation through dying dominates throughout, closely aligned with Seale's 'revivalist' (1998: 7) discourse where death is constructed as an opportunity for growth. The transcendence theme is very strong here but manifests somewhat differently in the various sub-genres. For dying women, salvation resides in relationship and sacrifice; they nurture their loved ones and achieve transcendence in knowing their lives go on through their partners and offspring, which is principally where their identity has been located in life. Dying gay men's salvation entails the conversion of homophobes, the eradication of fear and prejudice constituting transcendence. The political mobilization of their communities is another measure of liberation resulting from their experience of dying. Frequently not experiencing death in filmic portrayals and with their dying course less readily identifiable, older people's salvation is more difficult to locate. An intimate relationship is usually core to their narrative, and it is sustaining this and their identities that much of the plots revolve around. Death-row inmates are redeemed via confession or other forms of conversion prior to their executions, encapsulated in the doomed prisoner's declaration, 'it figures I'd have to die to find love.' Celebrities die bravely and selflessly; nonentities can achieve celebrity by conspicuous, transcendent heroism in the face of dying. In the process they achieve immortality in instructing lesser mortals in how they might achieve such exemplary conduct.

While ostensibly encouraging us to reflect on mortality, films of this genre paradoxically serve to *distance* us from an engagement with the inevitability of dying, so divorced are they from reality in general and the chronic illnesses and dependence in old age that are the likely end of life's journey for most. Given the media's ubiquity and our continued sequestration from the social realities of dying and death, this is significant. Media consumers are not 'cultural dopes'; however, our experiences here are heavily mediated; we can only select our constructions and inform our understandings from the materials at hand. Bauman (1992: 16) argues that we use 'magic and irrationality' to escape the threat that death represents; if so, cinematic portrayals of dying would appear to support this activity. Given the growing interest in utilizing media depictions to teach about dying and death (Johnson and Jackson 2005), the limitations of this particular medium warrant acknowledgement. I am not arguing here for absolute realism, a documentary approach to filmic depictions of dying or that life lessons cannot be learned from fantasy portrayals. However, its sheer breadth of superficial and ideologically driven plotlines and characterizations suggests that this cinematic genre offers little for death-quarantined Westerners other than a further estrangement from the reality of our shared destiny.

References

Albom, M. (1997) *Tuesdays with Morrie*, New York: Doubleday.

Andersen, K., Launer, L., Dewey, M., Letenneur, L. and Ott, A. et al. (1999) 'Gender Differences in the Incidence of AD and Vascular Dementia: the EURODEM Studies', *Neurology*, 53 (9): 1992–7.

Ariès, P. (1981) *The Hour of Our Death*, London: Allen Lane.

Bauman, Z. (1992) *Mortality, Immortality and Other Life Strategies*, Palo Alto, Calif.: Stanford University Press.

Baxendale, S. (2003) 'Epilepsy at the Movies: Possession to Presidential Assassination', *The Lancet Neurology*, 2 (12): 764–70.

Bazzini, D. G., McIntosh, W. D., Smith, S. M., Cook, S. and Harris, C. (1997) 'The Ageing Woman in Popular Film: Underrepresented, Unattractive, Unfriendly, and Unintelligent', *Sex Roles*, 36 (7–8): 531–43.

Chapman, S. and Lupton, D. (1994) 'Freaks, Moral Tales and Medical Marvels: Health and Medical Stories on Australian Television', *Media Information Australia*, 72 (May): 94–103.

Clarke, J. (2006) 'The Case of the Missing Person: Alzheimer's Disease in Mass Print Magazines, 1991–2001', *Heath Communication*, 19 (3): 269–76.

Colaizzi, G. (2004) 'The Cinematic Act: Image Ideology and Gender Issue', *Semiotica*, 148 (1): 361–77.

Combe, K. and Schmader, K. (1999) 'Naturalizing Myths of Aging: Reading Popular Culture', *Journal of Aging and Identity*, 4 (2): 79–109.

Durkin, K. (2003) 'Death, Dying and the Dead in Popular Culture', in C. D. Bryant (ed.), *Handbook of Death and Dying*, Vol. I, Thousand Oaks, Calif.: Sage, pp. 43–9.

Ellis, C. (2005) '"There Are Survivors": Telling a Story of Sudden Death', *Sociological Quarterly*, 34 (4): 711–30.

Flagg, F. (1987) *Fried Green Tomatoes at the Whistlestop Café*, New York: Random House.

Foltyn, J. (2008) 'Dead Famous and Dead Sexy: Popular Culture, Forensics, and the Rise of the Corpse', *Mortality*, 13 (2): 153–73.

Fowler, R. (1991) *Language in the News: Discourse and Ideology in the Press*, London: Routledge.

Gaugler, J., Anderson, K., Leach, C., Smith, C., Schmitt F. and Mendiondo, M. (2004) 'The Emotional Ramifications of Unmet Need in Dementia Caregiving', *American Journal of Alzheimer's Disease and Other Dementias*, 19 (6): 369.

Gibson, M. (2007) 'Death and Mourning in Technologically Mediated Culture', *Health Sociology Review*, 16 (5) : 415–24.

Glaser, B. and Strauss, A. (2005) *Awareness of Dying*, London: Aldine. (First published 1965.)

Grunier, A., Mor, V., Weitzen, S., Truchil, R. and Teno, J. (2007) 'Where People Die: A Multilevel Approach to Understanding Influences on Site of Death in America', *Medical Care Research and Review*, 64 (4): 351–78.

hooks, b. (1994) 'Sorrowful Black Death Is Not a Hot Ticket', *Sight and Sound*, 4 (8): 10–14.

Hooks, E. (2001) 'Adrenaline Moments and Conflict: Two Essentials for Good Storytelling', *Computer Graphics*, 35 (2): 40–1.

Johnson, A. and Jackson, D. (2005) 'Using the Arts and Humanities to Support Learning About Loss, Suffering and Death', *International Journal of Palliative Nursing*, **11** (8): 438–43.

Kessler, E., Rakoczy, K. and Staudinger, U. (2004) 'The Portrayal of Older People in Prime Time Television Series: The Match with Gerontological Evidence', *Ageing and Society*, **24** (4): 531–52.

King, S. (1996) *The Green Mile*, London: Orion.

Klass, D., Silverman, P. and Nickman, S. (1996) *Continuing Bonds: New Understandings of Grief*, London: Taylor & Francis.

Knox, S. (2006) 'Death, Afterlife, and the Eschatology of Consciousness: Themes in Contemporary Cinema', *Mortality*, **11** (3): 232–52.

Lerner, B. (2006) *When Illness Goes Public: Celebrity Patients and How We Look at Medicine*, Baltimore, Md.: Johns Hopkins University Press.

McIlwain, C. (2005) *When Death Goes Pop: Death, Media and the Remaking of Community*, New York: Peter Lang.

McInerney, F. (2006) 'Heroic Frames: Discursive Constructions Around the Requested Death Movement in Australia in the Late 1990s', *Social Science and Medicine*, **62** (3): 654–67.

McNamara, B. and Rosenwax, L. (2007) 'Factors Affecting Place of Death in Western Australia', *Health and Place*, **13** (2): 356–67.

Mahon, M. (2000) 'The Visible Evidence of Cultural Producers', *Annual Review of Anthropology*, **29** : 467–92.

Meyer, T. (2005) 'Media Portrayals of Death and Dying', *The Forum*, **31** (2): 3–4.

Pausch, R. (2008) *The Last Lecture*, Sydney: Hachette.

Pickering, M., Littlewood, J. and Walter, T. (1997) 'Beauty and the Beast: Sex and Death in the Tabloid Press', in D. Field, J. Hockey and N. Small (eds.), *Death, Gender and Ethnicity*, London: Routledge, pp. 124–41.

Prejean, H. (1994) *Dead Man Walking*, New York: Vintage Books.

Quindlen, A. (1994) *One True Thing*, New York: Dell Publishing.

Schultz, N. and Huet, L. (2000–1) 'Sensational! Violent! Popular! Death in American Movies', *Omega*, **42** (2): 137–49.

Seale, C. (1998) *Constructing Death: The Sociology of Dying and Bereavement*, Cambridge: Cambridge University Press.

——— (2004) 'Media Constructions of Dying Alone: A Form of "Bad Death"', *Social Science and Medicine*, **58** (5): 967–74.

Segers, K. (2007) 'Degenerative Dementias and Their Medical Care in the Movies', *Alzheimer's Disease and Associated Disorders*, **21** (1): 55–9.

Van Fuqua, J. (1996) '"Can You Feel It, Joe?" Male Melodrama and the Feeling Man', *The Velvet Light Trap*, **38** (Autumn): 28–38.

Waites, K. (2006) 'Invisible Woman: Harbert Ross' Boys on the Side Puts HIV/AIDS and Women in Their Place', *The Journal of Popular Culture*, **39** (3): 479–92.

Wijdicks, E. and Wijdicks, C. (2006) 'The Portrayal of Coma in Contemporary Motion Pictures', *Neurology*, **66** (9): 1300–3.

Williams, A. (2006) 'Perspectives on Spirituality at the End of Life: A Meta-Summary', *Palliative and Supportive Care*, **4** (4): 407–17.

11 | Dying in the Judaeo-Christian tradition

DOUGLAS DAVIES

Dying and the dynamics of living

While this chapter's prime focus is upon dying within Christianity it is important to acknowledge Jewish cultural roots evident in ideas of suffering, death, resurrection and atonement related to Jesus. Viewed, at first, by his disciples as the Jewish Messiah, his identity develops over several centuries until he is described in Christian creeds as the divine Son of God. His act of dying came to constitute Christianity's core belief in salvation understood as a deliverance from death through an act of atonement with God. Accounts of Jesus's betrayal, trial, scourging and crucifixion, as well as his last words from the cross, his abandonment and final breath, have all contributed to a poignantly personal narrative of the end of a life that has, paradoxically, been taken as the source of hope for dying Christians. As we shall see, the two prime Christian rituals of Holy Baptism and the Holy Communion, amongst the most extensively practised rites in world history, have dying at their core. Yet, true to the sense of hope that fires Christian belief, such dying is always penultimate. The concern with ultimate fates belongs to new birth and new life, whether understood as an eternal afterlife or as a new quality of existence experienced on earth. These facts, along with the lives of many acknowledged saints and martyrs, their relics and the churches and cemeteries of the Christian dead provide an ongoing tradition against which to consider Kellehear's seven themes derived from a relatively recent period of social, human and life-science analyses of dying. Taking these briefly in turn it is clear that the theme of agency is alien to Christianity in the sense that God alone and not the human individual is the prime agent in the giving and taking of life. The idea that people are 'in control of their fate' can be identified as radically secular. The issue of linearity, by sharp contrast, reflects the deeply rooted Christian sense of life as a journey, albeit a journey into God. Kellehear's theme of fluctuation

233

is also not without its Christian counterpart in the sense that, as one funeral rite has long expressed it, 'in the midst of life we are in death', an acknowledgement of the oscillating uncertainty of life in which even the man whose successful investment has yielded much profit may be dead the morning after a new property development (Luke 12:15–21). The theme of disengagement is, itself, more complex in terms of how its forms might be valued. Disengagement from 'the world' can be positively viewed when paralleled, for example, by an engagement with the divine, as in the Wisdom literature reflected in the Book of Job whose central character also shares, to a degree, in the theme of disintegration. He will not curse God even when scraping the sores from his boil-infested body and even as he mourns the death of all his children and the loss of all his property (Job 2:4–10). From another perspective, the sense of dying as collapse pervades the final suffering and death of Jesus. As for the theme of indeterminacy or disenfranchised dying, this is alien to Christianity and is a mark of secularization of life whose narratives of worth fail to draw from the resources of death to which Christianity has brought positive values in the notion of salvation. By the sharpest of contrasts, Kellehear's theme of transcendence is, essentially, one that echoes traditional Christianity's notion of dying as transformation that we detail in the remainder of this chapter.

Dying to self

A dominant theme of Christian spirituality is that life is a form of dying to self and living to God. While literally evident in martyrs, its more metaphorical force affects the way believers seek to live in relation to God and others. Of deep relevance is the fact that Christian worship and liturgy give voice to these ideas of dying both in terms of the person of Jesus and in terms of the personal life of believers. Here doctrinal, symbolic and existential realms vitalize each other as baptism, Eucharist and daily devotion become manifest in an ethics of self-sacrifice for the good of others and in the worship of Almighty God. A non-morbid sense of dying comes to underlie a positive way of life that need not fear death. The crux of contemporary Christianity relates to those for whom this traditional perspective remains as a basis for belief in a life after death and those who interpret it more existentially as a basis for constructing an attitude towards this earthly life. For both, the motif of Jesus as the dying and rising saviour plays a foundational role, albeit differently interpreted. So it is that 2,000 years of Christianity, preceded by a millennium of Jewish thought and practice, witnessed the rise of an overarching belief in a self-revealing deity who is both creator and saviour. This theologically driven cultural capital has influenced millions in their self-understanding of living and dying and in their pastoral care and community support of the dying and bereaved long before the psychological and sociological models of the twentieth century. However, the secularization of intellectual minorities, especially from the later nineteenth century, along with a more popular secular shift in Western-influenced societies of the twentieth century, called many of these beliefs into question at the very time when social-medical sciences proffered alternative explanations.

Jewish roots

Though not the oldest Jewish text, Genesis underlies the biblical themes of life and death as Adam, tempted to eat the forbidden fruit in Eden's Paradise, is doomed to death, made from the earth, to it he will return: earth to earth and dust to dust (Genesis 3:19). This Adam motif is framed by the idea of covenant that locates agency in a binding vow of promise between God and his chosen people. Taking human frailty and sin into account it sets the scene for an immense journey into the future. The journey from Eden, from which Adam and Eve are expelled, and the alienation from the Earth itself which befalls Cain as a penalty for fratricide, possesses its goal in a promised land of refuge and plenty. This covenanted territory parallels other covenant signs framing death and life in the Genesis myths. God 'dresses' Adam and Eve when banishing them from Eden; Cain is set a wandering but given a 'mark' – the mark of Cain – to protect even this murderer from those who would assail him. Noah is 'shut into' his protective ark during the catastrophic flood but, on emerging onto the purified Earth he encounters the rainbow, a visible sign explicitly described as a mark of covenant between God and Noah. Soon, God commands the less transient covenant mark of circumcision upon Abraham and his sons that continues amongst Jews to this day. Levenson (1993) controversially argued that circumcision was a substitute sacrifice rooted in ancient Israelite sacrifice of the first-born son to God. Nevertheless, agency within a journey narrative involving life and death constitutes an ongoing Jewish sense of corporate identity in tribes and families of 'Israel'. Directed by divine law, the Torah, inspired and warned by prophets and ritually served by priests, Israel developed in its ideas of destiny. Early Jews hoped for a God-given long life with many offspring and a name of high repute to continue through their descendants: the righteous would flourish whilst the wicked would die childless, remembered no more. The living pondered the dead as shadow figures in the undesired domain of *Sheol*, 'half a hope and half a dread' (Nairne 1928: 165). Some argue that its emergent monotheism prompted Jews to oppose ideas of ancestors: if they existed they were not to be contacted (Blenkinsopp 2004). Life was for the living and for worshipping God, not for seeking after ancestral ghosts. With time, however, the dead became reclassified as awaiting a resurrection that partnered belief in a future kingdom of God on Earth. Death transcendence moves from the flourishing of old age and memorial-descendants to a new world order evident in Ezekiel's valley of dry bones which echoes the Genesis creation myth's dry ground before the Lord moistened it with mist prior to fashioning the wet earth into humanity (Ezekiel 37:1–14).

Resurrection ideas involved a growing need to vindicate the dying of righteous people, especially heroic martyrs for God, notably in the Maccabean Revolt two centuries before Christ. Because righteous lives could not be squandered, the idea of the resurrection and, in some of these texts, also of an ongoing soul, prayers for the dead and the role of personal suffering in achieving atonement contributed in a fundamental way to the Jewish world into which Jesus came as evident in the four books of Maccabees. Early Jewish rites often involved double burial, with a cave-tomb burial followed by bone-placement in ossuary boxes whose design motifs such as ships have been interpreted as symbolizing the journey of the dead into their future (Kraemer 2000: 17). Since then, Jews have undergone two millennia of transformation within a Diaspora of communities and the rise of the State of Israel following the devastating Nazi Holocaust of the Second World War. Kraemer suggests that one reason why that catastrophe – *Shoah* – impacted on Jews more than any previous onslaught was because the previous century had witnessed a growing disbelief in any sort of afterlife amongst many Jews. '*The Holocaust did not precipitate a crisis of faith. A prior crisis of faith made the Holocaust the theological watershed it has become'* (Kraemer 2000: 148; emphasis in original). This poignantly indicates the role of afterlife hope within a culture and might, for example, contrast the hope-engendering belief in resurrection amidst the second-century BC Maccabean slaughter with the dispiriting effect of the Nazi Holocaust.

Whether believing in afterlife or not, Jewish communities have continued to encourage ritual burial, a focused period of mourning *Shiva* ('seven' days) with community support before returning to the duties of daily life, including periodic memorials of the dead.

Christian developments

Jewish resurrection beliefs came to sharp focus within early Christianity in the thought that God vindicated Jesus's righteous life by raising him from the dead as a kind of new creation. This integrated the themes of living and dying in the spirituality of early Christians. The profound historical influence of Judaism continued within traditional Christianity's theologically paired concepts of creation and salvation that bring a strong sense of moral meaning to life and a shape to human destiny. Underlying it has been the sense of dying as both shame and glory. One established expression of this duality lies in the double-Adam motif leading from the mythical-doctrinal Adam in the Garden of Eden to the historical Jesus depicted as the second Adam whose death by crucifixion holds near-centre stage in Christianity's emergence from Judaism with the claim that, as Messiah, Jesus had risen from the dead. This Christian emphasis upon death's transcendence through the resurrection of Jesus Christ became foundational for Christian faith and underpinned the regular ritual practice of baptism and Eucharist which, together, established a matrix for funeral rites. From its Mediterranean birthplace, Christianity's expansion influenced the art, architecture, music and literature, as well as the philosophy of entire world cultures but always with its pervasive sense of death's conquest. This provided both a sense of individual hope of post-mortal survival in an even fuller heavenly existence and a means of constructing this-worldly existential reflections as in Kierkegaard's 'Sickness unto Death' (1968). Christianity's genius lay in an embodied hope personified in Jesus and contextualized in outgoing worship rather than in some philosophical preoccupation with death as in Heidegger (Macquarie 1973: 120). Christianity aligned faith with death transcendence in a spirituality of daily 'dying with Christ'. It integrated the key issues of human wickedness, the knowledge of mortality, the fear of death and the sense of hope that both empowers human survival and anticipates the possibility of transcending death itself. These ideas belonged to a social world that invested life with moral value, including the later Jewish notion that death involved a process of atoning for sin. Formerly explicit in the sacrifice of animals, dying as atonement came to apply to human beings on the basis that death is a kind of suffering and, 'according to the common rabbinic view, suffering effects atonement' (Kraemer 2000: 98).

Christianity exported these Jewish ideas worldwide by focusing atonement for humanity's sin on Jesus's suffering and death. Viewing his resurrection as a vindication of his righteous life, and describing its new-found energy as the activity of the Holy Spirit, Christianity's success was fostered by a new and inclusive community. The Gentile world was to be the arena of triumph of Christ's resurrection, especially after Emperor Constantine espoused the faith in the fourth century, and subsequent expansionism established Christian afterlife beliefs. The sheer cultural power of Christian state administration, often aligned with architectural programmes of church-building and cemeteries, helped legitimate death and afterlife doctrines by ritually framing life's journey from this world to the next, ultimately from baptism to last rites. Christian dying was a core act and not a marginal event.

Life was under divine control, albeit managed through church leaders. Christianity took up the theme of the Book of Job, whose titular hero lost all he had through accident, famine and bereavement yet could utter: 'the Lord gives and the Lord takes away: blessed be the name of the Lord' (Job 1:21). In developed Christian thought, this capacity was associated with the Holy Spirit, described in one creed as 'the Lord and Giver of Life'. This theological commitment came to underlie the very idea of life as a gift from God, a life that should not be 'taken' by human beings, whether in murder, as one of the Ten Commandments asserted, or in suicide, which was long considered a serious sin. From the sixth century until the twentieth, the Catholic tradition treated the death of suicides as problematic and largely forbad them a normal Christian funeral. The very idea of 'playing God' as expressed in current contemporary ethical debates over euthanasia and assisted suicide has continued this line of thought. In the most real sense, death lay in God's hands and not in the individual's control. Dying itself could be framed by Christian pastoral oversight with the notion of last rites or rites for the dying coming to assume a significant place in pastoral care. Most certainly, that closing part of life was often conceived of in terms of a journey but one that had its origin early in earthly life, regularly marked by baptism. That sacrament, a sacred rite that brought divine benefits to the individual as part of the worldwide church, was complemented by the Eucharist or mass that assisted individuals in their earthly life and found a natural reinforcement in the availability and administration of Holy Communion prior to death. Its Latin name of *viaticum* indicated food for a journey and explicitly spoke of the Christian's onward progress towards God. From its Jewish root of Adam's exile from Eden, and the subsequent journey through wilderness and desert to a promised land of covenant, Christianity took up the motif of life as a journey. That idiom had profound cultural effect, reflected in the very first lines of Dante's early fourteenth-century *Divine Comedy* (1971: 67).

> Midway along the journey of our life
> I woke to find myself in a dark wood,
> For I had wandered off from the straight path.

In the quite different religious world of the late seventeenth century, *The Pilgrim's Progress* by John Bunyan (1628–88) would also depict life as a journey to Heaven, passing through death en route. The hymnody of Christendom is, similarly, replete with journey motifs as in the familiar 'Guide Me, O Thou Great Jehovah' of 1745 by the Welsh poet-evangelist William Williams, which speaks of Christian believers as pilgrims analogous to ancient Jews leaving Egyptian captivity and wandering in the wilderness before crossing the river Jordan to enter the promised land. The petition that God might 'lead me all my journey through' draws on Old Testament imagery of the divine 'crystal fountain' of water that sustained the thirsting pilgrims and of the 'fiery cloudy pillar' that provided direction. At the journey's end, death becomes entry to the Promised Land, and appropriate emotions are addressed.

> When I tread the verge of Jordan,
> Bid my anxious fears subside:

Death of death, and hell's destruction,
Land me safe on Canaan's side.
                    (Bailey 1950: 110)

   In that safe landing, the pilgrim vows ever to give 'Songs of praises'
to God. This hymn has long been associated with funerals with a
popularity that extended to its use for several Welsh generations at
international rugby matches, a cultural reminder that hymns, songs
and music, do not gain and sustain such widespread support unless
they echo an emotional chord. Perhaps one reason for this felt affinity
with journey motifs lies in the idiom's power to touch individual lives.
As in Dante's astute description, it is often 'Midway along the journey of our life' that we wake up to realize the passing of time and find
ourselves in some strange place, for him the 'dark wood'. It takes time
for the experience of the ageing and death of our seniors and, indeed,
of the birth and ageing of our juniors, to impinge upon ourselves and
our peers (Young 2002). We awake to become aware of the passage
of time that is made intellectually and emotionally sensible by the
image of a journey. Christian funerary rites often mark this by call-
ing mourners to consider the time they have left in this life, exhorting
them to live faithfully in it.

Ritual dying

Complementing the linear salvation history from creation to the
future 'new heavens and new earth' marked by baptism and funeral
rites, Christendom also provides cyclical rites that embrace forms of
dying, notably in the Eucharist. In this sense, Kellehear's motif of
'dying as oscillation' can be understood as an oscillation between a
sense of one's mortality and a sense of one's commitment to vitality.
Baptism long treated ordinary life as life 'in the flesh' that needs to be
transformed into a form of life directed 'by the Spirit'. The Anglican
Book of Common Prayer of 1662, for example, included the prayerful
invocation of God: 'O Merciful God, grant that the old Adam in this
Child may be so buried, that the new man may be raised up in him.
Amen.' In later liturgies, too, motifs of death and rebirth are common
and are linked to the multivocal use of the word 'water'. One modern
'prayer over the water' refers to the waters of Genesis over which the
Spirit of God 'moved at the beginning of creation', as well as to passing

through water in moving from slavery to 'freedom in the Promised Land'. In fact, this journey motif becomes the dominant model in the Church of England's *Common Worship* book of 2000 whose 'pastoral introduction' to baptism begins with the words: 'Baptism marks the beginning of a journey with God' (Church of England 2000: 345). This introduction is, indeed, also stronger than any previous public statement on the water of baptism for it speaks of 'our "drowning" in the water of baptism, where we believe we die to sin and are raised to new life' (Church of England 2000: 345). Drowning is one of the strongest possible expressions of dying 'in the present tense'. The act of baptism 'unites us to Christ's dying and rising' (Church of England 2000: 345). This contemporary emphasis upon the dynamic of death and resurrection in baptism has a biblical tradition in Paul's idea that he 'dies daily' (1 Corinthians 15:31), a concept that makes sense when considered through the Eucharist as a death–life rite.

Eucharist

The Eucharist, the Christian rite using bread and wine, takes its origin in the early Christian account of the ritual meal – 'the Last Supper' – Jesus held with his disciples just before he was betrayed, arrested, tried and crucified. By tradition it was reckoned to be the Jewish event of Passover. Here, we have the prime link between the Jewish and Christian traditions with its whole grammar of discourse framed by death and life motifs. The Passover meal is, itself, a memorial of a time when the Jews were slaves in Egypt and of an event associated with their escape to freedom. God is said to have 'passed over' Egypt, killing the first-born sons of the Egyptians but leaving Jewish homes untouched. They had been instructed to kill and hurriedly eat a lamb, to eat unleavened bread and bitter herbs and to place the lamb's blood on their door as a sign to protect them from the destroying force. So it was that the Jews were delivered from captivity amidst a scene of death and grief to their Egyptian captors: 'for there was not a house where there was not one dead' (Exodus 12:30). This rite of Passover remains an annual Jewish festival. In a radically transformed nature it also became the regular, daily, weekly or periodical Christian rite variously called the Mass, the Holy Communion, the Eucharist, or the Lord's Supper. Biblical writers, especially in St John's Gospel, played on the symbolism of the event so that, for example, Jesus comes to be identified with the Passover lamb and temple sacrifices that existed to remove sin. He becomes the 'Lamb of God that takes away the sin of the world' (John 1:29). The biblical story of the Exodus of the Jews as slaves – those escaping death, to a promised land of freedom and life – involves the account of their safe passage through the waters of the Red Sea (Exodus 14:22–31), the very story picked up and developed in some later Christian baptismal ritual: 'through water you led the children of Israel from slavery in Egypt to freedom in the Promised Land' (Church of England 2000: 355). So it is that the language of baptism interacts with that of the Eucharist to forge a Christian spirituality that helps provide a way of thinking and speaking about death.

The central rite of the Eucharist involves a memorial of the last supper of Jesus with his disciples, focused on the role of bread and wine as symbolic of his body and blood that will, soon, be subject to death. But these elements of bread and wine are, as the original text says and as they are now ritually framed, 'given for you' (Luke 22:19). Different Christian traditions place a variety of emphases upon these ideas. In more Catholic traditions, the mass becomes a kind of sacrifice in which the sacrificial death of Jesus on the cross is rehearsed, some would say repeated, by the priest as symbolic of Christ himself. The Catholic doctrine of transubstantiation, especially as developed philosophically by Aquinas in the twelfth to thirteenth centuries, went so far as to argue that the actual 'substance', or inner nature of the bread actually became the 'substance' or real nature of Christ's body, and so, too, with the wine and his blood, even though their outward appearance, or 'accidents', retained those of bread and wine eaten and drunk by the faithful. The power of this has been enormous both in terms of world culture-history, with significant repercussions in sacred architecture, art and music, and also in the personal piety and spirituality of hundreds of millions of people. When given these elements, the faithful are addressed with words that link the body and blood of Christ 'given for you' with the person's eternal destiny – 'keep you in eternal life', or some such expression. More Protestant traditions seek to avoid this immediate sense of a sacrifice taking place upon an altar and opt for some sense of recalling or participating in a memory of Christ's death for them in a shared meal around a table. In either case, this is a ritual in which Christ's life, death and resurrection are linked with the life, death and eternal future of the believer. What is more, it is linked with a renewed sense of vitality for ongoing daily life. Life and death become integral to a practical spirituality.

Engaging with the dead

In many traditions, the Eucharist provides a place for considering the dead. Prayers for the dead play a regular role in the regular liturgy and, in practice, even allow the living to gain a sense of the presence of their dead relatives, an issue that is seldom appreciated for ordinary worshippers but which is related, formally, to the doctrine of the Communion of Saints. That concept is a wide one, open to numerous interpretations, but at least it allows the living to think of themselves as part of an extended community of the faithful, both living and 'dead', and of God. Protestant traditions have tended to avoid this spectrum of doctrine on the basis that human destiny is worked out between the individual and God and that prayers for the 'dead' cannot influence it. Regular prayers for the dead may, in one sense, also counteract a disengagement from the dying, if it is believed that prayers with them are a substantial element in their final period of living and motivate pastoral care at the closing of life.

In many Christian traditions there are other periods, too, that focus on the dead and on the way the living relate to them whilst also reflecting upon their own death. The annual commemoration of the feasts of All Saints followed by All Souls, on 1 and 2 November, respectively, give an explicit focus to the departed in slightly different guises. The latter is also a reminder that for much of its history Christianity has paid attention to the relationship between the living and the departed through various forms of prayer related to them. The medieval period was, in particular, especially important in the way the living could pay for masses to be said for the dead to assist them in some way in the afterlife and to remind the living of the way their own moral state might influence their own post-mortem destiny. The idea of Purgatory as a state in which the sinful lives of Christians could be purged prior to the pure vision of God in Heaven was aligned with these clustered beliefs and was one element that catalysed the Protestant Reformation as it opposed the idea of the possibility of purchasing indulgences that allowed the departed an easier or earlier exit from Purgatory into Heaven. In the well-known popular rites of the Day of the Dead in Catholic Mexico, for example, the All Souls period involves a complex interplay of local ideas of the interplay of the dead and the living associated with celebrations at cemeteries as well as playful jesting with images of death.

One sharply focused sense of a death–life oscillation within Christendom falls on Ash Wednesday, the day that leads into the ascetic period of Lent that runs up until Easter's celebration of resurrection. In the Catholic tradition, the rite that gives its name to this event involves placing ashes on the head of penitent believers with words such as 'dust you are and to dust you will return', an expression derived from the Genesis myth of Adam's fall from divine grace when God reminded Adam of his origin from the earth and of his destiny in returning to it (Genesis 3:19). This symbolic event tells believers that they are dying. It calls them into a period of repentance and of relative bodily abstinence through fasting. As this fasting period of some forty days moves towards its climactic final week, many in the Christian tradition practise various rites that mark Christ's life on the brink of his betrayal and death. Two of these merit attention here, one taking place on Maundy Thursday and another on Good Friday.

Betrayal and dying

The final Thursday before Easter is called Maundy Thursday from the Latin *mandatum* or commandment focused on the 'commandment' to 'love one another' and to be a servant of each other symbolized in John's Gospel when Christ washed his disciples' feet (John 13:34). John places the betrayal within the Last Supper, aligning it with the intimacy of the meal and with Satan's entry into Judas (John 13:2, 21–7), while the Synoptic Gospels focus betrayal on Judas Iscariot betraying Jesus with a kiss in the Garden of Gethsemane (Matthew 26:49; Mark 14:45; Luke 22:48). Subsequently, Jesus is arrested, tried, flogged and crucified. The commandment of love was, then, set in the period of the Jewish Passover, and later interpretation saw it as an alignment of Passover and Eucharist already mentioned above. The human emotion and divine pathos involved in the texts surrounding these events is great as they focus on the issue of betrayal and love and of Christ's agony in the Garden of Gethsemane, an episode of great significance for the Christian spirituality of death. Jesus asks his closest disciples to watch with him while he approaches God as his Father and asks that, if it is possible, this 'cup' be removed from him. This 'cup', a symbol of his death, appears in many later representations of this event and provides a complex symbol that echoes 'the cup' of the Last Supper which he has shared with the disciples and of subsequent Christian Eucharists (Mark 14:24). It haunts myths of the 'Holy Grail'. Jesus, in effect, prays that his impending death might be avoided (e.g. Matthew 26:36–46). Here there is a stark juxtaposition between, on the one hand, the 'cup' in the Last Supper that all have been bidden to drink and the anticipated mutual drinking that will occur in the coming Kingdom of God (e.g. Matthew 26:29) and, on the other, the 'cup' of suffering and death now before him. But Christ adds the famous words, 'not my will, but thine, be done' (Luke 22:42). In Luke's Gospel (22:44), there is in some, but not all, ancient texts an additional description of Christ's agony in which his earnest prayer results in a sweat that resembles 'great drops of blood falling down to the ground'. Then, in the gospel narratives, Jesus goes to the disciples only to find them sleeping. Luke's description of them as 'sleeping for sorrow' is, in a sense, kind, for it indicates their distress and their reaction to what they saw in Jesus. Luke is, by tradition, described as a doctor (Colossians 4:14). Such sleep for sorrow will not be unknown to many who have watched alongside those they love. The support Jesus does get is ascribed to an angel (Luke 22:43). The whole context of the Last Supper and this Gethsemane episode is, in the three Synoptic Gospels, one of deep sorrow. And that emotion of sorrow coupled with impending pain and grief moves onward, both in the biblical texts and in contemporary Christian liturgy and spirituality, into Good Friday. In some churches, the rite of the stripping of the altar leaves the focal part of a church's sacred space bare of its normal decoration, the lights are dimmed to allow darkness to make its own symbolic message clear while the singing of a psalm such as Psalm 22 adds its own poignant message of a servant of God abandoned by God, including the words 'My God, my God, look upon me; why hast thou forsaken me: and art so far from my health, and from the words of my complaint?' – words which are also part of the tradition of Jesus's words from the cross, 'My God, my God, why hast thou forsaken me?' (Mark 15:34).

Good Friday, or 'Great Friday' in the Orthodox Church, the day following, takes up these sentiments, only to intensify them in this, the day of Jesus's death. In any and all of these rites, the historical past or the theological constructs posited upon biblical passages of some 2,000 years ago pass into the devotional present tense. It is in the here and now that emotions are elicited in close alliance with biblical texts, liturgical formulae, prayer and sermons. And all are embedded in the fact of death. But what is important from the Christian perspective is that the overriding theological message is purposeful. From the imposition of ashes on Ash Wednesday, through the relative asceticism of Lent, to Maundy Thursday's love and betrayal and Good Friday's suffering and death, the individual's life is caught up in the suffering of Jesus. So many factors conduce to highlighting the mutual bond of believer and saviour. The focus on the cross as the place of death is central to the architecture and art of most churches. In many historic traditions the very cruciform plan of the church building symbolizes the crucifixion, some even reflect the falling of the dead Christ's head to one side in a shift in the long axis of the church building while the music and silence that, mutually, fill it bring their own dynamism to bear on individual and corporate life.

In Catholic and some other traditions not only will stained-glass windows and paintings portray many of these scenes of Christ's passion but walls may also carry the Stations of the Cross. These have an origin in the experience of pilgrims to Jerusalem who followed a pilgrimage route from the house of Pilate, who tried Jesus, through to his crucifixion at Calvary. This route, and the piety associated with meditations on events befalling Jesus on it, becomes ritualized into some fourteen cameos comprising the Stations of the Cross. Popularized in Europe in the Middle Ages, these underlie a devotional practice of moving from one to another along with appropriate prayer and meditation that focuses believers on the last day in the earthly life of Jesus. Many Christian churches have also developed their own focus in services on that day as in the Anglican adoption of a Catholic three-hour service from noon until three in the afternoon, a period deemed to be that matching Christ's period of crucifixion. This involves prayers and hymns and, often, meditations on Christ's 'words from the cross'. Such services often create a deep mood of engagement with the suffering and death of Jesus and, inevitably, stimulate individuals to ponder their own suffering and future death, as well as recalling those features in the lives of those they have known and loved.

Death's glory

This spirituality of participation in Christ's passion continues in a strangely liminal Saturday until the first Eucharist of Easter strikes the note of resurrection. 'Christ is risen! He is risen indeed, hallelu-jah!' is one traditional form of Easter greeting. Ceremonies are some-times held very early on Easter Day, allowing the theological message of the conquest of death by Jesus, the Son of God, to coincide with the literal rising of the sun and the dispelling of night's darkness. New fire may be kindled and candles lit. The Paschal Candle, a large can-dle symbolizing Christ himself, is sometimes marked so as to recall Christ's wounds of crucifixion, before being lit and carried in pro-cession and placed in church to mark the presence of the risen Christ amongst his people. Easter was the traditional time for the baptism of those who underwent instruction during Lent and who now became full members of the Christian community; this allows the motifs of death and rebirth discussed above for baptism to be intensified in the context of Easter worship.

The complex theological and liturgical nature of Christianity does not, however, end with Easter. For the liturgical calendar moves into the Ascension of Jesus which reflects the traditional belief that Jesus as a resurrected being spent a period with his disciples before departing from them when he 'ascended into Heaven'. This is duly followed by the Feast of Pentecost or the coming of the divine power of the Holy Spirit, something often regarded as the actual beginning of the Christian Church. The significance of this in the present con-text is twofold. First, that the Holy Spirit is described in the Niceno-Constantinopolitan Creed as 'The Lord and Giver of Life' and that Christianity is, essentially, a corporate and not an individualist ven-ture. In other words, Christians are part of a wide community embra-cing both the living and the departed, a community that comprises the 'body of Christ', animated by the divine Spirit. Ideas of support and inspiration are associated with the Holy Spirit, often called the Comforter, while afterlife beliefs add their own sustenance as when John's Jesus says, 'In my Father's house are many mansions ... I go to prepare a place for you', a text well known in the context of some Christian funerals (John 14:2).

Underlying all that has been said so far lies the major theme of the total Judaeo-Christian tradition that promises a fulfilment of destiny despite human failing. Its proper theological description is salvation, and its focus lies in Jesus, whose Jewish identity and the scriptural resources of the Hebrew Bible became Christianity's focal point. Salvation is a complex idea that embraces a cluster of associated

concepts such as deliverance, a notion that implies a negative power
from which someone is saved, a power never better symbolized than
that of death. The fulfilment that deliverance brings is, itself, grounded
in the will of God for people and for the world in which they are set,
often understood in terms of God's Kingdom and of a sense of justice
that will pervade it. One presupposition of this anticipated kingdom
is that life as actually experienced now is flawed, lacking in this sense
of just rule. This tradition has its own explanation of the flaw in existence which is depicted in the Genesis accounts of Adam and Eve and
their disobedience of divine commandment. Whether interpreted in a
literal sense or, much more often, in a radically existential sense, these
accounts explain human experience for any age, as myths that see the
world in terms of commandment, human wilfulness, life and death.

Transformations

Paul, regarded by many as Christianity's founder, developed Jewish
themes of dying to a remarkable degree in writings now regarded as
sacred scripture. His Chapter 15 of his First Letter to the Corinthians
emerged as a charter text on dying and resurrection. Paul, a highly
trained religious teacher, believed he had met the risen Jesus whilst in
the very act of persecuting Christians. His conversion, reflected in his
name change from Saul to Paul, produced a man who now expected
Jesus, the Christ, to return very soon, on the clouds of Heaven, to
redeem God's people from oppression on a renewed Earth and in the
kind of kingdom described above. The Earth itself would be transformed; indeed, his conversion engendered an affinity with transformation motifs, and his theology typifies change. Just as Jesus died
and was resurrected so would Christians die and be resurrected. The
first and second Adam theme described above is, essentially, Pauline.
His Corinthians rhetorical debate was against those who denied resurrection. He speaks of the fleshly body that is buried and the spiritual body that is resurrected, using analogies of the different kinds
of flesh in beasts, birds and fishes and the different orders of glory
of sun, moon and stars. At the divinely appointed time, the trum-
pet shall sound and the dead be raised incorruptible as the mortal
puts on immortality and as 'death is swallowed up in victory'. The
Synoptic Gospel tradition of the empty tomb, itself a powerful prompt
for belief in early Christianity, has regularly been complemented and,

indeed, overtaken by this image of the resurrected and glorified Jesus. One problem was that some Christians were dying before this prom- ised event occurred. Paul responded to this issue in his First Letter to the Thessalonians. Those who had died, who 'are asleep' as he put it, will come with Jesus when he arrives and would not, in fact, be forgotten or somehow upstaged by Christians still alive at Christ's second coming. Indeed, when Christ arrives 'in the clouds ... the dead in Christ shall rise first', and then the living Christians will be caught up with them in the clouds 'to meet the Lord in the air'. Paul said this, in part, so that believers who had suffered bereavement might 'comfort one another with these words' (1 Thessalonians 4:13–18). This theme that many Christians would not die at all but be instant- aneously transformed and caught up to meet Jesus amidst the clouds has, sporadically, re-emerged in Christian history as amongst mil- lions of late-twentieth and early twenty-first-century Americans in what has come to be called the Rapture. In Lahaye and Jenkins' *Left Behind* novels, as well as in film, this 'rapture' motif depicts a wicked world having true believers mysteriously disappearing, leaving the rest to bear the brunt of the Devil's oppression. This version of American disaster movies can be interpreted in many ways, but one of them is to see the 'rapture' idea, in which believers do not die at all, as one step on from an American way of death that came to hide death behind the cosmetic preparation of corpses. Both cases could be seen as forms of disenfranchised dying and exemplify the extreme possibilities avail- able to a Christianly informed culture. By the beginning of this cen- tury, this series of books had sold some 50 million copies. Some have interpreted it as a form of 'terror rhetoric' (Jackson 2007: 52), others as a misguided interpretation of scripture (DeMar 2001).

However, Paul's accommodation to the fact that Christ's second coming with its attendant rapture did not occur in his day led him to advise new Christians that they were not to be worried by its non- arrival. The day would come, sooner or later, when the dead would rise and be changed, becoming incorruptible and would be 'with Christ' for ever. His view of death, and it is one that has been extremely influential upon the entire Christian world, was embedded within his sense of the religious life as one of moral conflict. He wanted to do and be good but found himself at odds with those desires. This led him to speak of his body as something dissolvable or open to dis- sociation, as something that is not his ultimate home (2 Corinthians

5:1–6). He was not dismayed by this, despite his 'groaning' in this state, because he anticipated a future 'clothing' of deliverance that would come through Christ in God's good time. Meanwhile, he had to bear the forces of death at work within him as they existed in conflict with the forces of life reckoned to be the work of God's Holy Spirit. That same Spirit could 'groan' alongside Paul as he lived in this 'body of death', itself subject to the 'bondage of corruption' (Romans 8:26, 21, respectively). Christian life, itself, was a dynamic oscillation between the forces of death and of life; each Christian was, in a sense, an intersection of the old and new Adams, the Adam of the 'flesh', and the Adam of the 'Spirit'. The history of Christian art has not been slow to portray this sense of the wastedness of the body because of sin. Portrayals of Christ, especially in medieval crucifixion art, leave no doubt as to the pain of human embodiment, itself reflected in many tombstones, not least the double structures in which the glory of human status is shown in clothing and looks whilst the lower level reveals the skeletal decay of earthly destiny. In practical, pastoral, terms, there has been a long tradition of Christian engagement with this human frailty exemplified in hospital/hospice care and in religious orders dedicated to the socially disenfranchised, the old, decaying and dying typified in medieval London in the twelfth-century St Bartholomew's Hospital and, more recently, by Mother Teresa.

Greater love

One final view, from the twentieth century, also reveals the potential of a Christian theology to remove the sting of death at a cultural level and followed the First and Second World Wars in what has been called the 'greater love' motif employed when engaging with the millions of dead soldiers of these wars. In John's Gospel, Jesus is reckoned to say 'Greater love hath no man than this, that a man lay down his life for his friends' (John 15:30). This text came to be inscribed on innumerable war memorials in Britain. This 'greater love' motif developed in a way that created its own form of popular spirituality underlying how people thought of the soldiers who had died, one that Jon Davies (1995) persuasively interpreted as a kind of Euro-Christianity, causing a shift in theological and pastoral outlooks, not least reducing remnants of earlier notions of Hell as a place of torment. The millions who died, often in conditions of abject slaughter, simply made it impossible, not least on the part of their bereaved families, to think of them in any traditional way as sinners going to Hell. Rather, their deaths became interpreted as sacrifices made for a greater good, with the biblical 'greater love' motif highlighted in a profound existential affinity. A couple of generations later, Marvin and Ingle (1999) could offer a different perspective on war death when arguing that, for Americans, military 'blood sacrifice' by US troops was necessary for national cohesion. The desire to establish positive interpretations of dying has been one of Christianity's major theological motivations. While, in former eras, this often related to the afterlife and Heaven, the post-war twentieth century witnessed a more radical this-worldly orientation of death concern. This has been particularly evident in respect of the deaths of millions of civilians in poverty, famine and war-related disaster where Christian groups have sought to provide material and personnel resources, motivated by the belief that God possesses a 'bias to the poor' and disinherited. Liberation theologians in South America as well as well-known people such as Albert Schweitzer in Africa, who developed his philosophy of the reverence for life, and Mother Teresa with her Missionaries of Charity in India are symbolic of a Christian engagement with ultimate ills and death. The Judaeo-Christian tradition continues to be a major project in death transcendence because of its worshipful engagement with a God who is transcendence itself. Its faith in the Holy Trinity brings an embodied focus of hope in Jesus the resurrected Son alongside a sense of divine power in the Holy Spirit that fosters love (1 Corinthians 13:13).

References

Bailey, A. E. (1950) *The Gospel in Hymns, Background and Interpretations*, New York: Charles Scribner's Sons.

Blenkinsopp, J. (2004) *Treasures Old and New: Essays in the Theology of the Pentateuch*, Grand Rapids, Mich.: Eerdmans.

Church of England (2000) *Common Worship*, London: Church House Publishing.

Dante, A. (1971) *Divine Comedy*, trans. Mark Musa, Harmondsworth: Penguin. (Written *c.* 1300).

Davies, D. (2008) *The Theology of Death*, London: T. & T. Clark.

Davies, J. (1995) *The Christian Warrior in the Twentieth Century*, Lampeter: Mellen Press.

DeMar, G. (2001) *End Times Fiction: A Biblical Consideration of the Left Behind Theology*, Nashville: Thomas Nelson Publishers.

Jackson, B. (2007) 'Jonathan Edwards Goes to Hell (House): Fear Appeals in American Evangelism', *Rhetoric Review*, **26** (1): 42–59.

Kierkegaard, S. (1968) *Fear and Trembling and Sickness unto Death*, trans. and ed. Walter Lowrie, Princeton, NJ: Princeton University Press. (First published 1849.)

Kraemer, D. (2000) *The Meanings of Death in Rabbinic Judaism*, London and New York: Routledge.

LaHaye, T. and Jenkins, J.B. (2001) *Desecration: Antichrist takes the Throne*, Wheaton, Ill.: Tyndale House.

Levenson, Jon D. (1993) *The Death and Resurrection of the Beloved Son: The Transformation of Child Sacrifice in Judaism and Christianity*, New Haven, Conn.: Yale University Press.

Macquarie, J. (1973) *An Existentialist Theology: A Comparison of Heidegger and Bultmann*, Harmondsworth: Penguin. (First published 1955.)

Marvin, C. and Ingle, D.W. (1999) *Blood Sacrifice and the Nation*, Cambridge: Cambridge University Press.

Nairne, A. (1928) *The Life Eternal: Here and Now*, London: Longman, Green & Co.

Young, K. (2002) 'The Memory of the Flesh', *Body and Society*, **8** (3): 25–48.

12 | Near-death experiences and deathbed visions

BRUCE GREYSON

When some people come close to death, they go through a profound experience in which they believe they leave their bodies and enter some other realm or dimension, transcending the boundaries of the ego and the ordinary confines of time and space. Such experiences had been described sporadically in the medical literature since the nineteenth century (Greyson 1998) and had been identified as a discrete syndrome more than a century ago (Heim 1892). Moody (1975) introduced the term 'near-death experiences' (NDEs) for these phenomena. Many scholars use the plural term 'near-death experiences' rather than talk about 'the [singular] near-death experience', because NDEs may be not one unitary phenomenon but rather a class of related phenomena (Kellehear 2007a). Be that as it may, in his initial description of NDEs, Moody outlines fifteen characteristic features commonly reported by American survivors. These fifteen features, which have come to define NDEs both among the academic community and in the popular imagination, include ineffability, hearing the news of one's death, overwhelming feelings of peace, hearing a noise, seeing a tunnel, a sensation of being out of the body, meeting non-physical beings, a 'Being of Light', a life review, a border or point of no return, coming back to life, telling others about the experience, effects on lives, new views of death and corroboration of knowledge not acquired through normal perception (Moody 1975).

Ring (1980) proposes a structured temporal sequence of NDE features involving, sequentially, peace, separation from the body, the tunnel, seeing the light and merging with the light. A sophisticated statistical scaling model shows that NDEs, with increasing intensity, reflected peace, joy and harmony, followed by insight and mystical or religious experiences, while the most intense NDEs involved an awareness of things occurring in a different place or time (Lange et al. 2004). Descriptions of the experience and the sequence of features within it did not vary across gender, age, age at the time of the experience, time elapsed since the experience and intensity of the experience.

Research on NDEs

One of the problems with research into NDEs is that, with a few notable exceptions, almost all NDE research has been retrospective, raising the question of the reliability of the experiencer's memories (French 2001). Embellishment of NDE accounts, if it occurred, would diminish their importance and theoretical challenge. Autobiographical memories are subject to distortion over years, and memories of unusual or traumatic events may be particularly unreliable as a result of emotional influences. To test the reliability of NDE accounts, Greyson (2007) administered a quantitative measure of NDEs to the same experiencers on two occasions about twenty years apart, in the early 1980s and then again in the 2000s. Contrary to concerns that NDE accounts are embellished over time, there were no statistically significant differences between the NDE accounts on the two administrations, and changes were not significantly associated with the elapsed time interval. This evidence that accounts of NDEs are reliable over a period of two decades supports the validity of studies of such experiences that had occurred years prior to their investigation.

Researchers have identified very few personal traits or variables that can predict who will have an NDE or what kind of NDE a person may have. Retrospective studies of NDErs have shown them collectively to be psychologically healthy individuals who do not differ from comparison groups in age, gender, race, religion, religiosity or mental health (Ring 1980; Sabom 1982; Gabbard and Twemlow 1984; Irwin 1985; Greyson 1991a). NDErs are indistinguishable from others in intelligence, neuroticism, extroversion, trait and state anxiety and relevant Rorschach measures (Locke and Shontz 1983). However, some studies have suggested that NDErs tend to be good hypnotic subjects, remember their dreams more often and are adept at using mental imagery (Irwin 1985) and tend to acknowledge significantly more childhood trauma and resultant dissociative tendencies (Ring 1992) than others. It is not clear, however, whether these distinguishing personality traits are the results of having had an NDE or whether people who already have those characteristics are more prone to have NDEs when they come close to death.

A common assumption has been that an inadequate supply of oxygen to the brain, as a common final pathway to brain death, must be implicated in NDEs (Rodin 1980; Blackmore 1993). However, NDEs occur without impaired oxygen supply, as in non-life-threatening illnesses and near-accidents. Furthermore, inadequate brain oxygen generally produces idiosyncratic, frightening hallucinations and leads to agitation and belligerence, quite unlike the peaceful NDE with consistent, universal features. Furthermore, studies of people near death have shown that those who have NDEs do not have lower oxygen levels than those who do not have NDEs (Sabom 1982; Van Lommel et al. 2001). Similar considerations apply to the theory that high levels of carbon dioxide may contribute to NDEs (Morse et al. 1989; Jansen 1997). NDE-like features that have been reported with high carbon-dioxide levels are rare and isolated, and NDEs are reported by patients in whom carbon-dioxide levels were not elevated (Sabom 1982; Morse et al. 1989; Parnia et al. 2001).

NDEs have also been attributed to hallucinations produced either by medications given to dying patients or by metabolic disturbances or brain malfunctions as a person approaches death. However, many NDEs are recounted by individuals who had no metabolic or organic malfunctions that might have caused hallucinations, and patients who receive medications in fact report fewer NDEs than do patients who receive no medication (Osis and Haraldsson 1977; Sabom 1982; Greyson 1990). Furthermore, brain malfunctions generally produce clouded thinking, irritability, fear, belligerence and idiosyncratic visions, quite unlike the exceptionally clear thinking, peacefulness, calmness and predictable content that typify the NDE. Visions in patients with delirium are generally of living persons, whereas those of patients who are thinking clearly as they approached death are almost invariably of deceased persons (Osis and Haraldsson 1977). Patients who had fevers when near death reported fewer NDEs and less elaborate experiences than did patients with normal temperatures (Osis and Haraldsson 1977; Ring 1980; Sabom 1982). Such findings may suggest that either drug-induced or metabolically induced delirium rather than causing NDEs in fact inhibits them from occurring (Kelly et al. 2007).

NDEs have been speculatively attributed to a number of neurotransmitters in the brain, most frequently endorphins or other endogenous opioids released under stress (Carr 1982; Saavedra-Aguilar

Gómez-Jeria 1989; and Blackmore 1993). Other models have implicated serotonin, adrenaline, vasopressin and glutamate (Morse et al. 1989; Saavedra-Aguilar and Gómez-Jeria 1989; Jansen 1997). These speculations are based on hypothetical endogenous chemicals or effects that have not been shown to exist and are not supported by any empirical data.

NDEs have also been speculatively linked to a number of anatomic locations in the brain, most often the right temporal lobe (Morse et al. 1989; Saavedra-Aguilar and Gómez-Jeria 1989). However, NDE-like phenomena are almost never seen in temporal lobe seizures (Devinsky et al. 1989; Rodin 1989), and electrical stimulation of the temporal lobes elicits experiences quite different from NDEs (Horowitz and Adams 1970; Gloor 1990). Reports of phenomena induced by magnetic stimulation of the temporal lobes that bear vague resemblance to NDE-like phenomena (Persinger 1994) could not be replicated by other researchers and seem to have been due to suggestion (Granqvist et al. 2005). Although psychophysiological factors may indeed interact in complicated ways with sociocultural ones in NDEs, theories proposed thus far consist largely of unsupported speculations about the dying process, some of which are inconsistent with the data we do have (Kelly et al. 2007).

Deathbed visions

Deathbed visions are comparable to NDEs but occur to people on their deathbed who do not recover, though they are able to relate their experiences to others at the bedside as they are dying (Cobbe 1882; Bozzano 1906, 1923; Hyslop 1907; Barrett 1926; Osis and Haraldsson 1977; Rogo 1978; Callanan and Kelley 1993; Alvarado 2006). Dying persons may suddenly awaken from comas or states of severe cognitive impairment and with apparent lucidity describe seeing deceased loved ones and otherworldly visions.

These deathbed visions usually precede death by minutes or hours and transform the dying persons' attitudes and affects in the remaining time. Obviously, deathbed visions cannot produce the long-term aftereffects in the subsequent life of the experiencer that NDEs do, but they appear to influence beliefs and values comparably in the moments before death. Deathbed visions might be expected to affect the bereavement of loved ones left behind and the attitudes and behaviour of caregivers, but little research has been done on this topic (Houran 1997; Ethier 2005; Brayne et al. 2006).

NDEs and the study of dying

The focus of this volume is on dying as a particular form of social life and experience that goes beyond, yet provides context to, illness, death and the attempt to make sense and meaning out of both. NDEs as 'pseudodeaths' mimic dying in their apparent transition from life, perhaps into a post-mortem realm; yet they gainsay dying in their return to the social world of the living. NDEs are a common feature of the dying process: recent research suggests that NDEs are reported by 12 per cent to 18 per cent of cardiac arrest survivors (Parnia et al. 2001; Van Lommel et al. 2001; Greyson 2003). However, NDEs have been neglected by many scholars because of their associations in the popular media with parapsychology and 'New Age' culture. But despite this popular association, much of the scholarly literature on NDEs has focused on practical clinical aspects. The theoretical portion of that literature has been polarized between medical explanations that reduce NDE features to physiological or psychological mechanisms and transcendental explanations beyond currently established physical mechanisms. The latter may suggest new medical understandings of the brain–mind relationship or may situate NDEs among religious and spiritual traditions suggesting the possibility of mind surviving bodily death.

Much of the debate in the NDE literature has focused on how close the experiencers had actually been to death, or whether in fact some had actually met the criteria for clinical death. That debate has assumed a sharp dividing line between life and death, something that does not exist in nature (Kellehear 2008a). This irresolvable debate can be bypassed by considering death and dying as social relationships rather than simply biological experiences. Social perceptions of death are fluid, permitting varying degrees and combinations of death-associated relationships. Indeed, it may be meaningless to declare a person dead without specifying who has made that determination and for what purpose (Sassower and Grodin 1986). People who may not be physiologically near death may be socially dead when their relationships with the outside world are irrevocably terminated. And, conversely, people who meet criteria for irreversible brain death may remain socially alive when their bonds with the living remain strong and appear reciprocal (Kellehear 2008a).

Applying the social-relationship perspective to NDEs resolves the apparent paradox of phenomenologically complex NDEs occurring to people who are not near *physiological* death: all NDEs occur to people who are near *social* death. Studying NDEs phenomenologically as a social process obviates getting bogged down in either the untestable eschatological assumptions of religion or the equally untestable neurophysiological assumptions of biomedicine. Considerations of NDEs as social relationships are meaningful regardless of whether NDEs are the results of neurochemical changes or actual perceptions of a transcendental dimension. In Thomas and Thomas's famous dictum, 'If men define situations as real, they are real in their consequences' (1928: 572).

NDEs are important to social scientists because they precipitate pervasive and durable changes in beliefs, attitudes and values. However, sociological contributions to our understanding of NDEs have been relatively neglected (Flynn 1986; Sutherland 1992; McClenon 1994; Kellehear 1996). Much of the sociological input has focused on the role of expectation and the impossibility of separating language from experience (Kellehear 2007a). It is certainly plausible that NDEs are products of the imagination, constructed from one's personal and cultural expectations, to protect oneself from facing the threat of death (Rodin 1980; Greyson 1983b). Comparisons of NDE accounts from different cultures suggest that prior beliefs have some influence on the kind of experience a person will report following a close brush with death (Kellehear 1993, 1996, 2008b; Augustine 2007). However, it is unclear whether cultural beliefs affect the experience itself, or merely its recall and retelling, or the investigators' collection of the accounts. Some of the cross-cultural differences observed may reflect not differences in the experiences themselves but rather the ways in which people interpret what they have experienced. Any common underlying core experience must inevitably be cast in the images, concepts and symbols available to the individual (Roberts and Owen 1988).

The influence of expectancy on NDEs has obvious limits. Individuals often report experiences that conflict with their specific religious and personal expectations of death (Ring 1984). Furthermore, people who had no prior knowledge about NDEs describe the same kinds of experiences as do people who are quite familiar with the phenomenon, and the knowledge individuals had about NDEs previously does not seem to influence the details of their own experiences (Greyson and Stevenson 1980; Ring 1980; Sabom 1982; Greyson 1991a). Experiences that were reported before 1975, when Moody coined the term 'near-death experience' and popularized the phenomenon do not differ from those that were reported since that date (Athappilly et al. 2006). And young children, who are less likely to have developed expectations about death, report NDEs with features similar to those of adults (Bush 1983; Gabbard and Twemlow 1984; Herzog and Herrin 1985; Morse et al. 1985; Serdahely 1990), although Kellehear (2007a) has pointed out that children do not represent socially 'uncontaminated' NDErs because their experiences are inevitably transmitted through adults and cannot be understood separate from the language used to describe them.

Theories of dying applied to NDEs

In his introductory chapter in this volume, Kellehear outlines a more robust model for understanding sociological features of dying, outlining seven recurring insights culled from his systematic review of the literature on dying. These complementary models of dying may provide a valuable framework for understanding NDEs. Kellehear cites NDEs as exemplars of the theme of dying as transcendence, and indeed they are that. But NDEs also incorporate to varying degrees all seven themes of agency, linearity, oscillation, disengagement, disintegration, disenfranchisement and transformation. How these themes play out in NDEs differs in some ways from how they may manifest in other dying experiences. With dying individuals, the primary question is how each theme influences the social roles of the dying individual and of significant others *during the dying process*. With NDEs, there is the added question of how these themes influence social roles *after the individual has 'returned'* to the social world of the living. Furthermore, some of these themes are fully manifested only over time and are necessarily attenuated by the acute time course of the near-death event.

Agency: dying as personal control

Kellehear describes the theme of agency as the most common view of dying, in which dying people are in control of their fate, enabling them to orchestrate a 'good death' (Kastenbaum 1979). However, agency is rarely encountered in NDEs. The predominant theme in NDEs is surrender of personal control. Many experiencers credit this surrender with the powerful therapeutic impact of their NDE. After a lifetime spent fearing loss of control, they felt control involuntarily stripped from them and experienced a sense of overwhelming wellbeing that reduced their need for control after their 'return' (Greyson 1991b).

NDErs do sometimes manifest the theme of agency as they sense the approach of death. Indeed, many experiencers describe struggling to remain in control during the early part of the dying process. NDEs tend to occur quite late in the dying trajectory and often do not begin to unfold until after the individual relinquishes efforts to remain in control.

A secondary aspect of the theme of agency is the effort of dying individuals to maintain their personal identities (Matthews 1979). Maintenance of personal identity is a complex issue in NDEs. Many experiencers describe an altered sense of identity in which they have a sense of merging with something greater than the self. This may be expressed as a paradoxical state of retaining some form of personal identity while still becoming part of the greater being (Ring 1984).

A third feature of the theme of agency involves reinforcing the importance of the dying person's lifelong investment in activities and obligations. Many NDErs undergo a life review in which they relive their entire lives, sometimes coming to a reassessment of the value of different activities and relationships. This reassessment may contribute to subsequent life changes when the experiencer attempts to reintegrate into the social world of the living (Ring 1980, 1984; Flynn 1986; Greyson 1991b; Ring and Valarino 1998; Fox 2003).

Linearity: dying as a journey

Kellehear notes that dying may involve the socially constructed life stages of separation, transition or liminality and incorporation. Dying viewed as a transition from 'living person' to 'dead person' is an important social device for family and healthcare workers caring for the dying individual.

This theme of linearity fits the description of NDE as a special kind of status passage (Kellehear 1990). If we consider the social features of NDEs to include sudden and unexpected separation from relationships, a transition period involving the expectation of death and a sudden return to the original social networks but with inexorably altered behaviors, then they can be viewed as a 'status passage' or a change from one social identity to a different one (Glaser and Strauss 1971). Like the more common life transitions such as puberty, marriage, career change and parenthood, NDEs involve separation from one social status, a period of transitional reorientation and recognition of a new status. However, Kellehear (1990) argues that unlike those more common status passages, the relational aspects of NDEs have gone unrecognized. Their stigmatization as medical or psychological aberrations, their marginal position as unsought and uncontrolled status passages, and the common refusal of experiencers to reintegrate into established social roles have inhibited both experiencers and scholars from discussing their relational aspects. NDEs have been marginalized by social scientists not only because they are not structural or normative paths to social change but also because they often represent powerful criticism of established social roles and controls (Kellehear 1990).

All life changes – puberty, marriage, parenthood and so on – are socially constructed by the community and not simply biologically determined (Van Gennep 1969). Kübler-Ross's (1969) familiar stages of dying – denial, anger, bargaining, depression and acceptance – are interactive in that they represent a linear trajectory that may describe the dying person's relationship to caregivers or prescribe certain responses from caregivers. In contrast, Ring's (1980) familiar stages of NDEs – peace, separation from the body, the tunnel, seeing the light and merging with the light – reflect processes that are internal to the experiencer or interactive between the experiencer and otherworldly beings. The linear stages of NDEs do not become social constructs until they are described by the experiencer after 'returning'.

Fluctuation: dying as oscillation

Kellehear describes the theme of fluctuation in the context of chronic illness, in which dying people may cycle between disability and improvement over time. This oscillating course of cycling between health and illness is typical of dying in old age (Moss et al. 2003). NDEs, by contrast, are acute events that often occur to otherwise healthy individuals; as such, they do not lend themselves to oscillation. Nevertheless,

the general concept that dying as an identity is not always an uninterrupted trajectory of decline is relevant to NDEs, in which the characteristic trajectory is a journey through decline and back to recovery.

Following NDEs, survivors face varying challenges in reintegrating
with their social networks. Sutherland (1992) studied NDErs' paths
through this process and delineates four clear types of integration
trajectory, some with subtypes. Some experiencers had an 'accelerated
trajectory', particularly when their NDEs confirmed prior life experiences and social relationships, enabling a rapid reintegration. Others
had a 'steady trajectory', with a much slower yet consistent progression towards reintegration. Still others had an 'arrested trajectory',
in which integration was impeded by contextual situations and oscil-
lated as the experiencers sought support from various social networks.
Finally, there were some who had a 'blocked trajectory', in which the
NDEs were never integrated into the experiencers' social relationships. Sutherland's work highlights the variability among integration
trajectories, in which fluctuations are related not to cycling between
health and illness but rather to oscillating social interactions.

Disengagement: dying as withdrawal

Kellehear describes the theme of disengagement as involving a withdrawal of attention from the affairs of the wide world, which is applicable not only to physical dying but more broadly to 'social death'
(Sudnow 1967). This withdrawal from the world of the living is a
typical feature of NDEs, which can occur not only when people are
physiologically near death but also in situations in which people fear
they are going to die but are not physiologically endangered at all, as
when they have full-blown NDEs during falls from heights or while
barely avoiding potentially fatal automobile accidents.

Kellehear suggests that disengagement may be a socially appropriate response of aged persons who anticipate declining health and
severe illness. Because NDEs are acute events that are not anticipated,
they rarely permit the acculturation into the group experience of dying
that may occur with an ageing population. However, with increasing
cultural familiarity with NDEs, participants in our society may be
learning what to expect during a close brush with death (Augustine
2007), so that when that acute event occurs, we accept disengagement
from the world of the living as a socially appropriate acute response.

Kellehear notes that the theme of disengagement may be played out not only in withdrawal of interest in world interests but in reengagement with other activities, values and concerns. This is exactly what many NDErs describe: it is not that they 'lose interest' in life but that the features of another existence, an 'afterlife', begin to take precedence. NDErs disengage from life only when they engage with their apparent disembodied states, their life reviews and the transcendental features of lights and otherworldly entities and environs (Ring 1980, 1984). Kellehear notes that at some point in any dying process, the individual shifts attention to 'what comes next', and this appears to be the driving force in NDEs.

Disintegration: dying as collapse

Kellehear describes the theme of disintegration as a focus on the deterioration of the physical body, to which both the dying persons and their social networks are passive observers, sometimes labelled 'dirty dying' (Lawton 2000). A large proportion of patients die in pain, many in some form of delirium or dementia (Sullivan 2002). A characteristic of NDEs is separation of the sense of self from the physical body, and with that separation patients often describe transcending the physical deterioration of the body. Experiencers typically report cessation of all pain when they leave their bodies, and most also report an enhancement of their thought processes (Kelly et al. 2007). Anecdotal reports from physicians suggest that on rare occasions patients with chronic dementia or coma caused by advanced brain cancer may become lucid in their dying moments, regaining lost mental abilities as they appear to separate from their compromised brains (Osis and Haraldsson 1977; Haig 2007). In their escape from the disintegrating body, NDErs avoid experiencing their death and collapse.

Some sociologists argue that an integral part of the dying process is coming to terms with our bodily vulnerability and developing sociopsychological defences against this harsh realization (Seale 1998). Survivors of NDEs do not deny this somatic fragility but cease to identify with it. Many report an emotional distance from their bodies as they viewed them from an apparently extracorporeal visual perspective, and they return with a strong sense of personal identity that was independent of the body and, by implication, will survive

eventual bodily disintegration (Kelly et al. 2007). Whereas sociological perspectives on dying as collapse have contrasted acceptance
of physical decline with struggle against disease and death, NDEs
offer a third alternative, that of transcending disease and decline
by identifying with a self that will not disintegrate when the body
collapses.

Indeterminacy: Disenfranchised dying

Kellehear reviewed the disenfranchising effects of the medicalization of death in the twentieth century that hid dying patients away
in hospitals, out of sight of their families, and often hid fatal diagnoses and life expectancies from patients themselves (Ariès 1974).
The past half-century has seen a reversal of this trend among hospital staff but that enhanced attention on dying has not extended
to those dying out of hospital, either from violence or from chronic
illness such as AIDS or dementia at home or in nursing homes.
Much of the experience of dying by these 'disenfranchised' populations remains unacknowledged by medical, political and academic
authorities (Kellehear 2007b). The reclassification of these groups
as victims, or chronically ill, or anything else other than 'dying persons' has impeded research into their experiences and contributed to
this disenfranchisement.

Similarly, NDErs have been disenfranchised by the indeterminate
status of NDEs. Whereas most experiencers regard their NDEs as the
most profound events of their lives, these experiences are generally
discounted by medical and academic authorities as hallucinations,
delirious ramblings of a sick brain and fantasies based on wishful
thinking. Blackmore (1993) and Woerlee (2004) typify the medicopsy-
chological dismissal of NDEs as imaginary productions of a failing
brain. Among religious scholars, Zaleski (1987) suggests that many
theologians felt more comfortable regarding NDEs as metaphors or
literary motifs rather than as actual encounters with the divine, and
Couliano (1991) places NDEs within the tradition of fantastic accounts
of otherworld journeys. The reluctance of the medical and academic
establishments to take their concerns seriously and to acknowledge
the powerful impact of NDEs has disenfranchised NDErs, inhibited
them from discussing their NDEs and alienated them from their social
networks (Greyson and Harris 1987; Greyson 1997).

Transcendence: dying as transformation

Kellehear notes that experiences of dying are not all about physical collapse and social disengagement but that some dying experiences may involve transcending these losses to arrive at a new status with dramatically altered consciousness and social relationships. He cites NDEs and deathbed visions as exemplars of dying as transformation. Regardless of the physiological mechanisms underlying NDEs and deathbed visions or the eschatological implications of these experiences, there is abundant evidence of their powerful impact both on personal values, beliefs and attitudes and on social roles, relationships and behaviours. The literature on the after-effects of NDEs has focused on the beneficial personal transformations that often follow. After-effects typically reported include increases in spirituality, concern for others and appreciation of life, and decreases in fear of death, materialism and competitiveness (Sabom 1982).

Studies comparing NDErs' attitudes before and after their NDEs report reduced fear of death, a sense of relative invulnerability, a feeling of special importance or destiny and a strengthened belief in post-mortem existence (Noyes 1980). They also report greater appreciation for life, a renewed sense of purpose, greater confidence and flexibility in coping with life's vicissitudes, increased value of love and service and decreased concern with personal status and material possessions, greater compassion for others, a heightened sense of spiritual purpose and a greatly reduced fear of death (Ring 1980, 1984). NDEs lead to significant positive changes in the purpose and meaning of life and in death acceptance (Bauer 1985). These profound changes in attitudes and behaviour have been corroborated in long-term studies of NDErs and in interviews with their significant others (Ring 1984).

Compared to non-experiencers, NDErs report greatly increased concern for others, decreased fear of death, increased belief in an afterlife, increased religious interest and feeling and lessened desire for material success and approval of others (Flynn 1982). Compared to persons who have come as close to death but not had NDEs, experiencers place significantly lower value on social status, professional and material success and fame (Greyson 1983a) and find death less threatening (Greyson 1992).

The changes in social status following NDEs are not all positive, and the emphasis in the popular media on the positive benefits of NDEs inhibits those who are having problems from seeking help. Sometimes people who have had NDEs may doubt their sanity, yet they are often afraid of rejection or ridicule if they discuss this fear with friends or professionals. Sometimes NDErs do receive negative reactions from professionals when they describe their experiences, which discourages them even further from seeking help in understanding the experience (Greyson and Harris 1987; Greyson 1997).

Most NDErs gradually adjust on their own to their experience and its effects. However, that adjustment often requires them to adopt new values, attitudes and interests. Family and friends may then find it difficult to understand the NDEr's new beliefs and behaviour. On the one hand, family and friends may avoid the NDEr, who they feel has come under some unwelcome influence. On the other hand, family and friends influenced by the popular publicity about the positive effects of NDEs may place the experiencer on a pedestal and expect unrealistic changes. Sometimes, friends expect superhuman patience and forgiveness from the NDEr or miraculous healing and prophetic powers; they may then reject the NDEr who does not live up to these unrealistic expectations (Greyson and Harris 1987; Greyson 1997).

Emotional problems after NDEs include anger and depression at having been resuscitated or 'sent back', perhaps unwillingly. NDErs often have problems reconciling the experience with their traditional religious beliefs or their previous values and lifestyles. Because the experience seems so central to their sense of self and seems to set them apart from other people around them, NDErs may come to define themselves exclusively as experiencers. Because many of their new attitudes and beliefs are so different from those around them, NDErs can overcome the worry that they are somehow abnormal only by redefining for themselves what is normal. NDErs may feel a sense of distance or separation from people who have not had similar experiences and may fear being ridiculed or rejected by others – sometimes, of course, with good reason. Difficulty reconciling the new attitudes and beliefs with the expectations of family and friends can interfere with maintaining old roles and lifestyle, which no longer have the same meaning. NDErs may find it impossible to communicate to others the meaning and impact of the NDE on their lives. Frequently, having experienced a sense of unconditional love in the NDE, the experiencer cannot accept the conditions and limitations of human relationships (Greyson and Harris 1987; Greyson 1997).

In reviewing social systems disrupted by death, Vernon (1970) notes that conflict is more likely to arise when prior planning had not established shared expectations, such as in sudden, unexpected deaths of family members. Because NDEs are rarely if ever anticipated, they might be expected to provoke similar interactional conflicts. Researchers have noted that the value incongruities between NDErs and their families lead to a relatively high divorce rate (Bush 1991). The 'social death' that occurs when the familiar personality of an NDEr dies can be as disruptive to a family as the physical death of that person (Insinger 1991). The effects of an NDE 'may include long-term depression, broken relationships, disrupted career, feelings of severe alienation, an inability to function in the world, long years of struggling with the keen sense of altered reality' (Bush 1991: 7).

Concluding reflections

NDEs and deathbed visions have received extensive phenomenological investigation, and they have been widely discussed as manifestations of a dysfunctional brain or as glimpses of an otherworldly realm. The impact of these experiences on social relationships and on larger-scale societal interactions has received relatively little attention. A review of this literature suggests that NDEs and deathbed visions share many social processes with more mundane dying experiences, but it also highlights both the empirical and the conceptual gaps in our understanding of the dying process.

As increasingly acknowledged varieties of dying experience, NDEs and deathbed visions can be viewed in terms of the seven themes Kellehear describes in his introductory chapter to this volume. Some of these themes are typically manifested over time and are necessarily attenuated in NDEs and deathbed visions by the acuteness of those experiences. On the other hand, the return to the world of the living after NDEs allows consideration of how these themes are manifested not only in dying behaviour but also in behaviour as the experiencers reintegrate into their social networks. Just as each of these theories may offer some insight into the social processes of NDEs and deathbed visions, so too might near-death and deathbed visionary experiences permit additional insights into the social consequences of other varieties of dying experience.

The theme of agency is manifested in NDEs in the personal reassessment of life review, though the applicability of this theme in maintenance of personal identity and personal control is more complex. The theme of linearity is played out in the depiction of NDEs as a kind of status passage. The theme of fluctuation may be seen in the characteristic trajectory in NDEs through decline and back to recovery, as well as through complex oscillation in integration trajectories following NDEs. The theme of disengagement is relevant to NDErs and deathbed visionaries in their decathexis of the physical world as they begin to interact in a seemingly otherworldly venue. The theme of disintegration appears in NDEs and deathbed visions not as a focus on bodily collapse but as separation of the sense of self from the deteriorating body; its model of coming to terms with our vulnerability by transcendence may provide insights into coping with disintegration in other forms of dying experience. The theme of indeterminacy is echoed in the ambiguous status of NDEs and deathbed visions and the reluctance of medical and societal authorities to acknowledge them as valid experiences of dying. And finally, the theme of transcendence finds it highest expression in NDEs, in which survivors almost universally report profound transformations in values, beliefs, attitudes and social relationships.

Although the above discussion has focused on the impact of NDEs and deathbed visions on the experiencers themselves, NDEs may have a significant impact on people who do not experience them but only encounter them indirectly. Flynn (1986) describes a project in which his college students, after having studied NDEs, practised unconditional love and were themselves transformed by the exercise. Ring (Ring and Valarino 1998) describes the spiritual meaning and 'soulmaking' significance of NDEs. Like Flynn, he reports that his students, having studied NDEs, also became more empathic and spiritually oriented through applying the lessons of NDEs: that death is not fearsome, that life continues beyond, that love is more important than material possessions and that everything happens for a reason.

There are also suggestions that NDEs may have more widespread cultural implications. Some enthusiasts have written messianically about the potential of NDEs to transform society. Twentieth-century social critics as diverse as British historian Arnold Toynbee, Swiss psychiatrist Carl Jung and German theologian and medical missionary Albert Schweitzer have written that 'nothing short of a worldwide spiritual revolution will suffice' to save human civilization (Lorimer 1990: 259). Ring suggests 'that the NDE can be viewed as an *evolutionary device* to bring about this transformation' (1984: 7) and that NDEs and similar mystical experiences may point the way towards unlocking humankind's dormant spiritual potential. Ring (1984) speculates that, with increasing resuscitation technology enabling more and more individuals to return from the brink of death, the cumulative impact of their uplifting testimonies may foster the spiritual evolution of the collective consciousness of humanity. The title of his book on the after-effects of NDE, *Heading Towards Omega,* comes from French Jesuit philosopher and scientist Pierre Teilhard de Chardin's notion of the 'Omega point', a hypothetical end point in human history representing an evolutionary culmination in the highest strivings of human culture.

Badham (1997) argues that NDEs revitalize society's belief in God and hope for an afterlife. Although Fox correctly concludes that 'NDEs cannot unambiguously be used as apologetic tools for the propagation of any one particular religious or spiritual tradition or be somehow fitted into any one tradition to the exclusion of all others' (2003: 339), these experiences may foster cultural change by leading us to question some of our basic assumptions about mind and brain; about our relationship to other individuals, social networks, and the divine; and about human society and our role in it. Those insights will not come from the limited perspective of any one discipline viewing NDEs and deathbed visions through the limited lens of neurophysiology, psychology, theology or sociology. A fuller understanding of NDEs, as indeed of all varieties of dying experience, requires interdisciplinary collaboration and a humble appreciation of the profound impact of the experience on individual, interpersonal and social processes.

References

Alvarado, C. S. (2006) 'Neglected Near-Death Phenomena', *Journal of Near-Death Studies*, **24** (3): 131–51.

Ariès, P. (1974) *Western Attitudes Towards Death: From the Middle Ages to the Present*, Baltimore, Md.: Johns Hopkins University Press.

Athappilly, G. K., Greyson, B. and Stevenson, I. (2006) 'Do Prevailing Societal Models Influence Reports of Near-Death Experiences?

Comparison of Accounts Reported Before and After 1975', *Journal of Nervous and Mental Disease*, **194** (3): 218–22.

Augustine, K. (2007) 'Psychophysiological and Cultural Correlates Undermining a Survivalist Interpretation of Near-Death Experiences', *Journal of Near-Death Studies*, **26** (2): 89–125.

Badham, P. (1997) 'Religious and Near-Death Experience in Relation to Belief in a Future Life', *Mortality*, **2** (1): 7–21.

Barrett, W. F. (1926) *Deathbed Visions: The Psychical Experiences of the Dying*, London: Methuen.

Bauer, M. (1985) 'Near-Death Experiences and Attitude Change', *Anabiosis: Journal of Near-Death Studies*, **5** (1): 39–47.

Blackmore, S. J. (1993) *Dying to Live: Science and the Near-Death Experience*, London: Grafton.

Bozzano, E. (1906) 'Apparitions of Deceased Persons at Deathbeds', *Annals of Psychical Science*, **3** (2): 67–100.

(1923) *Phenomenes psychiques au moment de la mort*, Paris: Editions de la Bibliothèque de Philosophie Spiritualiste.

Brayne, S., Farnham, C. and Fenwick, P. (2006) 'Deathbed Phenomena and Their Effect on a Palliative Care Team: A Pilot Study', *American Journal of Hospice and Palliative Care*, **23** (1): 17–24.

Bush, N. E. (1983) 'The Near-Death Experience in Children: Shades of the Prison-House Reopening', *Anabiosis: Journal of Near-Death Studies*, **3** (2): 77–193.

(1991) 'Is Ten Years a Life Review?', *Journal of Near-Death Studies*, **10** (1): 5–9.

Callanan, M. and Kelley, P. (1993) *Final Gifts: Understanding the Special Awareness, Needs, and Communications of the Dying*, New York: Poseidon.

Carr, D. (1982) 'Pathophysiology of Stress-Induced Limbic Lobe Dysfunction: A Hypothesis for NDEs', *Anabiosis: Journal of Near-Death Studies*, **2** (1): 75–89.

Cobbe, F. P. (1882) *Peak in Darien*, London: Williams & Norgate.

Couliano, I. (1991) *Out of This World: Otherworld Journeys from Gilgamesh to Albert Einstein*, Boston, Mass.: Shambhala.

Devinsky, O., Feldmann, E., Burrowes, K. and Bromfield, E. (1989) 'Autoscopic Phenomena with Seizures', *Archives of Neurology*, **46** (10): 1080–8.

Ethier, A. M. (2005) 'Death-Related Sensory Experiences', *Journal of Pediatric Oncology Nursing*, **22** (2): 104–11.

Flynn, C. P. (1982) 'Meanings and Implications of NDEr Transformations: Some Preliminary Findings and Implications', *Anabiosis: Journal of Near-Death Studies*, **2** (1): 3–13.

(1986) *After the Beyond: Human Transformation and the Near-Death Experience*, Englewood Cliffs, NJ: Prentice-Hall.

Fox, M. (2003) *Religion, Spirituality and the Near-Death Experience*, London: Routledge.

French, C. C. (2001) 'Dying to Know the Truth: Visions of a Dying Brain, or False Memories?', *Lancet*, **358** (358): 2010–11.

Gabbard, G. O. and Twemlow, S. W. (1984) *With the Eyes of the Mind: An Empirical Analysis of Out-of-Body States*, New York: Praeger.

Glaser, B. G. and Strauss, A. L. (1971) *Status Passage*, London: Routledge & Kegan Paul.

Gloor, P. (1990) 'Experiential Phenomena of Temporal Lobe Epilepsy', *Brain*, **113** (6): 1673–94.

Granqvist, P., Fredrikson, M., Unge, P., Hagenfeldt, A., Valind, S., Larhammar, D. and Larsson, M. (2005) 'Sensed Presence and Mystical Experiences Are Predicted by Suggestibility, Not by the Application of Transcranial Weak Complex Magnetic Fields', *Neuroscience Letters*, **379** (1): 1–6.

Greyson, B. (1983a) 'Near-Death Experiences and Personal Values', *American Journal of Psychiatry*, **140** (5): 618–20.

(1983b) 'The Psychodynamics of Near-Death Experiences', *Journal of Nervous and Mental Disease*, **171** (6): 376–81.

(1990) 'Near-Death Encounters With and Without Near-Death Experiences: Comparative NDE Scale Profiles', *Journal of Near-Death Studies*, **8** (3): 151–61.

(1991a) 'Near-Death Experiences Precipitated by Suicide Attempt: Lack of Influence of Psychopathology, Religion, and Expectations', *Journal of Near-Death Studies*, **9** (3): 183–8.

(1991b) 'Near-Death Experiences and Systems Theories: A Biosociological Approach to Mystical States', *Journal of Mind and Behavior*, **12** (4): 487–508.

(1992) 'Reduced Death Threat in Near-Death Experiencers', *Death Studies*, **16** (6): 533–46.

(1997) 'The Near-Death Experience as a Focus of Clinical Attention', *Journal of Nervous and Mental Disease*, **185** (5): 327–34.

(1998) 'The Incidence of Near-Death Experiences', *Medicine and Psychiatry*, **1** (2): 92–9.

(2003) 'Incidence and Correlates of Near-Death Experiences on a Cardiac Care Unit', *General Hospital Psychiatry*, **25** (4): 269–76.

(2007) 'Consistency of Near-Death Experience Accounts over Two Decades: Are Reports Embellished over Time?', *Resuscitation*, **73** (3): 407–41.

Greyson, B. and Harris, B. (1987) 'Clinical Approaches to the Near-Death Experiencer', *Journal of Near-Death Studies*, **6** (1): 41–52.

Greyson, B. and Stevenson, I. (1980) 'The Phenomenology of Near-Death Experiences', *American Journal of Psychiatry*, **137** (10): 1193–6.

Haig, S. (2007) 'The Power of Hope', *Time*, **169** (5): 118–19.

Heim, A. von St. G. (1892) 'Notizen Über Den Tod Durch Absturz' ('Remarks on Fatal Falls'), *Jahrbuch Des Schweitzerischen Alpenclub* (*Yearbook of the Swiss Alpine Club*), **27**: 327–37.

Herzog, D. B. and Herrin, J. T. (1985) 'Near-Death Experiences in the Very Young', *Critical Care Medicine*, **13** (12): 1074–5.

Horowitz, M. J. and Adams, J. E. (1970) 'Hallucinations on Brain Stimulation: Evidence for Revision of the Penfield Hypothesis', in W. Keup (ed.), *Origin and Mechanisms of Hallucinations*, New York: Plenum, pp. 13–22.

Houran, J. (1997) 'Hallucinations That Comfort: Contextual Mediation of Deathbed Visions', *Perceptual and Motor Skills*, **84** (3, Part II): 1491–504.

Hyslop, J. (1907) 'Visions of the Dying', *Journal of the American Society for Psychical Research*, **1** (1): 45–55.

Insinger, M. (1991) 'The Impact of a Near-Death Experience on Family Relationships', *Journal of Near-Death Studies*, **9** (3): 141–81.

Irwin, H. J. (1985) *Flight of Mind: A Psychological Study of the Out-of-Body Experience*, Metuchen, NJ: Scarecrow Press.

Jansen, K. L. R. (1997) 'The Ketamine Model of the Near-Death Experience: A Central Role for the N-Methyl-D-Aspartate Receptor', *Journal of Near-Death Studies*, **16**: 5–26.

Kastenbaum, R. (1979) 'Healthy Dying: A Paradoxical Quest Continues', *Journal of Social Issues*, **35** (1): 185–206.

Kellehear, A. (1990) 'The Near-Death Experience as Status Passage', *Social Science and Medicine*, **31** (8): 933–9.

(1993) 'Culture, Biology, and the Near-Death Experience', *Journal of Nervous and Mental Disease*, **181** (3): 148–56.

(1996) *Experiences Near-Death: Beyond Medicine and Religion*, New York: Oxford University Press.

(2007a) 'Culture and the Near Death Experience: Comments on Keith Augustine's "Psychophysiological and Cultural Correlates Undermining a Survivalist Interpretation of Near-Death Experiences"', *Journal of Near-Death Studies*, **26** (2): 147–53.

(2007b) *A Social History of Dying*, Cambridge: Cambridge University Press.

(2008a) 'Dying as a Social Relationship: A Sociological Review of Debates on the Determination of Death', *Social Science and Medicine*, **66** (7): 1533–44.

(2008b) 'Census of Non-Western Near-Death Experiences to 2005: Overview of the Current Data', *Journal of Near-Death Studies*, **26** (4): 249–65.

Kelly, E.W., Greyson, B. and Kelly, E.F. (2007) 'Unusual Experiences Near Death and Related Phenomena', in E.F. Kelly, E.W. Kelly, A. Crabtree, A. Gauld, M. Grosso and B. Greyson, *Irreducible Mind: Towards a Psychology for the 21st Century*, Lanham, Md.: Rowman & Littlefield, pp. 367–421.

Kübler-Ross, E. (1969) *On Death and Dying*, New York: Macmillan.

Lange, R., Greyson, B. and Houran, J. (2004) 'A Rasch Scaling Validation of a "Core" Near-Death Experience', *British Journal of Psychology*, **95** (2): 161–77.

Lawton, J. (2000) *The Dying Process: Patients' Experiences of Palliative Care*, London: Routledge.

Locke, T.P. and Shontz, F.C. (1983) 'Personality Correlates of the Near-Death Experience: A Preliminary Study', *Journal of the American Society for Psychical Research*, **77** (4): 311–18.

Lorimer, D. (1990) *Whole in One: the Near-Death Experience and the Ethic of Interconnectedness*, London: Arkana.

McClenon, J. (1994) *Wondrous Events: Foundations of Religious Belief*, Philadelphia, Pa.: University of Pennsylvania Press.

Matthews, S.H. (1979) *The Social World of Old Women: Management of Self-Identity*, Beverly Hills, Calif.: Sage.

Moody, R.A. (1975) *Life after Life*, Covington, Ga.: Mockingbird Books.

Morse, M.L., Conner, D. and Tyler, D. (1985) 'Near-Death Experiences in a Pediatric Population', *American Journal of Diseases of Children*, **139** (6): 595–600.

Morse, M.L., Venecia, D. and Milstein, J. (1989) 'Near-Death Experiences: A Neurophysiological Explanatory Model', *Journal of Near-Death Studies*, **8** (1): 45–53.

Moss, M.S., Moss, S.Z. and Connor, S.R. (2003) 'Dying in Long Term Care Facilities in the US', in J.S. Katz and S. Peace (eds.), *End of Life Care in Care Homes: A Palliative Approach*, Oxford: Oxford University Press, pp. 157–73.

Noyes, R. (1980) 'Attitude Change Following Near-Death Experience', *Psychiatry*, **43** (3): 234–42.

Osis, K. and Haraldsson, E. (1977) *At the Hour of Death*, New York: Avon.

Parnia, S., Waller, D.G., Yeates, R. and Fenwick, P. (2001) 'A Qualitative and Quantitative Study of the Incidence, Features and Aetiology of Near Death Experiences in Cardiac Arrest Survivors', *Resuscitation*, **48** (2): 149–56.

Persinger, M. A. (1994) 'Near-Death Experiences: Determining the Neuroanatomical Pathways by Experiential Patterns and Simulation in Experimental Settings', in L. Bessette (ed.), *Healing: Beyond Suffering or Death*, Chabanel, Québec: Publications MNH, pp. 277–86.

Ring, K. (1980) *Life at Death: A Scientific Investigation of the Near-Death Experience*, New York: Coward, McCann, & Geoghegan.

—— (1984) *Heading Towards Omega: In Search of the Meaning of the Near-Death Experience*, New York: William Morrow.

—— (1992) *The Omega Project: Near-Death Experiences, UFO Encounters, and Mind at Large*, New York: William Morrow.

Ring, K. and Valarino, E. E. (1998) *Lessons from the Light: What We Can Learn from the Near-Death Experience*, New York: Plenum/Insight.

Roberts, G. and Owen, J. (1988) 'The Near-Death Experience', *British Journal of Psychiatry*, 153 (5): 607–17.

Rodin, E. A. (1980) 'The Reality of Death Experiences: A Personal Perspective', *Journal of Nervous and Mental Disease*, 168 (5): 259–63.

—— (1989) 'Comments on "A Neurobiological Model for Near-Death Experiences"', *Journal of Near-Death Studies*, 7 (4): 255–9.

Rogo, D. S. (1978) 'Research on Deathbed Experiences: Some Contemporary and Historical Perspectives', *Parapsychology Review*, 9 (1): 20–7.

Saavedra-Aguilar, J. C. and Gómez-Jeria, J. S. (1989) 'A Neurobiological Model for Near-Death Experiences', *Journal of Near-Death Studies*, 7 (4): 205–22.

Sabom, M. B. (1982) *Recollections of Death: A Medical Investigation*, New York: Harper & Row.

Sassower, R. and Grodin, M. A. (1986) 'Epistemological Questions Concerning Death', *Death Studies*, 10 (4): 341–53.

Seale, C. (1998) *Constructing Death: The Sociology of Dying and Bereavement*, Cambridge: Cambridge University Press.

Serdahely, W. J. (1990) 'Pediatric Near-Death Experiences', *Journal of Near-Death Studies*, 9 (1): 33–9.

Sudnow, D. (1967) *Passing On: The Social Organization of Dying*, Englewood Cliffs, NJ: Prentice-Hall.

Sullivan, M. D. (2002) 'The Illusion of Patient Choice in End-of-Life Decisions', *American Journal of Geriatric Psychiatry*, 10 (4): 365–72.

Sutherland, C. (1992) *Transformed by the Light: Life After Near-Death Experiences*, Sydney: Bantam.

Thomas, W. I. with Thomas, D. S. (1928) *The Child in America*, New York: Knopf.

Van Gennep, A. (1969) *Rites of Passage*, Chicago, Ill.: University of Chicago Press.

Van Lommel, P., Van Wees, R., Meyers, V. and Elfferich, I. (2001) 'Near-Death Experience in Survivors of Cardiac Arrest: A Prospective Study in the Netherlands', *Lancet*, 358 (9298): 2039–45.

Vernon, G. M. (1970) *The Sociology of Death*, New York: Ronald Press.

Woerlee, G. M. (2004) *Mortal Minds: a Biology of the Soul and the Dying Experience*, Utrecht: De Tijdstroom.

Zaleski, C. G. (1987) *Otherworld Journeys: Accounts of Near-Death Experience in Medieval and Modern Times*, New York: Oxford University Press.

Index